African Philosophy for the Twenty-First Century

African Philosophy for the Twenty-First Century

Acts of Transition

Edited by
Jean Godefroy Bidima and Laura Hengehold

ROWMAN & LITTLEFIELD
Lanham • Boulder • New York • London

Published by Rowman & Littlefield
An imprint of The Rowman & Littlefield Publishing Group, Inc.
4501 Forbes Boulevard, Suite 200, Lanham, Maryland 20706
www.rowman.com

86-90 Paul Street, London EC2A 4NE

British Library Cataloguing in Publication Information Available

Library of Congress Cataloging-in-Publication Data

Names: Bidima, Jean Godefroy, 1958- editor. | Hengehold, Laura, editor.
Title: African philosophy for the twenty-first century : acts of transition / edited by Jean
    Godefroy Bidima and Laura Hengehold.
Description: Lanham : Rowman & Littlefield, 2021. | Includes bibliographical references
    and index.
Identifiers: LCCN 2021037852 (print) | LCCN 2021037853 (ebook) |
    ISBN 9781538154168 (cloth) | ISBN 9781538154182 (paperback) |
    ISBN 9781538154175 (epub)
Subjects: LCSH: Philosophy, African—21st century.
Classification: LCC B5321 .A375 2021 (print) | LCC B5321 (ebook) |
    DDC 199.6—dc23
LC record available at https://lccn.loc.gov/2021037852
LC ebook record available at https://lccn.loc.gov/2021037853

Contents

Acknowledgments

I thank Abbé Benjamin Nkoé, my first professor of philosophy in Cameroon, for his commitment at the time to making young people like myself aware of the need to question ideologies—including those produced by Africans themselves. I also gratefully acknowledge Antoine Garapon, Magistrate, for his friendship and intellectual rigor, which helped me to be wary of ideologies that revolve around legal discourses. Nor could I forget to mention Nick Nesbitt, for the intellectual complicity and friendship which, over the course of many years, have not lost any of their luster. Finally, sincere thanks to the late professors Eloi Messi Metogo, OP. and Francis (Abiola) Irele.

Our thanks also go to the Baker-Nord Center for the Humanities at Case Western Reserve University for supporting Laura Hengehold's contributions to this volume in numerous ways. For their expert input and long-standing friendship, Laura expresses her deep appreciation to Cheryl Toman and Allison Moore, along with Brent Adkins and, on a more personal level, Joe Cairnes. We are both indebted to the inspiration and great patience of our editors, Sarah Campbell and Frankie Mace, and want to extend our gratitude to Nivethitha Tamilselvan and Elle Haag, without whom the last stages of this book would not have been possible.

Introduction

Laura Hengehold

"To do philosophy is to be *en route*," said the German philosopher Karl Jaspers. But this "route" is history with its accelerations, its imperatives and its twists, its different faces and its anticipated and unforeseen encounters.[1] Often the route has multiple lanes, and one traveler marks her speed with respect to those in other lanes, also moving; hence the impossibility of an absolute chronology. Philosophizing from and with Africa in a historical spirit means recognizing what one shares with these times even as one projects futures and pasts—ironically, awareness of coexistence with an event, particularly an event of incongruity or divergence, is presented as *topicality*.[2] Philosophizing also means being attentive to something *untimely* in the flow of events, something more like a tendency, an inkling, or a mirage on the surface of the pavement that has yet to blossom, vanish, or be integrated into a recognizable terrain.

The goal of this volume is to explore how a discipline expresses "transitional acts." With this expression, we mean on the one hand, the manner in which thought enters into a diacritical relation with history as it is in the process of being made, and on the other hand, the steps that this same thought must run through to assure its own renewal *in proposing provisional solutions to problems*. A *transitional act*, as Jean Godefroy Bidima explains, is one that expresses both the audacity of confrontation with the novelty of creation, prudence in the face of risks and anticipation, even eagerness, in the face of the unexpected.

The *timeliness* of African philosophy has often been assessed with reference to the rhythms of its religious practices, including Islam, and the waves of imperial domination by Europe that were justified by Christian evangelization. Other frames of analysis reflected the temporalities of postindependence nation-building and the Cold War, with their nuclear horizon. In the 1990s, the habits of ethnic belonging, renewal, and warfare rose to the foreground

1

against a field marked by increasing globalization of trade and the structural adjustment policies surrounding international debt, which both provoked such wars and were overshadowed by them. A longer view would examine changes in language, educational institutions, and mechanisms for the dissemination of ideas.[3] Attempts to solve the problems bequeathed by history should neither impede attention to the emergence of new ideas in relation to a specific terrain, nor encourage the artificial, advertising-driven frenzy for novelty which Olúfẹ́mi Táíwò associates with certain pitfalls of the European idea of modernity.[4]

As Hanétha Vété-Congolo describes in chapter 8, African philosophy as a global dialogue (rather than an indigenous dialogic practice, emerging from Islam, Christianity, or pagan oral tradition) began with European efforts to understand African beliefs with the goal of converting them more effectively to the colonizer's religion. Gradually, this dialogue was reclaimed as a subjective public *act* by Muntu, namely, human existence as understood from within African histories and their horizons. In the hands of Fanon, Senghor, Nyerere, and others, down to the era of Steve Biko, and in parallel with movements for racial equality elsewhere in the diasporic black world, this philosophical work attempted during the anticolonial era to synthesize liberatory European doctrines with African beliefs and aspirations on behalf of independent nations and continental unity. The relationship between individual critical creativity and collective values forced African thinkers to question who the individual of a liberated society had once been and would be in the future. This relationship was especially important given that the racism of European settlers and soldiers denied the individuality and rationality of colonized peoples. This philosophical work also called on the former colonial countries to challenge the "ethnophilosophical" presuppositions of their own scholarship and its pernicious effect on non-African peoples.[5]

At the end of the Cold War many Africans justifiably hoped that democratization would expand and that states would no longer be shackled by the self-serving geopolitical goals of American and Soviet-funded "development." Many philosophers during this period dedicated themselves to justifying or relativizing multiparty systems of governance and to participating in a global dialogue about individualist and communitarian strands of liberalism. They also sought a form of modernity that would bear witness to the changing aspirations of African populations and the ways that individual African cultures had historically grappled with that tension. In 1994, the inauguration of postapartheid South Africa seemed to promise a new era, but almost simultaneously the horrific genocide in Rwanda gave philosophers pause. The complicity of Western powers such as the United States and France revealed that the humanizing meaning of decolonization had not made the impact that it should have on Western consciousness. Reflection on the many sources of violent ethnic partisanship at that time went hand in hand with reflection on the nature of philosophy's purported universality and an attempt to situate universality in a positive way rather than merely to denounce Western thought's traditional indifference to location and historical situation.

During the early 2000s, partly provoked by the events in Rwanda, what some historians have called the Third World War spread across Central and Southern Africa, particularly the mineral-rich regions of Angola and the Democratic Republic of Congo. Often battles were fought (and continue to be fought) using arms given, sold, or smuggled into Africa as a result of the former US-Soviet standoff. Civil wars were among the results of falling prices for exported commodity foodstuffs, financial changes linked to the unification of European currency, and the weight of international debt accrued by African governments under highly coercive circumstances during the 1980s and 1990s. International agencies and governments demanded cuts in public education, cultural programs, and health spending or forced countries to accept services from international agencies funded by Northern governments rather than to pay their own doctors and teachers. This had a profound effect on African public spheres, including philosophical creativity and criticism, which often moved into exile—although this brought African thinkers closer to their counterparts in the American diaspora. It should be noted that the United States and other powerful governments who imposed these structural adjustment programs often demanded the intense privatization of intellectual work and publishing in their own countries, which has affected their academic culture and the freedom even of students and scholars who were, globally speaking, relatively privileged.

As we enter the second decade of the twenty-first century, the events that frame our philosophical timelines or provide us with topics include processes of migration and new forms of biological and medical experimentation, work, and communication. These are set in motion by a new geopolitical division in which Asia plays a significant role, while climate crisis, which already affects tropical countries directly, is also a grim horizon for thought in the global North. None of the former temporalities have vanished. For example, ghosts of the US-Soviet opposition continue to haunt the foreign policy and internal politics of former "proxy" states in Africa. Many of these ghosts seem to have been displaced into a wide-ranging and opportunistic crusade against Islam in the name of fighting terrorism, in which China participates elsewhere. Unfortunately, the Arab Spring of 2010 and 2011 was unable to mitigate the violent tensions between militarized radicals, constitutionalists, and authoritarians in Northern African countries, and international military intervention can only perpetuate crisis in Africa given Islam's coexistence with other religions along the Sahel. The older tones are displaced by new rhythms of urgency, new *topoi*, and new plateaus for philosophical reflection.

Meanwhile, the trajectory of philosophy itself, as a more or less global practice and profession, has been marked by new events. Even during the slave trade, black abolitionists and political thinkers in England, the United States, Liberia, and the English Caribbean, as well as revolutionary Haiti, were engaged in philosophical dialogue. V. Y. Mudimbe pointed to the liminal status of Edward Blyden as an international figure in the nineteenth century, prefiguring the pan-Africanism of Garvey and others; and in the twentieth, Fanon was read more widely in French Africa after he had been translated and appropriated by the American Black Power movement.[6] Thus, one can argue that the subject of African philosophy is empirically global as well as philosophically universal, in a continual reversal of "rootedness" and being "en route." Starting in 2002, the trans-American Caribbean Philosophy Association began meeting on a regular basis and Anglophone publishers began soliciting manuscripts in African and Caribbean thought.

Since the 1970s, in the work of Enrique Dussel (Mexico), Anibal Quijano (Peru), and Walter Mignolo (Argentina), Latin American thinkers have developed a philosophical critique of colonial modernity that seeks to clear ground for the needs and intellectual reflection of indigenous Americans as well as those of African descent. There has also been increased awareness in Brazil, for example, that high school and university curricula must redress the exclusion of African-descended peoples, a movement to which the Portuguese Boaventura de Sousa Santos has contributed with his numerous works on the decolonization of knowledge.[7] This South American intellectual activity influences philosophers in North America, including Canada. Given that the function of "race" and "blackness" as categories of social domination differs on both sides of the Atlantic, one of the most important contemporary questions is the extent to which African philosophy can and should be conceptually distinguished from a philosophy of race or antiracism, and what light it does or does not shed on racism against black, Arab, Asian, and indigenous people of different generations in the global North.

Both because of and despite the extended impact of the Bologna process governing the accreditation of European universities, academics in some African countries such as Senegal and Cameroon are forming regional associations. CODESRIA (in Dakar) is a powerful pan-African intellectual center with scholarship and publishing funds, as are some South African universities.[8] Since 1995, a Cercle Camerounais de la Philosophie has met regularly and so have some national and international societies like the International Association for African Philosophy and Studies.[9] The Rhodes Must Fall movement of 2015–2017, and its academic counterpart Fees Must Fall, shook South Africa with demands for a more prominent representation of African culture in public space, university curricula, faculty hiring, and financial aid policies.[10] It challenged the historically unchanging Eurocentrism of South African education and corresponded to a growing demand for greater accountability to the majority black population from elected leaders. At the level of the international academic elite, the 2016 *Ateliers de la pensée* in Dakar brought together prominent French and Francophone intellectuals with the goal of setting an internally fruitful horizon for African philosophy and exploring its relevance for diasporic Africans in France and Europe.[11]

These are just a few of the highly visible moments in philosophy's transition as an institution during the early years of the twenty-first century. They cannot substitute for the myriad unsung conversations or the *untimely* element which is still emerging from their shadows. Commitment to social analysis in terms of (neo) Marxist political economy, celebratory traditionalism, or the principles of global neoliberalism underlie some powerful national and generational differences of orientation among African philosophers and sometimes make for odd bedfellows. One can and must certainly ask how national and international funding sources for such institutions, even within Africa, promote certain strains of inquiry and research at the expense of others. Freedom of thought, inasmuch as it rightly includes the perspectives of others, may also less justly reflect their financial, religious, or ethnic priorities—and this goes for the global North as well as African countries. The extent to which philosophical discourse should reflect intellectual conversations in other countries, nation-building projects, the contribution of dissidents, or the practical needs of nonphilosophers remains subject to heated debate and poses moral dilemmas for each thinker who enters into African philosophy.

The politics of language, foregrounded in the 1980s by Ngũgĩ Wa Thiong'o,[12] remain as profound a barrier to wider philosophical dialogue as the difficulties posed by lack of popular access to the formal and informal tools of philosophical work. Souleymane Bachir Diagne has also pointed out that these conversations have not sufficiently integrated awareness of the written philosophical work that has been done for centuries by Islamic scholars in Northern and Western Africa, while the recently deceased Moroccan Mohammad al-Jabri and Egyptian Samir Amin are the best known secular thinkers from this region in recent times.[13] As Edwin Etieyibo and Jonathan O. Chimakonam found using a survey of universities throughout sub-Saharan Africa, and as Florence Piron has confirmed with her SOHA surveys regarding the use of digital media, the ability of African philosophers to flourish through dialogue in their own languages and on African soil has been hampered by lack of resources for communication, translation, and funding for university libraries as well as market distribution of books.[14] The philosophical work that is most relevant to the needs of local communities, including critical studies of others' work, may not even show up on the kind of schematic global horizon described here. But this certainly does not mean it is lacking in importance or creativity.

In the following chapters, the relationship between knowledges and imaginaries serves as a mobile point from which African philosophers and Africanists try to counteractualize or meet what is *untimely* in this historical process head-on.

Contributors from multiple countries and parts of the world begin from concrete experiences of transition—in the ways societies organize family, work, and emotional life; the ways that childhood and aging demarcate the times of a life and generation, and the ways that nonhuman nature and divinity are conceptualized in relation to the fleeting span of human existences. Above all, they ask how the meaning of human being, never a given, is changing and how Africans and other human beings are managing to find principles for navigating and selecting what is best among those transitions.[15] Some essays may contain the tools for critiquing an ideological or mystifying use of a concept from other essays; concepts which when taken in their untimely sense are crucial vehicles for African thought. Neither the meaning of humanism nor of philosophy remains unsettled.

Cultures around the world have often associated human existence with manhood, which is one reason that many philosophers in this collection have bucked the trend by beginning with the assumption that African humanity, but also female humanity, is paradigmatic. The equation of humanity with manhood orients political thought toward statecraft and men's economic (or military) activity rather than the economic and cultural activity of women, particularly the forms of nurturing governance they exercise at the heart of families. Nigerian philosopher Nkiru Nzegwu has argued that the structure of the family is an underappreciated resource for philosophical thought and that its presuppositions are presuppositions of thought.[16] The family is the context in which children are first inculcated into imaginaries and taught critical skills (along with a healthy dose of blind faith, in many cases); yet the family is not simply what we imagine. Women are imagined to be responsible for families, often without sufficient resources, but they are also subordinated within the family and their work is taken for granted by both the state and male relatives. One of the turning points in the historical as well as the philosophical processes that form a backdrop for this volume might be the 1985 United Nations World Conference in Nairobi, which concluded the Decade for Women, brought explicit global attention to the activism of African women, and provoked feminists in Northern countries to grapple with the Eurocentrism and American-centrism of the feminist scholarship that had hitherto occupied the public sphere when it came to women's lives. Unfortunately, it also justified the intensification of development programs aimed at African women from outside the continent.

In the opening chapter, "What Does Being in the World Mean? Thinking Life and Domestic Bonds in Twenty-First-Century Africa," Ivoirian philosopher and poet Tanella Boni describes how economic challenges have frayed men's and women's willingness to trust historical forms of the couple and family life, whether monogamous or polygamous, and threaten a financialization of all affective and educational activity. She rereads classic examples of modernist African literature by Sony Labou Tansi and Ahmadou Kourouma from the point of view of their female characters, to understand how such tendencies might be resisted, without falling into an uncritical embrace of either patriarchal or Western feminist priorities. The families whose transitions Boni describes had gone through changes during the colonial epoch and before, but these transitions were not considered historically significant. In the second chapter, "Probing Gender Injustices in Africa," Delphine Abadie addresses the ways in which African feminist efforts to confront the representation of African women in Western-centered development discourse and philosophical discourse both succeed at being timely and sometimes threaten to miss the untimeliness associated with power relations that claim tradition and language as their alibi. Just as (Western) feminist philosophy marked a change in Western philosophy's self-image, so too feminist self-understandings in Africa and elsewhere (like Latin America) are going to depend on the outcome of debates between African philosophers of gender such as Oyèrónkẹ́ Oyěwùmí and Bibi Bakare-Yusuf. Tsitsi Dangarembga's *Nervous Conditions* provides Abadie with a ground-level phenomenological description of the female circumstances which these theorists have put into geopolitical perspective.

The increase in migration, both within countries and between countries and continents, is one of the most obvious events at the start of the twenty-first century. A change of location, migration symptomatizes other changes—in the economic circumstances, particularly of rural people; in ecological circumstances, especially desertification; in the communication technology that makes it possible for people to learn about forms of life in far-flung regions and to remain in contact with families who have relocated far away; and certainly not least, dramatic changes in the disparity of access to a meaningful and settled life between North and South. Many migrants are also victims of war resulting from such pressures. Intercontinental migration makes the news, but migration within Africa is both a sign/cause of stress and an occasion for hospitality. Laws matter, and access to jobs, but so does the spirit in which such laws and forms of work are generated. In "Gender between Kinship and Utopia," Laura Hengehold examines the Cameroonian Werewere Liking's literary, artistic, and educational practices in the Ki-Yi Village of Côte d'Ivoire as a clue to changing the meaning of belonging, work, and spirituality. Insofar as family/kinship means bringing new beings into the world and finding a place for them, it incarnates the untimely. How can work be conceptualized in relation to creativity rather than in relation to the circulation of increasingly scarce goods? Not only African but also European migrants and the societies that are resisting their arrival could benefit from Liking's ideas.

In most of the world's countries, the work environment for artists and scholars has been utterly transformed by new technologies for generating and disseminating knowledge and creativity, at the same time as they have exposed the latter to new sorts of parasitism and exploitation. Access to such opportunities and pitfalls is also far from evenly distributed, from reasons ranging from lack of access to electricity or computing equipment to the culture of university teaching in different countries. The imaginary horizon and critical activity of philosophers, like others who are involved with creative production and education, are shaped by what anthropologist Florence Piron calls the world-system of knowledge in chapter 4, "The University, Cognitive Justice, and Human Development." The European university system, as she explains, prioritized forms of knowledge which were mutually supporting and supported the colonial and capitalist dominance of Europe. Despite decolonization, their assumptions and pedagogical strategies dominate African universities even today. Indeed, many graduates of African universities still travel to Europe and England for postgraduate training. Transmission of indigenous knowledge and research aimed at community development are discouraged in favor of research that extends a specific division of academic labor, wherein data from the South supports research financed, conceptualized, published, and exploited in the North. Here Piron is diagnosing a failed or lagging transition, a "nonevent" rather than a transition that is easy to pinpoint. She calls for a change in African practices of education, research, and dissemination as well as in the ways digital technology and education are monetized in the North, where students and teachers have vastly different conditions of access and support depending on their position in the academic hierarchy and their proximity to private or state funds.

The relationships between work and technology is also at the heart of Nick Nesbitt's chapter, "Specters of the Infinitesimal: Posthuman Francophone Worlds." Nesbitt reverses the standard Eurocentrism by which philosophical transitions in the diaspora are considered effects of what happens in French metropolitan thought. He assesses the conflict between existentialist humanism and structuralist antihumanism, roughly identified with French thought of the 1940s and 1960s, respectively, with respect to the continuity of Caribbean humanist philosophy, particularly the strain of social and economic thought which drove Aimé Césaire to first join and then, in 1957, break from the French Communist Party rather than betray. Nesbitt now returns to the essence of this Caribbean thought in light of the novel danger to humanity posed by "posthumanism," the rapidly decreasing importance of human labor of any kind in contemporary production processes. Posthumanism means an increasingly "superfluous" mass of humanity, located in the global South but also in significant pockets of the North, is consumed by the search for remunerative labor under ever more precarious conditions.

For Jean Godefroy Bidima, these are indeed questions of life and death. But Bidima is also cautious regarding the way that calls to arms in the name of "life or death" can impose their own deadly "blackmail," stultifying thought as well as diminishing the value of lives in the short term. In chapter 5, "Anthropocenes and New African Discourses: 'Dwelling in the World' with Poetry and Criticism," Bidima assesses the dangers of uncritical or reactionary thinking posed by philosophies of nature that are put forward as antidotes to the very real climate crisis which is affecting Africans. As during the Cold War, the rhetoric of urgency satisfies what Kant might call a "demand of Reason" for a stable, totalizing horizon against which different temporalities appear to be neutralized and reductive oppositions and identities can be tolerated, if not positively celebrated—with potentially dire consequences. In their dialogue with various philosophical antihumanisms, we should note that none of the philosophers in this collection presume to hold or to give any historical group the rights to a conclusive definition of the human; Bidima is concerned that we should avoid similarly reductive limits on Nature, even in the name of respecting or exalting the nonhuman. In lieu of divinizing Nature, or essentializing the human, Bidima urges us to develop a *conscience*.

For Séverine Kodjo-Grandvaux, one of the chief obstacles to an ethically robust ecological practice is the unthinking opposition between human and nonhuman nature which has spread worldwide in the wake of European colonial modernity. Just as Piron critiques positivist epistemology and the Humboldtian university model through which it is reproduced, Kodjo-Grandvaux's chapter "Rethinking the Living World in Light of African Philosophy: Toward an Animist Humanism" argues that many of the problems in contemporary philosophy of science, which have devastating technological effects, result from the historical tendency to associate intelligence, feeling, and communication only with the human being and a relatively small group of humans at that. The result of this opposition between humanism and naturalism is the degradation of humans as elements of nature. Cultures that can see a value worth protecting in nonhuman nature, she argues, are better prepared to grant more protections and more meaningful protections to human beings. The ontological and epistemological significance of feeling, which she identifies with some of Senghor's more notorious statements, takes on a new meaning in light of research into communication and sentience in the nonhuman biosphere and allows her to hope for a resurgence of humanism in an animist frame.

The perceived relationship between the human and the nonhuman is particularly important because one of the ways Africans in the diaspora were dehumanized was the attempted eradication of the intellectual anchors for their sense of personhood. In chapter 8, "From Muntu to Moun: An African Ethicalization of Caribbean Discourse," Hanétha Vété-Congolo carefully analyzes two texts by members of the eighteenth- and nineteenth-century enslaving class in the Caribbean. Put forward as exercises in translation between French, Creole, and the Congo language, the express purpose of these texts was to share techniques among French speakers for teaching newly enslaved Africans to think of themselves as less than human, as descended from the "inanimate," in their own native languages. Yet Vété-Congolo observes that this linguistic transition *failed* to take place, despite the myriad violent transformations of African lives on the shores of Martinique, Haiti, and Guadeloupe; for "mountu," the Congo word for "human," continues to live on as "moun" in contemporary Creole and would have provided those subject to bondage with a point for intellectual self-definition and resistance. This becoming-human of the supposedly inanimate through language has been and remains a becoming-ethical of language itself.

Chielozona Eze, finally, addresses the transition within African philosophy from a reading of past events and texts that focuses on racial and geopolitical conflict to one that focuses on the problems of intra-African injustice that not only made Africans vulnerable to colonization but more important, that render them vulnerable today. In "Nelson Mandela and the Topology of African Encounter with the World," Eze revisits Chinua Achebe's *Things Fall Apart* in order to attend more carefully to the moments when leaders made moral choices that sowed or enhanced divisions already present in traditional societies. While the focus on external conflict was morally and practically essential during decolonization and, in South Africa, the fight against apartheid, as a general principle Eze believes it must make way for forgiveness. He argues that the legacy of Mandela's handshake, stripped of the specifically Christian meanings with which Bishop Tutu surrounded it, is the best horizon against which to pose contemporary calls for the transformation of postapartheid South African society and injustices between Africans across the continent.

To say that we never inhabit just one temporality risks being a meaningless abstraction unless we imagine these temporalities are related through plurality and parallelism.[17] One can thus go further to propose that even when we confront a common topic/*topos*, none of us is ever from a single *place*. For some people, this is impossible to remember or even to discover, given the weight of mystification (often padded with comfort), while others find its pain viscerally impossible to forget or to ignore. No doubt, there are many structures and self-appointed authorities that profit from persuading us that we have no meaning outside of a single history and its organizing preoccupations—and all too often they have succeeded. Talk of intellectual trends, linear "modernity," or "development" are ways of trying to assign people to a temporality and better yet a specific time the way that racism and colonialism tried to assign them reductively to a (rejected) place. They resemble the contemptuous challenge that, as Vété-Congolo describes in her intricate topology/genealogy of modern Creole, was found in the translation manual of nineteenth-century enslaver Baudry des Loziéres: "What boat brought you?"

To say that even those of us whose families have been rooted for generations or millennia are not from a single place does not mean we fail to be situated in specific ways with respect to one another and with respect to one another's conflicts. Masculine, feminine, and other; younger and older; black African, Arab (including Arab African), Asian, and white; Christian and Muslim, animist and atheist are some of the names of those opposed *topoi* which participate in an unknown number of deeper transitions. Nor does such a claim mean any of us are from *everywhere*, as Descartes encouraged his European readers to believe their subjectivity was or ought to be universal *a priori*; nor that any of us has a right to make the world into a place where they would always be "at ease," in María Lugones's words, *never* feeling like a stranger or being called into question.[18] It means that despite these real and painful oppositions, we have a right to hope that our social location will *also* mean something else, as Foucault says, in the test of a future reflection.[19]

In an article from 2019, Jean Godefroy Bidima considers a reading of the art object as a witness to the aspects of history that escape the temporal expectations, attention span, or speed of the present.[20] But perhaps, he continues, witnessing is too irenic a stance. Thus, he goes on to argue for the superiority of a reading in which the art object is the site of the *crisis* in which those differing or conflicting time scales are revealed in the first place. "The crisis expressed by the art object," he explains, "permits regimes of historicity to be evaluated." In this collection, Boni, Nesbitt, Abadie, and Eze all appeal to literature as the art form in which a crisis between the expectations and forms of urgency characterizing the anticolonial and immediate postcolonial era and others now beginning to reveal themselves can be discerned. Likewise, the performing arts practiced by Werewere Liking and described in chapter 3 force us to rethink the relations that were once expected to obtain between work, belonging, and a publicly visible creative process that is neither entirely individual nor even entirely human, but which young people must have the right to join. Even Mandela's handshake is an artistic gesture in this sense, inviting invention. Crisis marks the moment when what is *new* is the subjectivity confronting these seemingly disparate temporalities, whose costs and stakes seem tallied in advance. It is situated, and constructive, and *conscient*.

Most of the essays in this book were written during the COVID-19 pandemic of 2020, an event whose duration, speeds, and geography have not yet been settled in the historical record and which manifestly transcends both human and nonhuman nature. Although every country on earth was touched by this catastrophe, which has both political and ecological causes, the brunt of suffering has and (as of writing) continues to be borne by people of African and Asian heritage. Their ideas about what makes us human—recontextualizing the old ways that humanisms and antihumanisms were once opposed—could still blossom in the pause, such as it is, that COVID-19 introduced in the global economy.

Traces of the pandemic are visible in the kinds of texts this book lacks, as well as those it includes. The loss of access to books, colleagues, conferences, and for some, sources of income, as well as anxiety regarding family relationships and the duty to care for those who were stranded alone, sick, or dying during this exceptional period have made many people aware of how different people's academic worlds look to one another even in a given country. They have forced those of us whose libraries remained open and who had the ability to afford home computers and printers to reflect more frequently on how difficult negotiating the university and its associated public spheres are for those excluded in ordinary times. In fact, and unfortunately, the broad outlines of the pre-pandemic world have barely changed in most places. What these outlines mean, however, has been stretched by violent accelerations and decelerations, contractions of supply and demand—in the time of a breath, which many were no longer able to take. This book is dedicated to Florence Piron, who escaped the virus but could not outrun her own body, and to the work of epistemic justice which she so fervently hoped to disseminate using today's technology in its most liberatory way.

NOTES

1. In response to, and with sincere thanks for, this phrasing of the problem by Jean Godefroy Bidima.

2. In *Time and Free Will,* Bergson famously denounced the act of confusing lived temporality—plural or multiple—with the spatial designations with which we communicate that experience. And yet *topoi* are unavoidable elements of reflection. See Henri Bergson, *Time and Free Will: An Essay on the Immediate Data of Consciousness,* trans. F. L. Pogson (Mineola, NY: Dover Publications, 2001), 226–231.

3. Achille Mbembe calls for such attention to the *longue durée* in *On the Postcolony* (Berkeley: University of California Press, 2001), 7–9.

4. Olúfẹ́mi Táíwò, *How Colonialism Pre-empted Modernity in Africa* (Bloomington: Indiana University Press, 2010).

5. For one early argument of this kind, see Kwasi Wiredu, "How Not to Compare African Traditional Thought with Western Thought (1976)," in *The Anniversary Issue: Selections from Transition, 1961–1976, Transition* 75/76 (1997), 320–327.

6. V. Y. Mudimbe, *The Invention of Africa: Gnosis, Philosophy, and the Order of Knowledge* (Bloomington: Indiana University Press, 1988), chapter 4; Françoise Lionnet and Shu-mei Shih, eds. *The Creolization of Theory* (Durham and London: Duke University Press, 2011), 19.

7. For an overview, see the articles collected in *Coloniality at Large: Latin America and the Postcolonial Debate*, ed. Mabel Moraña, Enrique D. Dussel, and Carlos A. Jáuregui (Durham: Duke University Press, 2008); Boaventura de Sousa Santos, *The End of the Cognitive Empire: The Coming Age of Epistemologies of the South* (Durham: Duke University Press, 2018).

8. Emnet Tadesse Woldegiorgis, "The Influence of the Bologna Process," in *Regionalization of African Higher Education*, ed. Jane Knight and Emnet Tadesse Woldegiorgis (Cham, Switzerland: Springer, 2017), 189–207.

9. https://cercaphi.org; https://isapss.com

10. Aretha Phiri, "Introduction: Re-reading the Canon, Re-reading Africa," in *African Philosophical and Literary Possibilities,* ed. Aretha Phiri (Lanham, MD and London: Lexington Books, 2020), xi–xix.

11. Achille Mbembe and Felwine Sarr, eds. *Écrire l'Afrique-Monde, Les Ateliers de la pensée* (Dakar: Philippe Rey/Jimsaan, 2016).

12. Ngũgĩ wa Thiong'o, *Decolonizing the Mind* (London: James Currey, 1986).

13. Mohammed Abed Al-Jabri, *The Formation of Arab Reason: Text, Tradition and the Construction of Modernity in the Arab World*, trans. Centre for Arab Unity Studies (London and New York: I.B. Tauris, 2011); Souleymane Bachir Diagne, "Precolonial Philosophy in Arabic," *A Companion to African Philosophy,* ed. Kwasi Wiredu (Malden, MA and Oxford: Blackwell, 2006), 66–77.

14. Edwin Etieyibo and Jonathan O. Chimakonam, "The State of African Philosophy in Africa," in *Method, Substance, and the Future of African Philosophy*, ed. Edwin Etieyibo (Cham, Switzerland: Palgrave MacMillan/Springer, 2018), 71–90; on SOHA (Sciences Ouvertes en Haïti et Afrique Francophone), see Florence Piron, *Justice cognitive, libre accès et savoirs locaux: Pour une science ouverte juste, au service du développement local durable,* ed. Florence Piron, Samuel Regulus, and Marie Sophie Dibounje Madiba (Quebec: Éditions sciences et bien commun, 2016), section V.

15. Perhaps this is why Senghor believed the universal was something to be constructed rather than presupposed (conceptually) or found (empirically). See, for example, Léopold Sédar Senghor, "Négritude et Civilisation de l'Universel," *Présence Africaine*, Nouvelle série 46 (2e trimestre 1963), 8–13. For a discussion of Césaire's views on the universal, see Jean Godefroy Bidima, "La traversée des mondes," *Esprit* 466 (July/Aug 2020), 79–91.

16. Nkiru Uwechia Nzegwu, *Family Matters: Feminist Concepts in African Philosophy of Culture* (Buffalo: SUNY Press, 2006).

17. For example, see Bado Ndoye, "Réenchanter le monde: Husserl en postcolonie," in *Écrire l'Afrique-Monde, Les Ateliers de la pensée,* ed. Achille Mbembe and Felwine Sarr (Dakar: Philippe Rey/Jimsaan, 2016), 364.

18. María Lugones, "Playfulness, World-Traveling, and Loving Perception," in *Pilgrimages/Peregrinajes: Theorizing Coalition Against Multiple Oppressions* (Lanham, MD: Rowman & Littlefield, 2003), 90–93.

19. Michel Foucault, *The Order of Things: An Archeology of the Human Sciences,* trans. Alan Sheridan (New York: Random House, 1970), 339.

20. Jean Godefroy Bidima, "Création, imagination, et sens esthétique," in *Philosophiques* 46, no. 2 (Fall 2019), 335.

BIBLIOGRAPHY

Al-Jabri, Mohammed Abed. *The Formation of Arab Reason: Text, Tradition and the Construction of Modernity in the Arab World.* Translated by the Centre for Arab Unity Studies (London and New York: I.B. Tauris, 2011).

Bergson, Henri. *Time and Free Will: An Essay on the Immediate Data of Consciousness* Translated by F. L. Pogson (Mineola, NY: Dover Publications, 2001).

Bidima, Jean Godefroy. "Création, imagination, et sens esthétique." *Philosophiques* 46, no. 2 (Fall 2019): 327–338.

———. "La traversée des mondes." *Esprit* 466 (July/Aug 2020): 79–91.

de Sousa Santos, Boaventura. *The End of the Cognitive Empire: The Coming Age of Epistemologies of the South* (Durham: Duke University Press, 2018).

Diagne, Souleymane Bachir. "Precolonial Philosophy in Arabic." In *A Companion to African Philosophy.* Edited by Kwasi Wiredu (Malden, MA and Oxford: Blackwell, 2006): 66–77.

Etieyibo, Edwin, and Jonathan O. Chimakonam. "The State of African Philosophy in Africa." In *Method, Substance, and the Future of African Philosophy.* Edited by Edwin Etieyibo (Cham, Switzerland: Palgrave MacMillan/Springer, 2018): 71–90.

Foucault, Michel. *The Order of Things: An Archeology of the Human Sciences.* Translated by Alan Sheridan (New York: Random House, 1970).

Lionnet, Françoise, and Shu-mei Shih, eds. *The Creolization of Theory* (Durham and London: Duke University Press, 2011).

Lugones, María. "Playfulness, World-Traveling, and Loving Perception." In *Pilgrimages/Peregrinajes: Theorizing Coalition Against Multiple Oppressions* (Lanham. MD: Rowman & Littlefield, 2003): 77–100.

Mbembe, Achille. *On the Postcolony* (Berkeley: University of California Press, 2001).

——— and Felwine Sarr, eds. *Écrire l'Afrique-Monde, Les Ateliers de la pensée* (Dakar: Philippe Rey/Jimsaan, 2016).

Moraña, Mabel, Enrique D. Dussel, and Carlos A. Jáuregui, eds., *Coloniality at Large: Latin America and the Postcolonial Debate* (Durham: Duke University Press, 2008).

Mudimbe, V. Y. *The Invention of Africa: Gnosis, Philosophy, and the Order of Knowledge* (Bloomington: Indiana University Press, 1988).

Ndoye, Bado. "Réenchanter le monde: Husserl en postcolonie." In *Écrire l'Afrique-Monde, Les Ateliers de la pensée.* Edited by Achille Mbembe and Felwine Sarr (Dakar: Philippe Rey/Jimsaan, 2016): 355–368.

Nzegwu, Nkiru Uwechia. *Family Matters: Feminist Concepts in African Philosophy of Culture* (Buffalo: SUNY Press, 2006).

Phiri, Aretha. "Introduction: Re-reading the Canon, Re-reading Africa." In *African Philosophical and Literary Possibilities.* Edited by Aretha Phiri (Lanham, MD and London: Lexington Books, 2020).

Piron, Florence. *Justice cognitive, libre accès et savoirs locaux: Pour une science ouverte juste, au service du développement local durable.* Edited by Florence Piron, Samuel Regulus, and Marie Sophie Dibounje Madiba (Quebec: Éditions sciences et bien commun, 2016).

Senghor, Léopold Sédar. "Négritude et Civilisation de l'Universel." *Présence Africaine*, Nouvelle série 46 (2e trimestre 1963): 8–13.

Táíwò, Olúfẹ́mi. *How Colonialism Pre-empted Modernity in Africa* (Bloomington: Indiana University Press, 2010).

wa Thiong'o, Ngũgĩ. *Decolonizing the Mind* (London: James Currey, 1986).

Wiredu, Kwasi. "How Not to Compare African Traditional Thought with Western Thought (1976)." In *The Anniversary Issue: Selections from Transition, 1961–1976. Transition* 75/76 (1997): 320–327.

Woldegiorgis, Emnet Tadesse. "The Influence of the Bologna Process." In *Regionalization of African Higher Education.* Edited by Jane Knight and Emnet Tadesse Woldegiorgis (Cham, Switzerland: Springer, 2017).

Chapter 1

What Does Being in the World Mean?

*Thinking Life and Domestic Bonds
in Twenty-First-Century Africa*

Tanella Boni

THINKING THE FAMILY MEANS
THINKING LIFE ITSELF

What types of bonds do individuals weave with one another to create a "world"? The word "individual" is not a given. If the word has a long history in the West, confirmed by and starting with the existence of the Cartesian cogito,[1] in West Africa, being an "individual" seems to mean taking on an "imported" attitude that would not fit well with local realities. The form of life to which it leads, individualism, would be synonymous with self-absorption. In some African countries, for example, in Côte d'Ivoire, the place of the group and above all the family is thought to be unquestionable. After all, the group is what raises, socializes, protects, and gives roots. Now, the consequences of policies that conflict with local realities, as well as the effects of economic and cultural globalization hitting African societies with full force, show how far social mutations that overturn the organization of familial bonds such as kinship, parenthood, and filiation can go. Conjugal and extraconjugal bonds are the first to be transformed. Henceforth, money is all powerful and counts as much if not more than love or attachment. While people in families help one another and protect one another against all sorts of sanitary, social, educational, or environmental insecurity, the constraints weighing on them become more and more numerous as soon as they must be adapted to transformations in lifestyle. Amid the vast web of familial relations, one wonders if noncommercial principles exist anymore and what place they occupy? Here I am talking about the extended family, the one whose members are too numerous to know, since kinship ties can be lost in the mists of time. They may never have existed because the word "family" is polysemous. It can refer to the idea of proximity or socializing for many years.

But let us come back to the idea of "family" as "ties" of kinship.

The family is not just any collectivity or group of individuals. One might imagine the family as a painting, a work of art, a valuable object, on which we find represented bonds that are often intangible, because they are living. It may be that the strongest or most intense of these bonds remains invisible in the artistic process. Unfinished or anchored in the shadows of chiaroscuro, they elude the eye. Houses, places of habitation for living characters each of whom plays his or her proper role, are visible on the canvas. However, there is reason to fear that some characters are mistaken for simple scenery. Most of the time, these are women who, wounded in the familial setting, must fight to find their place before they can even begin to fight other social and political battles. But for whose gaze is this painting composed, this perpetually unfinished work that recomposes or decomposes itself according to the circumstances? Does it come from within the family or from the outside world? Although many forms of brotherhood and sisterhood are functioning to keep the family alive, this shifting world has a rather hierarchical order. The principles of seniority and gerontocracy rest on inequalities that give meaning to familial and social lives. But then, what allows individuals united by family ties to be solidary with each other and to resist the exhaustion of time, if not the quality of their reciprocal attachment to one another?

In fact, to think the family is to think life itself, with its tranquil moments, its upheavals, or its branching points. Whatever qualifications one may invoke or whatever concept one may apply to it, life is not a linear experience; to think life requires that one take many parameters into account. Nor is it presented to analysis as a destiny marked by a—purely biological[2]—finitude, one beginning with the individual's birth and ending with his or her death. I start from the hypothesis that the lives and deaths in a family are multiple and varied. They are multiple and varied depending on the places where we live, the languages we speak, our status in society, the communities to which we belong, the political regime that governs us, culture, history, religion, and so on. In matters involving women, the lives and deaths are even more complex.

The family and domestic bonds are objects which are somewhat left to the side by a certain kind of philosophy taught in African universities, where they seem overshadowed by the study of the state and political regimes. In taking these objects as my interest, my question cannot be reduced, as Engels thought in his time, to a question about the family's origin.[3] I am talking about the family's transformations and the challenges it must overcome to remain alive. For there are sometimes real surprises hidden in this familial community, which one believes is autonomous because it is supposed to be self-sufficient. Sometimes the conditions of its formation are constrained or forced, that is, undesired. Even when a union is wished for, the freedom of the individuals involved may be limited by the sudden appearance of an exterior gaze. Then too, conflict between different types of laws—juridical, customary, social, and moral—renders conjugal relations and filial ties more fragile.[4] Finally, as the decades pass, commercial values are imposed as the unavoidable measure of the solidity of family bonds.

For these reasons, the domestic world is an object that is very difficult to apprehend. On the one hand, we have living beings: women and men, children and adults. On the other hand, we have laws: things that are intangible, fictive, abstract, principles whose goal is to present each person's place, to indicate his or her rights but also to determine his or her duties, in a word to establish the rules of communal life.[5] The complexity of such an object requires one to be situated at the crossroads of several disciplines.

The first pitfall I come up against is the fact that my academic specialty is not "African philosophy." We know that this expression deserves to be rethought with new freshness after having been the object of long debates during the 1970s and 1980s.[6] Maybe I never had the leisure to sequester myself within a specialty.[7] Now, if one is not already inscribed in the schema of university teaching divisions—a schema inherited from the French system in francophone Africa[8]—one can probably see some new paths open up, with their risks and perils; one reaches toward new horizons, even if these have already been breached and swept clear by others.[9] Therefore, I give myself the freedom to situate my remarks in the margin of academic philosophical research.

THE SITE OF MY SPEAKING

Now, while the question of the family brings us back to a house, a country, or a whole world that dwells in me and in which I dwell, the act of thinking just this tiny zone of Africa's immensity and contrasts would mean being confronted with a whole series of difficulties.[10] It is as if I found myself at the foot of a wall, behind a territorial border that I am trying to cross. The difficulties become even worse when one is a woman. However, although I am conscious of the vulnerability that comes from the "double alterity" of being a woman and an African, I give myself the right to take some distance with respect to my "négritude" and my "womanhood," since the task that weighs on me is not so much to deconstruct the presuppositions of a dominant or hegemonic form of thought as to propose some pathways in light of the common humanity we have yet to build. But isn't taking some distance actually the best stance if I want to see my familial and social condition more clearly, better understand my history, or observe the cartography of my surroundings?

Soumaya Mestiri spoke about "the idea of a border feminism" ["un feminisme à la frontière"].[11] I will go further and say that, so far as I am concerned, I am still looking for the proper word. It's a whole style of thought that finds itself "on the border," there where I learn to think between the partitions, between the disciplines. My horizon of expectation is a reciprocal dialogue with the world's vast territory.

For the moment, given that they are relegated to the margins of everything that seems to be making the world by turning around itself, Africa and its forms of knowledge are "decolonializing" in a confrontation with the West. Now, what does it mean to make a world these days? We are all contributing to the world's construction, whatever our histories, our geographies, and our more or less violent relationships with the dominating parts of this world, which usually take themselves not for the center of the world but for its totality.[12] How to soothe or bandage our memories once they have been wounded by so much historical violence? And what, today, are our proper resources, our capacities, those making our confrontation with the tests of life possible? Under the weight of unforeseen events, life can divide and take an improbable direction.

In fact, what interests me is the question of the resilience of individual lives that are worthy of being lived.[13] This is yet one more reason to continue thinking about local experiences and connecting them up with each other. Perhaps it is the most secure anchoring point from which to dialogue with women and men who forget our existence. In speaking of anchoring, I am obliged to use Simone Weil's term "rootedness" [*enracinement*], a concept she said could only be defined with difficulty.[14] Whatever we are, we carry it with us everywhere we go. Now what we are, even before we are conscious of the role played by our states, is our "houses" and our familial bonds. But all the same, let us not forget the question of the political powers that lie behind them.

Thus, the world on which I turn my gaze, in which families dwell, is the world of Africa in the twenty-first century—transforming itself endlessly, composing and recomposing itself from every point of view. This world lives on the border between the local and the global. If thinking Africa means questioning the realities in which individuals are born, are raised, work and die, it also means considering each person's capacity to realize him or herself and to give meaning to communal life from within a private space, the house, in parallel with the social and political forms of collective life. Meanwhile, can we use the word "domestic" for every familial bond? As the first step of our reflection, let's begin with the "couple" and see if the word is or is not suited to our realities. What is a couple, therefore, which can be transformed at a given moment into parents or abandon this role when it breaks down over the course of time? Since maternity seems to be a life ideal in many women's eyes, it can be assumed that there are mothers who carry children to term despite risks and dangers. To be sure, fathers exist. Now the question of fathers, particularly in the domain of children's upbringing, seems to be a real problem. In fact, the education of children falls to women most of the time in polygamous households. Each woman takes care of her own children. Sometimes she lives alone with them, the father living elsewhere.

OF THE COUPLE'S VIABILITY

There is a widespread idea, repeated endlessly, to the effect that *individuals* in most African countries live from day to day because their living conditions are so difficult. Certainly, like all humans, they are capable of forming projects, including the project of a communal life which could perhaps be called a "couple," but this is hardly for certain. When one observes women, men, and children everywhere in the streets and in dwelling spaces, one may wonder if they are "individuals" given the looming weight of the "family" that watches over everything. From ancestors whose presence is interiorized everywhere one goes, to living persons who have the right to look in on the life of those near and far to whom they are connected, we find a real spider's web in which one can easily get lost. The gaze of others weighs on everyone's lives and creates moral and social pressure. For this reason, the will to be an autonomous individual is a long-term project at which not everyone will succeed and which is not always understood by one's immediate circle. It can lead to the rupture of some familial bonds. Paradoxically, however, it is one of the *conditions* for weaving elective and thus, conjugal bonds. But this is not the only thing. The very word "individual" can be misunderstood. Just as the word "family" is easily accepted and utilized, so too the word "individual" remains uncomprehended.[15] Yet how can a couple be formed if there are no individuals present? Of course, there are human persons, which complicate the situation even further. However, I would like to point out that being in a coupled relationship does not immediately mean having a marital bond.

In fact, in the French of Côte d'Ivoire, the word "individual" has a pejorative connotation. Because to treat someone as "a kind of individual"—note the paradox of the expression—is to show that we are not entirely sure about him, that we find him bizarre or even dangerous. The individual is the recalcitrant one, the upstart of whom one is mistrustful. One does not spontaneously think that an "individual" might be a free, organized body, or a consciousness, a free spirit and will. An individual who can be an autonomous subject is characterized by completeness and indivisibility. However, the mistrust that is manifest with respect to "individuals" is doubtless a legacy of the colonial period when the French colonists used certain words to address Africans whose names they had forgotten, or which they did not feel like pronouncing.[16] Do today's children and adults imagine that being an individual is an indispensable condition for the formation of a couple? But even if a couple is formed by accident or under constraint, it results from the encounter and relationship with an individual other than oneself and aims to make a communal life possible. Let us pause for an instant to consider this idea of "communal life" and, in the company of some ancient thinkers, make a detour through the history of academic philosophy.

For example, we find the idea of communal life expressed by Plato, in Book 5 of the *Republic*, when the character of Socrates and his interlocutors discuss the possibility of a community of women and of children. In the ideal City that Plato proposes, there would be no private goods. Individualism would be fought against. However, here it is not truly a question of the "family," nor of the "couple," since the best among the women—in intelligence and all sorts of qualities—will have to be brought up just like the best among the men. The lives of these men and these women are planned out in great detail. The legislator foresees everything and watches over the acts and gestures of each individual who has been called to live in service to the City and raised with an eye to this service. These men and women will be useful to the City for a certain time: the time it takes to bring children into the world. These children will be desirable and satisfying: the handicapped ones will be kept out in one way or another. The women live together and eat their meal in common. Here, Plato is not thinking about the life of the couple because the true family is the City where children, raised by nurses at the City's expense, will live as brothers and sisters without knowing who their biological fathers and mothers are. These children are raised by many fathers and mothers, because the law authorizes them to do so. Here, the state plays its proper role as planner and general overseer while substituting itself for the no longer existent family.

The "community of women and children" thus strikes me as being at the opposite pole from any communal life which might resemble the "couple's life" whose possibility we were trying to bring to light while keeping African realities in mind. Meanwhile, Plato's *Symposium* [*Le Banquet*] shows us that we are on the right track. There we encounter a story and are touched by something beyond time and space. What if the couple was a question of love from the start, a fleeting but omnipresent affective bond in which lack or longing [*manque*] are expressed? A question of fundamental desire which, by definition, remains insatiable? The being cut from its other half spends its life trying to recover it. Let us therefore remember that the myth of the androgyne told by Plato in the *Symposium* is, without a doubt, concerned with the first truth of the couple. All the same, can the primordial lack on which the idea of the couple is based account for the idea of the family?

THE MARGINS OF THE COUPLE

Even before we move on to the complex world of the family, the possibility of forming a "couple" remains a genuine question. We wonder if it is the right word to designate an experience of communal life, whether ephemeral or lasting. In the word "couple," I am deliberately evoking the idea of two who tend toward being one, "comme-un," by who knows what operation, mysterious or rational. And does one then *naturally* form a couple? Or is it by *convention*? Must the law, whatever it may be, intervene in the formation of this terribly singular relationship that resembles no other? And why would it come from outside to rule over the life of two free wills?

It is difficult to describe the path followed by an amorous relationship which ends by being transformed into a familial bond or in disintegrating for want of sufficient intensity to remain alive. Often it is born outside constraints and lives outside norms. It may constitute the starting point for a descent into the hell of lovers who live henceforth under the sword of a nameless insecurity. From this point of view, literary texts do the greatest justice to the complexity of this kind of relationship, in which our gaze on the world in which we live is transformed.

Thus in *l'Anté-Peuple*, Sony Labou Tansi stages the life of "citizen Dadou," a civil servant with no history who falls in love with a student he believes is a mere child.[17] From the first moment when he takes her in his car, everything happens as if he were living an endless nightmare. On the one hand, he is a married man, comfortably settled in his apparently peaceful conjugal life. According to the law, in fact, he lives in a couple with his wife. Perhaps he balked at routine, this kind of time that turns endlessly and in which nothing new happens. Very quickly, his house becomes a place of house arrest under the watchful eye of Lola, his wife. He wants to protect himself, at all cost, from making a mistake that will lead him to certain disaster. As the novelist shows, Dadou wants to be a "virtuous" man; he aims at excellence in his actions and therefore conducts himself according to goodness and justice. In reality, the moral law that he has interiorized reveals the limit he must not transgress, the boundary between good and evil.

Dadou is therefore a lucid man, someone who sees clearly. This is precisely why he wants to flee the evil that he sees looming on the horizon or rather right next to him every time that the one whom he calls the "child" looks at him. The world surrounding him has become "ugly." Only the child and her senseless words and her intoxicating body, which he refuses to touch, raise themselves above the generalized ugliness. Desire is born and grows from both sides, but for Dadou, the exterior injunctions that take the form of the moral law and the social law are very strong. Desire will remain unquenched. It will become longing. The bond which takes up residence between them will finish tragically with the child's suicide. The spouse will also die, after leaving a packet of letters for her husband. Dadou, scrambled by the dissolution of the marital and extramarital bonds that made his life meaningful, falls into alcohol. A second woman, the "child's" cousin, who is old enough to be more reassuring, but whom he does not really love, leads him little by little to get a grip on himself. However, something in him is broken. He has lost his job and his social status. How is he going to save his masculine dignity? He will become politically committed by joining the underground or rather the forest where some rebels are living. The family dismantled and Dadou morally and physically destroyed, it is a different character who is reborn, resilient, in a different world. Even if he gets himself taken for a "madman," the form of lucidity he acquired after the failure of his amorous and familial experiences is different. *L'Anté-peuple* is one of these novels that do not really tell a story but which rather present some truths regarding the uncertain times in which we live.

THE FAMILY'S COMPLEXITY

The family I am talking about is obviously not the little unit consisting of a mother, father, and child. It is a matter of the household where servants also work to assist the family. For example, in the middle or affluent classes, don't housemaids and gardeners or drivers also participate in family life? The catch is that their place is usually found on the sidelines. There is also the extended family who come to visit, quite large, and commonly referred to with the term "parents." Thus, the family refers to the complexity of life in a dwelling place, where moods are provoked and exchanged between people even when they are incompatible, and where silences or secrets are as numerous and voluble as words. It may happen that people do not really talk with each other because the communication is invisible. Now to talk with one another, does not this mean giving bonds, whatever they are, an opportunity to resist time and unexpected events? At the same time, we must consider the living spaces that multiply along with the alliances and the nature of conjugal, extramarital, or nameless bonds. Sometimes the members of a single family never meet one another, because they live in partitioned worlds, separated by heavy secrets. But let us start by seeing what the first welcoming space of the family, the house, consists of.

There is no doubt that one of Aristotle's texts, Book I of the *Politics*, refers to the banality of everyday life that cuts across cultures and ages. By banality of everyday life, I mean the time during which one has the impression that nothing new is happening and that everything, without respite, is down to earth. However, this is one of the rare times that the life of woman and man is evoked in a philosophical text as the inaugural moment of something more important: the City. But one notices that the first bonds to be woven rest on unequal relationships. The head of the family is the man fit for exercising all the powers that come to him not by "right" but from "nature," since the latter "never does anything in vain."

What interests the philosopher here is thus the genesis of the City which he conceives as a finished community. Now the first step shows the place of the family in this City, which is also the place of domestic economy. Although this text begins by demonstrating the existence of a "man" and a "woman," the philosopher also mentions the slave and the ox. The slave will work when no "ox" can be found or at the same time as the animal. We are introduced to the ominous idea that, among the "Barbarians," there might be no differ-ence between the woman and the slave.[18] When it is a question of producing the means of subsistence, it is the slave's work that produces it; he is the one whose body is naturally made to obey. The family is administered by a head: husband, father, and master. These three forms of authority correspond to three types of dissimilar domestic bonds. Man and woman are naturally united—since nature does things so well—for the sake of procreation. One wonders if there is any "attachment" or bond whatsoever. The family is thought as a domestic organization to bring about equilibrium in economic life.

In this "unfinished" community where every member is found in his or her place, there is but one head who exercises his power differently depending on the nature of the individual with whom he is dealing. Although man and woman come together for the sake of procreation, they are never comparable to a single body or a single soul. They are always two examples of individual-ity, one of whom (the man) dominates the other (the woman). We know how many times since that distant epoch that this schema of marital life has been imposed on the Western world and still governs its imaginaries. Aristotle seeks the stability of familial life and he conceives rules for it that take the family's dwelling place into account. The life of the couple as desire or one person's attachment to another is nowhere to be found. The philosopher gives us no room for dreams when he insists on the idea of marital authority and identifies the place of the conjugal relationship: the house where production must aim at subsistence rather than the accumulation of wealth.

With this we recognize, as Simone de Beauvoir noted at the start of *Le Deuxième Sexe*, that Aristotle belongs on the long list of philosophers who justify masculine domination—at the same time that he justifies slavery.[19] This domination is a concept that needs to be rethought today.

In fact, leaving Aristotle's world and returning to the realities that surround me, I wonder in what sense "masculine domination" is or is not all powerful. I try to see its weaknesses, its limits, where exactly the problem lies. We find some paths for reflection in a now-classic literary text. Ahmadou Kourouma's novel *Les Soleils des Indépendances* makes reference to Côte d'Ivoire at the start of the 1960s, but its truth, with some qualifications, is still valid in the twenty-first century.

The novelist tells the story of a "sovereign" husband, deprived of his social and political sovereignty but under the illusion that he governs his household. However, things seem to escape him. He believed his couple is well established, but something eludes the eye: his wife bears no children. Seemingly by chance, the sovereign is called Fama, as if the idea of sovereignty and grandeur were inscribed in a name belonging to him alone rather than referring to his clan name—Doumbouya—and to his home region—the Horodougou. To be a "sovereign" is part of his identity, while his wife Salimata is "purity" and "integrity" incarnate, as her own given name, which is moreover a popular name in the context being described, would also indicate. Meanwhile, between Fama the great man and Salimata the ordinary woman, communal life is not what we might imagine. Despite the drama that subtends their shared history and the twenty odd years they have lived together, it is as if the dynamics of the couple had not disappeared. For example, in the middle of the night, the "sovereign" husband delivers "donkey kicks" to his wife and Salimata, enraged, gives her husband a "spanking." Thereby, she behaves like a mother with respect to an unruly child while continuing her own reflections on her life as a woman, as if nothing had happened. They are still capable of playing together, they know one another as well as "the little carp and the crocodile living in the same ditch."[20] The conjugal bond holds up against economic, social, and even political problems. The man and the woman evolve together in the interval between a past which no longer exists anywhere but memories and a future nowhere to be found. In this uncertain universe, there is no great man—here a dethroned prince—without an ordinary woman endowed with a great soul on whom he can count, even if the political decline which strikes him under the "suns of independence" is a small thing compared to the dishonor that he must endure socially after his failure to beget. In fact, even if her husband does not want to know about it, Salimata knows that she is not the one who is sterile; the problem is Fama, who has lost the vigor of youth.

However, the ordinary woman Salimata has not come to the end of her difficulties. Given the circumstances and above all due to the weight of appearances and customary rules, Fama will become a bigamist. Although he thinks of Salimata continually, he will go back to his home village to find a second wife, Mariame. Henceforth, Salimata will learn to divide up the "nights" with her co-wife, a young widow, beautiful and seductive. The idea of "sharing nights," widespread in the social strata where polygamy is practiced, consists in anticipating a timeslot for each wife. The husband shares the bed of each of his wives according to this schedule. In reality, the schedule is not just about the sharing of beds. The day's household work, particularly the cooking, is divided according to the same principle. This work does not aim at material wealth. No one pays for it even if women may expect some generosity from their husbands. It is part of the chores that must be done and the time that must be given to taking care of others, in order to find one's own place, not in a couple but nevertheless in a web of complex relationships called family.

THE FAMILY'S METAMORPHOSES

In rereading *Les Soleils des Indépendances*, I see clearly that most of the evils described by Kourouma have not disappeared. The character Salimata endured an excision, a rape, and two early marriages before she escaped all that with the man of her dreams, the man who became her "sovereign" husband, and with whom she wanted to live and to have children. While excision remains a struggle for the associations of feminist activists, rape also continues to break many women's lives, for example, in armed conflict zones, as presented in the testimony gathered by Etelle Higonnet and the report she edited on the rapes in Côte d'Ivoire during the 2000s[21] (Higonnet 2007). As for early and forced marriages, they are more common than ever. The figures are alarming:

> In 2014, the number of women married before the age of 18 is estimated at 700 million, and more than one in three of them did so before turning 15. The majority of early marriages take place in developing countries. West Africa is the region of the world with the highest prevalence. Among the ten countries reporting the highest rates of early marriage, half are situated in this region. Niger and Mali are the most affected, with respectively 77% and 61% of marriages falling into this category.[22] (Aïssa Diarra, *Le Monde*, November 29, 2018)

One wonders for what reason girls who have barely reached puberty have to be married against their will even if they have gone to school. Under social pressure, they leave school to take care of a family where, most of the time, they are not a "first wife." It is a matter of ancestral practices that endure despite written laws. An article that appeared in the newspaper *Le Monde* relates:

> Fatimetou, a Mauritanian, was 13 years old. Married to an "*old man*"—the most widespread scenario—whose bed her mother forced her to share, she ran away repeatedly. Her family returned her to her husband. She sleeps in the street, and sticks to her studies despite everything. Today she waits for a judge to give her a divorce. Fatimetou is one of the 35% of girls married before the age of 18 and

the 15% married before 15 in Mauritania, where this practice is nonetheless banned.[23] (*Le Monde*, November 26, 2015)

These practices rest on a certain number of fears and religious beliefs, including deculturation by the school where children acquire values, languages, and forms of knowledge that are not those of their original culture. The low level of parental education and their precarious standard of living bring them to imagine solutions that endanger the lives of their children and particularly their daughters. Another frequently mentioned fear is that of sexual freedom. Thus, parents who want to be foresighted marry their daughter to prevent her from creating "bastards," children born outside marriage, and a source of supreme dishonor and shame for a self-respecting family. From this point of view, "bastardy" does not question the absence of fathers as much as their moral weakness or their powerlessness to play the proper role. Because fathers who are held by no legal obligation or social or moral law disappear. Many young single mothers raise their children alone, with the assistance of their own families, in the absence of biological fathers who, sometimes, burst into the life of their children only to disappear more thoroughly. This does not permit the formation of those reciprocal bonds of kinship and filiation on which an attachment would be based.[24]

It is obvious that these are the children who, at a moment when social mutations are picking up speed, suffer the dramatic consequences of prejudice or the constraints of another world to which their parents remain attached. The latter want to find solutions to their problems of everyday survival and they hope that the adult or the "old man" who will take over their daughter's life represents a favorable opportunity. On this subject, UNICEF mentions that "certain families give their daughters in marriage to lighten the economic burden that weighs on them or to draw a benefit from it. Others believe that marriage is a way to assure their daughters' future and to protect them."[25]

However, in the middle or wealthier classes, other preoccupations are at work. Polygamy may not mean what we expect it to mean: a matrimonial regime in which the man shares his life with two or more spouses in broad daylight and with everyone's knowledge. It so happens that in certain countries—like Côte d'Ivoire—this regime is forbidden by law. But, in recalling that they came from families in which traditional polygamy was the norm, men unconsciously reproduce forms of life that were believed to be quickly dying off. They organize what I call parallel lives or families. By parallel life I mean one that an individual creates in the margin of his official life, which obeys the rules established by the civil code. In this way, a man can live with several women at one time even if they do not all have the same social status. He is legally married to one woman. With the others, he gives himself the right to have children and therefore to found other families. These families avoid meeting and living together. As Ahmadou Kourouma says, "One does not gather birds when one fears the noise of wings."[26]

For the foundation on which the formation of parallel families rests is the secret. Such a man must be sufficiently skillful and deceitful to construct waterproof partitions between different families. But under such circumstances, this skill, which requires the intelligent manipulation of multiple fictions, is transformed into sneakiness or into hypocrisy, since the same character has to be capable of wearing this or that mask according to the occasion if he is to play his proper role as the faithful, reliable man with integrity. Paulina Chiziane's very beautiful novel *Le Parlement Conjugal* portrays the discovery of such a secret with great humor[27] (Chiziane 2006). Once the secret has gotten out, the fragile networks which supported familial bonds stretch, initially in the first family. Then each of the families bursts apart or decomposes. Hatreds are brought out into the open because each family member finds him or herself affected, profoundly hurt by the betrayal. Inheritances become impossible to manage because most of the time, no formal wills exist. Even if they existed, this would neither facilitate a communal life among the inheritors nor solid bonds between half-brothers and half-sisters. The power of Chiziane's novel comes from its ability to step back slightly from this sad reality and imagine the wives of a single man assembled in Parliament to tell the story of his bad behavior in his presence.

However, despite the wickedness that can take arise in polygamous families formed according to customary laws or founded on juridical principles in the countries where this matrimonial regime is accepted, one wonders if the old forms of polygamy, which rested on other types of considerations and preoccupations (including the view of women and children as a labor force), were not more just and respectful of the humanity of women and children. Certainly, the relations between father and mothers, between children but also between children and parents, were difficult to live with. At the same time, one could imagine a minimum of clarity and trust between the members of this kind of pyramidal family composed of a father, several mothers, and many children.

In the old forms of polygamy, a woman knows what to expect. She knows that her husband, referring to a religion or a customary practice, will take one or more women as his wives. In some countries, such as Senegal, the matrimonial regime (monogamy or polygamy) is chosen from the outset, at the time of a first marriage. However, can we know if this choice is respected? And if it is not respected, are there any penalties? In Côte d'Ivoire, this choice is not possible. The law advocates the regime of monogamy, but many examples involve unofficial practices of polygamy.

Now today, what seems to be missing is trust, which resembles the precious clay that permits solid familial bonds to be constructed. Trust is what breaks down in the case of hidden *postcolonial* polygamies, these parallel or disorderly lives that are never acknowledged as such. However, the construction of parallel lives that rest on secrets and the capacity for fabrication are not the prerogative of men. In this domain, women are not poor victims. We have yet to explore this form of inventiveness at the heart of the couple's decline and the breakdown of families.

A CONCLUDING WORD

To deepen the ideas of "making a couple" and "founding a family" means to consider new forms of inventiveness at the heart of African societies undergoing mutation. My thoughts here are incomplete. We must still think through the question of endangered childhood: these children who have no other houses than the streets or those who, for one or another reason, become adults before their time. Because to question the new familial bonds, those which are not based on traditional values such as one's word of honor, trust, or family solidarity, is also to think about "cut-off/put-off" [*coupé-decalé*] lifestyles and the growing influence of the internet and social networks.[28] Meanwhile, a fundamental question remains: How are we going to live in the world if we relativize the meaning of life?

Translated by Laura Hengehold

NOTES

    1. But already with Aristotle, the individual is the organized and indivisible living being from a biological point of view. See Aristote, *La Politique* (Paris: Vrin, 1995).
    2. As we know, this idea of "finitude" sometimes comes up in literary texts. I am thinking of the start of Ahmadou Kourouma's novel, *Les Soleils des Indépendances* (Paris: Seuil, 1970), where the novelist says, "Koné Ibrahima was finite/finished" (*fini*), literally transposing the Malinké word "bana" (finished) which means here, "is dead."
    3. Friedrich Engels, *L'origine de la famille, de la propriété privée et de l'Etat* (Montreuil: Le Temps des Cerises, 2015 [1884]).
    4. The written law, a tradition inherited from colonization, often comes into conflict with customary laws that have not disappeared. Moreover, there usually seems to be a gap between universal principles and local practices.
    5. Even if, as Simone Weil says, "It makes no sense to say that men have rights on the one hand and duties on the other." Simone Weil, *L'enracinement* (Paris: Gallimard, 1949), 6.
    6. See, among others, Niamkey-Koffi, *Controverses sur la philosophie africaine* (Paris: Harmattan, 2018).

7. In fact, this leisure does not exist when one is constantly tormented by the necessities of life and confronted with short time spans in which we are led to do ever more, and therefore a thousand things, all at the same time. This makes the activity of thinking uncomfortable. One might recall the idea defended by Aristotle to the effect that in every inquiry there are two possible paths: that of specialization—the technical knowledge of the thing itself—and the other, more global, of culture (Aristote, *Parties des Animaux* I, 1, 639a).

8. The drama is that African universities are always playing catch-up when the French system evolves.

9. It seems to me, in fact, that the task incumbent on every philosopher is to think by oneself, to organize one's fields of inquiry as one wants, to choose the paradigms, the concepts, and the objects to be thought. But to think by oneself is not to play the "lone ranger" as Descartes hoped. Peers and teachers are present, even if one does not name them. Philosophical thought being, if I can say, an affair of friendship that is cultivated, a friendship (philia) for which one must take care.

10. I often use the metaphor of the wall because the issue of migration is one that I try to imagine. To be "at the foot of a wall" means to be confronted with a difficulty which does not depend on us. This is a difficulty that affects our ability to think. We must therefore make an effort to overcome, just as a migrant stuck at the border of two countries must find a strategy to continue on his way.

11. Soumaya Mestiri, *Décoloniser le féminisme: une approche transculturelle* (Paris: Vrin, 2016).

12. In reality, this "world" is not order and beauty, the "cosmos" that the Greek philosophers imagine. It may be chaotic and marked by violence in all its forms, as we observe today.

13. How to overcome the traumas that break our lives, which diminish our capacities, our physical and intellectual abilities? How can one adapt to violence and to war, to events of extreme urgency in today's Africa? Beginning with private, domestic lives, in which women must fight to remain standing from every point of view.

14.   Rootedness is perhaps the most important and the most misrecognized need of the human soul. It is one of the most difficult to define. A human being has a root by virtue of his or her real, active, and natural participation in the existence of a collectivity which preserves certain treasures of the past and certain premonitions of the future in living form. Natural participation, that means to be led automatically by place, birth, profession, social environment. Each human being needs to receive almost everything about his or her moral, intellectual, and spiritual life through the mediation of the environments in which he or she naturally participates. (Weil, *L'enracinement*, 36)

15. *Ma famille*, television series (Côte d'Ivoire) produced and directed by Akissi Delta.

16. There are many such words.

17. Sony Labou Tansi (1947–1995), Congolese playwright, novelist, and poet. With his novel *L'Anté-Peuple* (Paris: Seuil, 1983), he won the Grand prix littéraire d'Afrique noire.

18. The Barbarians'—non-Greeks who speak like birds—language and customs make the difference in such a context.

19. Simone de Beauvoir, *Le Deuxième Sexe* (Paris: Gallimard, 1949).

20. Kourouma, *Les Soleils des Indépendances*, 92.

21. Etelle Higonnet, *Mon cœur est coupé. Violences sexuelles commises par les forces rebelles et progouvernementales en Côte d'Ivoire* (New York: Human Rights Watch, 2007).

22. Aïssa Diarra, *Le Monde*, 29 November 2018.

23. *Le Monde* of 26 November 2015.

24. According to the sociologist Serge Paugam, there exist four types of social bonds which include the bond of filiation. There also exist four types of regimes of attachment including the familialist regime which is regulated by the bond of filiation. Serge Paugam, *Le lien social* (Paris: PUF-Que sais-je? 2018).

25. UNICEF website: https://www.unicef.org/.

26. Kourouma, *Les Soleils des Indépendances*, 153.

27. Paulina Chiziane, *Le Parlement conjugal, Une histoire de polygamie* (Arles: Actes Sud, 2006).

28. The *coupé-décalé* was originally a popular musical style. Today, the word also designates cheating or betrayal that one did not expect from someone that one believed was honest.

BIBLIOGRAPHY

Aristote. *La Politique* (Paris: Vrin, 1995).

———. *Parties des Animaux* I, trans. and ed, Pierre Louis (Paris: Collection des Universités de France, Editions Les Belles Lettres, Paris (première édition 1957; édition utilisée 2002)).

Beauvoir, Simone de. *Le Deuxième Sexe* (Paris: Gallimard, 1949).

Boni, Tanella. "L'Amour dans *l'Anté-Peuple* de Sony Labou Tansi," in D. G. Lezou and P. Nda, eds., *Sony Labou Tansi témoin de son temps* (Limoges: Pulim, 2003): 199–212.

———. "Autour de Salimata: Violences et insécurité dans *Les Soleils des Indépendances* d'Ahmadou Kourouma," in Patrick Voisin, ed., *Ahmadou Kourouma: entre poétique romanesque et littérature politique* (Paris: Classiques Garnier, 2015): 111–135.

Chiziane, Paulina. *Le Parlement Conjugal, Une histoire de polygamie* (Arles: Actes Sud, 2006).

Diarra, Aïssa. *Le Monde*, 29 November 2018.

Engels, Friedrich. *L'origine de la famille, de la propriété privée et de l'Etat* (Montreuil: Le Temps des Cerises, 2015 [1884]).

Higonnet, Etelle. *Mon cœur est coupé. Violences sexuelles commises par les forces rebelles et progouvernementales en Côte d'Ivoire* (New York: Human Rights Watch, 2007).

Kourouma, Ahmadou. *Les Soleils des Indépendances* (Paris: Seuil, 1970).

Labou Tansi, Sony. *L'Anté-Peuple* (Paris: Seuil, 1983).

Niamkey-Koffi. *Controverses sur la philosophie africaine* (Paris: Harmattan, 2018).

Paugam, Serge. *Le lien social* (Paris: PUF-Que sais-je? 2018).

Platon. *Le Banquet* (Paris: GF-Flammarion, 2007).

———. *La République* (Paris: GF Flammarion, 2016).

Weil, Simone. *L'enracinement* (Paris: Gallimard, 1949).

Chapter 2

Probing Gender Injustices in Africa

Delphine Abadie

Although equality of the sexes became a central dimension for institutional transformations on the continent during the past few decades, feminism continues despite everything to be perceived by many African women and men as an imported idea, foreign to their cultural environment and to their historical experience. A vast body of social scientific research exists on African women, but it only rarely touches on the question of injustices specific to gender. On the African continent, as elsewhere in countries of the global South, the notion of "gender" was actually introduced by development sciences, following the theoretical presuppositions of analyses elaborated from the historical condition of women in the West. African women had been quickly identified by outsiders as objects and as sites for discursive elaboration, therefore, even before they had really conceptualized their position as subjects and actors in social relations between the sexes within their own societies.[1]

During these recent decades, a new generation of philosophers has contested the invisibility of problematics raised by the singularity of female existence in the discipline of philosophy at large. In the African context, mistrust vis-à-vis the traditional problematics of feminism also affected the philosophical project of working out a critical interrogation of gender. The very tiny presence of women in African philosophy has also, unquestionably, inhibited the development of African feminist philosophy. Moreover, the theoretical enterprise of some African intellectuals who do take the problematic of gender seriously seems confined to the negative task of deconstructing the conceptual presuppositions and the epistemic imperialism stamped on it by Western feminist thought. While not uninteresting in terms of the negative analysis they provide, these contributions are not necessarily very useful in offering prospective alternatives for the future of practical feminist struggles and for the development of endogenous models for female emancipation.

35

The starting point for most of these approaches consists in recognizing the profound transformations introduced by colonization in terms of the gendered division of labor. The contemporary use of the Western feminist paradigm, they continue—its concepts, its theories, and its presuppositions—allows this racist domination to be perpetuated and reinforced. The future of African women's liberation, therefore, would come from reactivating egalitarian precolonial social relations and from radically rethinking the epistemic utility of certain feminist notions in African contexts. Can we truly claim without further investigation, like Western feminist thought, that social relations are universally organized around biological sexual difference? That the male body is the normative marker in every society in the world, the one in relation to which the attributes of the female are defined, in the mode of a lack or of a difference? Put otherwise, are "gender" or "patriarchy" ethnocentric constructions that must be relativized? What are the stakes for an endogenous feminist theory purged of such distorting assumptions?

Developed by Oyèrónkẹ́ Oyěwùmí, the thesis of the "invention of gender" has gone beyond the field of research on African women since it was taken up by the Argentine philosopher María Lugones to elaborate her notion of the "coloniality of gender." In beginning with some of the most representative arguments of this current of critical thought on women in Africa as well as their refutations, the following pages attempt to clear a methodological and theoretical horizon for the future of philosophical research on gender injustices in Africa.

The first section, "The Invention of Gender," will review Oyěwùmí's main arguments for why, in analyzing the relations of power within African societies, the principle of gender should be abandoned in favor of the principle of seniority. The second section, "Reincarnating Gender," will formulate an initial critique, by pointing out inconsistencies into which one may fall when undertaking the analysis of gender identity in terms of ideal normative criteria, regardless of the way in which these are—or are not—put to work in real situations. The third section, "Coloniality, Postcolonial Power, and Gender Identity," is interested in the way that beliefs, customs, and traditions on which collective identity is founded are themselves shaped from within by power. This argument undermines the relevance of the culturalist response that takes a negationist stance toward gender. Finally, the last section of this text, "Embracing the Complexity," will propose methodological paths and sketch a two-level theoretical frame capable of faithfully doing justice to the lived experience of contemporary African women and of correctly interpreting injustices endured specifically by women in postcolonial Africa.

THE INVENTION OF GENDER

In her widely discussed work, *The Invention of Women: Making an African Sense of Western Gender Discourses* (1997), the Nigerian American author Oyèrónké Oyěwùmí defends the argument that, in the African context, starting an analysis of women's oppression with the prism of "gender" is a form of epistemic and scholarly domination to which we are subjected by the appeal of feminist studies from the North.[2] For this reason, feminist thought must be rejected for Africa. Aside from the marks of biology, there would never have existed a common criterion (interests, desires, social positions, etc.) capable of characterizing a given group as "women" prior to colonization. Different logics, namely, seniority, continue even today to rule over intersubjectivity and the assignment of familial, social, political, or juridical phenomena. The distorting reading of social phenomena that results from adopting dominant feminist philosophy's grid of intelligibility condemns every theoretical project bearing on the institution of the family, conjugal experience, or examples of African community life to epistemic extraversion.

According to Oyěwùmí, Western feminist theories as a whole assume the existence of the *nuclear family* as the primordial social institution.[3] The nuclear family household consists of a single family, articulated around a patriarchal man, his wife (a devoted and subordinate spouse), and their children. Supposed to coincide with biological sex, gender is the principal organizing factor in the bourgeois nuclear family. In prescribing moral and social roles, the institution of the nuclear family produces a gendered division of labor: the man, provider of the household's material needs, is involved with economic production and with maintaining civic life; as for woman, she is responsible for raising children, domestic tasks, *care* work—in short, the whole economy of reproduction. Gender is therefore essential not only for the family's smooth functioning but also for that of society: the private sphere, socially static, for women and public life, social mobility, and power for men. Now, this familial configuration is historically and spatially determined.

> Despite the fact that feminism has gone global, it is the Western nuclear family that provides the grounding for much of feminist theory. Thus the three central concepts that have been the mainstay of feminism: woman, gender, and sisterhood, are only intelligible with careful attention to the nuclear family from which they emerged.[4]

In Africa, the promotion of the nuclear family, the emergence of a category of women identifiable by anatomy, and their subordination to men resulted from the colonial state's policies. Under colonial administration, women saw their rights to inherit land withdrawn. They were excluded from leadership roles and confined to tasks associated with care and reproduction. In fact, historical research shows that in many precolonial contexts, women occupied roles of the first rank, particularly where agriculture was practiced. With the introduction of the monetized economy and the rationalization of farming practices, women were relegated to the unpaid domestic labor of keeping up gardens for home consumption, while men, under white patronage, were given the necessary training to become members of a paid workforce. In places where women had possessed certain kinds of political power, whether in virtue of their age, social status, or economic clout, it was henceforth lost. The colonial administrators also denied women's roles in some of their own institutions, such as initiatory societies, merchant associations, and village councils. While policies concerning gender varied from one colonizing power to the next and were not always coherent, they all reflected the same distrust for women's potential initiatives.[5]

Despite this, emphasizes Oyěwùmí, postcolonial Africa remains attached to traditional models of alliance, including the family lineage. Here, "lineage" means a group of individuals forming a clan in which they mutually recognize one another as descendants of a common ancestor. In countries where memory is transmitted orally, lineage can go back into the past as far as the ninth or tenth generation, connecting a considerable number of relatives dispersed across multiple branches. Moreover, biological filiation is not a necessary condition for membership in a lineage: its numbers expand over the course of generations by integrating the descendants of people close to the family, social partners, and adopted or fostered children, all of whom are treated as complete members of the family.[6]

Running contrary to African sociological realities, flawed analyses may occur when African women's and men's lives are translated into concepts from Western feminist thought that reinforce models of reasoning in terms of sexual binarism. Oyěwùmí gives the example of marriage practices and linguistic usage in the Oyo-Yoruba region to illustrate her claim that the African family is a non-gendered institution. Thus, the substantive *obinrin*, poorly translated into English as "woman," designates the individual whose anatomical attributes are those of the human biological female, what she calls the "anafemale"; in the same way, *okunrin* designates the "anamale" and not "man." The "child" (*omo*), the younger sibling (*aburo*), and the older sibling (*egbon*) are non-gendered categories. More fundamentally, the terms *oko* or *iyawo*, badly translated, respectively, as "husband" and "wife," designate "spouse" without gender distinction. Their difference appears not in terms of gender, but of lineage, *oko* being the individual who enters into the family lineage by marriage while the *iyawo* is someone who already belonged to it. While individuals from the said lineage already occupy a place and a social role determined by their birth order, the *iyawo*'s entry by marriage marks the year zero of his or her seniority in the lineage.[7]

In Africa and in lineage societies more broadly, seniority—and not gender—would be the principle that structures the organization of community and assigns attitudes, occupations, and identities. Seniority positions a subject within the structure of kinship that determines the social expectations regarding his or her identity, behavior, and responsibilities. In contrast with the gendered Western family, the privileges around which age-based examples of subordination are organized are never definitive. For those who are native to the group, chronological age difference marks the year zero of seniority, while the seniority of those who enter by matrimonial alliance follows that of all the children who are already members of the extended lineage. Thus, it follows that lineage is a web of complex relations within which seniority is always relative: "no one is permanently in a senior or junior position; it all depends on who is present in any given situation."[8] If an older sibling from family X marries Y, therefore, she becomes the younger sibling for the other members of her spouse's (Y's) lineage, but continues to receive honors linked to her right of seniority in X, her own birth family.

Now, Oyěwùmí tells us, in a society where the organizing principle of seniority precedes and supplants other social markers like gender, nothing prevents the existence of forms of social status authorizing female power. The Igbo and Yoruba queens and queen-mothers, the "male daughters" and "female husbands," the Amazons or the headwomen among the Flup of Casamance, the Mende and the Sherba of Sierra Leone or in the Ashanti kingdom would be examples of such status.[9] This means that in Africa, men and women maintain equivalent, complementary, interchangeable statuses and that no role is predetermined by the community expectations or the moral socialization of gender. Whether from the side of men or that of women, parallel gender-specific spheres, rituals, monarchical structures, and secret societies are deployed with complementarity, in such a way as to benefit the community as a whole.

REINCARNATING GENDER

The thesis of the invention of gender defended by Oyěwùmí is very popular in the diaspora and within globalized academic feminism. Meanwhile, it has become the object of important critiques in works enjoying less widespread diffusion. In "Yorubas Don't Do Gender: A Critical Review" (2004) and "Beyond Determinism" (2003), the Nigerian philosopher and editor Bibi Bakare-Yusuf distinguishes herself by the precision and originality of her refutation but also by the methodological precautions and the frame of analysis that she proposes (see section IV). According to her, the principle of seniority advanced by Oyěwùmí allows other interesting avenues to be opened up. At the same time, it rests on a simplistic and static conception of postcolonial power which supposes that a particular variable of oppression (seniority) can produce an action on the individual independent from a total situation and apart from other variables at work (such as gender), and this supposition leads to significant contradictions.

For example, it is always biological women, the anafemales, who are expected to move in with their spouse's lineage—thus far from their own lineage—and never the anamales. The anafemales are the one who enter into the lineage of their spouse, and in leaving their birth lineage to enter into the patrilineage of the husband's family, they lose, *in their everyday lives*, all the privileges associated with the years of seniority in their family of origin. One consequence of this is that the seniority of anafemale spouses is systematically compromised, since they become subordinates within their new lineage, which is always that of their (anamale) spouse.[10] As for traditionally matrilineal societies, while historical research tends to confirm that these were generally more egalitarian, the transmission of inheritance was still very rarely passed from mother to daughter, but rather from an uncle to a nephew who is his sister's son. "This did not give women [much] power apart from transmitting this power to the family's males."[11] Once again, behind seniority we would find gender.

Oyěwùmí's appeal to the non-gendered character of African languages is just as misleading, according to Bakare-Yusuf. In concentrating on the level of the symbols circulated by language, this appeal ignores the gap that exists between concepts, norms, discourses, and their uses (in all languages). Put otherwise, that language should be non-gendered tells us nothing about the ways in which gender difference manifests itself in social reality. Focusing our analysis on the sexual neutrality of status designations such as spouse, child, elder, younger person, and others prevents us from considering the social perception of the body which endows them with signification. These significations escape the formalism of language.

Even if a linguistic analysis might enable us to establish, for example, that *okunrin* and *obinrin* designate nothing more than an anatomical difference, still nothing would let us affirm that this has *always* been the case. To sustain such an argument, we would have to presuppose an original and primordial meaning to words, to which we would have access by some means, in scraping away the residue of their contemporary corruption. This kind of etymological stance could only function if one presumes that no discontinuity, no paradigmatic resignification should have disturbed the peaceful stability of meaning and language across time and culture. Bakare-Yusuf adds that any claim to seek a sort of anhistorical essence is particularly illusory in the case of Yoruba culture, which has been so heavily overlaid with a profusion of contradictory customary stories about origins.

One also finds this rivalry between the formalism of symbols and their social incarnation in the works of Ifi Amadiume, notably in her book *Male Daughters, Female Husbands* (1987). Amadiume defends the idea that sexual binarism in the African context is situated only on the normative level. The symbolic structure that supports social organization is based on a cosmogony of genders which is indeed dichotomous (man/woman), but this opposition of feminine and masculine principles is not necessarily attached to the anatomical body. The social value accorded to sexual binarism is not situated on the side of biological power but on that of its metaphysical significance.

For example, an (elder) daughter would frequently "take the place" of the eldest son in acquiring the father's property, land, and livestock, becoming thereby the head of a farming operation. Her status (*obi*) is translated in English by the phrase "male daughter." The *obi* then finds herself in a position to contract a "marriage" (*igba ohu*) with other women, thereby acquiring the title "female husband." Similarly, the cultural function linked to the adoration of Idemili, a central goddess of the Nnobi pantheon, is occupied by a woman, the *ekwe*, who exercises influence over "her wives." These polyandric unions are not formalizing a homosexual relationship in the strict sense: to heighten the *ekwe*'s prestige, her wives also get married either within or outside their patrilineage, raising the children that come from their marriage with a man or from occasional liaisons. Finally, the eldest of the female husbands, the *agba ekwe*, exercises a political function within the women's council, her word having authority over the other women of the village as a group. Put otherwise, the *ekwe* exercises the traditional authority of the male over other women.

Responsible for society's regeneration, the female principle is sacralized, which is why "mother is the preferred and cherished self-identity of many African women."[12] Bibi Bakare-Yusuf refers to the distinction established by Adrienne Rich (1979) between, on the one hand, maternity as domain of the possible for all women, in relation to their reproductive potential (the desire for maternity); and on the other hand, maternity as an institution that seeks to assure that men remain in control of this potential in each woman (the injunction to maternity). In connection with this second meaning, only a patriarchal conception of maternity can reduce the female social identity to her procreative functions.[13] It reaffirms the biologization of gender.

Thus, the schizophrenia between the level of symbols and women's real lived experiences conceals the fact that girls might previously have been socialized to desire marriage and child bearing as their chief life project, without being able to find them satisfying in their current forms. This kind of apolitical conception of maternity does not allow us to consider the specificity of certain injustices, for example, those linked to sterility, which are most often endured by women, even in the case where the male reproductive apparatus is the dysfunctional one. Put differently, we cannot valorize maternal identity without including an examination of the institutional schemas, social relations, regimes of power, and mechanisms of socialization by which women have a tendency to define their identity from the start as mothers, and the ways in which these arrangements ultimately support patriarchal social organization.

COLONIALITY, POSTCOLONIAL POWER, AND GENDER IDENTITY

The "gender-negationist" theses circulate widely in the research on transnational feminism. They provide a starting point for many works, including the majority of contributions to the important journal *JENdA: A Journal of Culture and African Women Studies*. The celebrated Argentine feminist philosopher María Lugones relies on Oyěwùmí's conclusions (and those of the indigenous essayist Paula Gunn-Allen) when working out her concept of the "coloniality of gender."[14] Her approach can also be found front and center in the feminist arguments of decolonial philosophers writing in French, particularly Soumaya Mestiri (2016) and Hourya Benthouami-Molino.[15]

Lugones adopts the notion of coloniality developed by the Peruvian sociologist Anibal Quijano (2000) in order to show how the specific oppression associated with gender helps us account for the invasive character of colonial violence in the postcolonial context.[16] Relying on Oyěwùmí's analyses with respect to the Yoruba, Lugones concludes that, despite being so foreign to precolonial cultures, the heterosexual and patriarchal organization of reproductive labor and the principle of sexual binarism underlying them expanded steadily until decolonization. This is why she speaks of the "coloniality of gender." "From then on," "to decolonize gender," Soumaya Mestiri tells us in her *Décoloniser le féminisme* (2016) "means to escape this double historico-theoretical compromise and to rehabilitate a strictly factual truth . . . that so-called primitive societies [*sic*] rested on equality."[17]

In the Yoruba and Nnobi contexts studied by Oyěwùmí and Amadiume, the claims inherent to gender such as it is understood by Western feminist theories appear to be particularly unsuited for decoding the complexity of African women's social realities. The authors are also right when they stress how relations between men and women were profoundly disorganized by colonial policies. In this respect, negationist theories do a splendid job at pointing to the poor fit and the oppressive character of these models developed by and for Western contexts.

However, customs and beliefs are not always vehicles of emancipation. Certain anthropologists have noted, for example, that among the Yoruba studied by Oyěwùmí, the rule of respect for seniority is constraining to such a point that it translates into genuflection before elders[18] (Iman et al., 2004 (1997)). Seniority also supports hierarchical social institutions. It is romanticizing to conclude that by contrast to modern behavior, customary practice rests on a principle of equality. In her contribution, "Challenging Subjects: Gender and Power in African Contexts" (2001), Amina Mama stresses the difficulties inherent in responding to the emancipatory aspirations of African women and men with a culturalist interpretation of identity (including gender identity). Appealing to the well-known conclusions of Benedict Anderson and, in Africa, Valentin-Yves Mudimbe, she recalls that the characteristics said to be primordial, myths, and grandiose histories which are claimed by movements waving the flag of identity have in fact been constructed. Even when they are presented as the neutral data of anthropology, identities are always political before all else, and permeated by power, whether precolonial, postcolonial, or colonial.

In this respect, the rewriting of mythologies regarding gender has played a structuring role in African nation-building.[19] Citing Partha Chatterjee, Sanya Osha sets up a parallel between the mechanisms of different nationalisms.[20] Much as we find in Amadiume's theories, nation-building discourses constructed a universe of significations articulated around the binarisms of female/male and material/spiritual, allowing for the recovery of a cultural dignity violated by colonial repudiation. In this order, women, symbols of specific virtues, quasi-saints, and goddesses, elevate civilizational values and metaphysics in a restorative way: "protected . . . from the purely material pursuits of securing livelihood in the external world, women express in their appearance and behavior the spiritual qualities which are characteristics of civilized and refined society."[21] In the absence of this superior morality, the bodies of women in the lowest conditions remain sites for the display of brutal physical patriarchal violence.

In Zaire, it was in their role as mothers and wives that Mobutu Sese Seko very publicly promoted women's status for the sake of national unity: "Reasserting the subjugation of women appealed to the ordinary men who might have felt emasculated by their own experience of Mobutu-style patriarchy."[22] In Zimbabwe, Robert Mugabe defended the civil rights of women and lauded their role in the war of liberation, only to quickly change his mind. Beginning in the 1990s, the courts systematically refused to recognize their right to inheritance or to property, invariably appealing to an incompatibility with customary laws.[23] "For many of us in Africa today, [to describe tradition and African cultures as necessarily humanist and communitarian] is too simplistic, too homogenizing and too romantic a vision. Political elites have too

often brandished the argument of 'African culture and tradition' to counter
women's interests."[24]

Chielozona Eze stresses that in these theories of the invention of gender,
emancipation is thought on the basis of an oversimplification of history and
social relations, in which a past, necessarily glorious, is recuperated for the
future of decolonial liberation.[25] In the process, Western imperialism alone is
held responsible for contemporary misogynist deviations. In this linear three-
stage sequence, no space is left for an analysis of endogenous conceptions
of social relations between the sexes, past and present, that have diminished
women.

Jean Godefroy Bidima holds a similar position in "Womanism et autoréflexion."[26] The emancipatory thought formulated by the negationist authors expels
domination and heterogeneity from group identity so as to protect a certain idea
of unity, including sexual non-binarism, non-dominating forms of gender, and
the simultaneous liberation of black women and men. Implicit in this imagery,
once again we find the idea that without external disturbances, social relations
in Africa would be exempt from conflicts, with nonantagonistic individualities
blossoming to form a whole. This homogeneous perspective on "us" leads to
the adoption of an ideological conception of the other, in which any perceived
division could only have been introduced from outside: by colonists, capitalism, slavery, neocolonialism, other ethnicities, and so on. Liberation therefore
requires the eviction of the foreign enemy. To accomplish this, the variable of
space-time is methodologically invalidated, and both women and Africanity
are essentialized, projected into a changeless, metaphysical space.

EMBRACING THE COMPLEXITY

The consequences of rejecting gender, feminist tools and their explanatory power in the African context are not simply theoretical. According to
feminist activists, these proposals lead to disruptive effects on the ground.
In her essay, "We are all feminists," taken from her resoundingly successful
TEDx presentation, Chimamanda Ngozi Adichie recounts a story in which
a Nigerian professor tries to correct her by reminding her that feminism and
its vocabulary are imported notions.[27] Although African feminists have long
performed their own appropriative work and rigorous reinterpretations of
Western feminism, nevertheless many people report examples of white colleagues subtly reminding them that the notion of patriarchy is imported and
that African women must therefore be vigilant with regard to these notions
that are "foreign" to the continent's cultural landscape. Lacking concepts
with which to identify the problems, the struggle against patriarchal exclusion
is deprived of necessary tools for political action.

Nevertheless, forms of Western epistemic domination do obviously exist when it comes to the question of gender in Africa. In fact, a critical apparatus for endogenous feminism would have to be able to take account of many levels when analyzing injustices involving gender, micropolitical and macropolitical, and the way in which these levels interfere and interact with one another. The specific injustices that African women live with seem to be situated at the crossroads of influences that are both local (political instrumentalization of women's issues, the pressure of custom, and patriarchy—traditional as well as modern) and foreign (maternalism of Northern feminists, racism, neocolonialism, etc.).

From a methodological point of view, Pinkie Mekgwe remarks quite rightly that fictional literature is a much more fertile ground than African philosophy to support our understanding of the diverse sources of injustice affecting women.[28] In "Old Wives' Tales and Philosophical Delusions," Louise Du Toit puts forward the idea that female African intellectuals who wished to affirm their singular experience and their strategies of resistance to patriarchy might have even preferred this genre to philosophy.[29] In the margins of the institutional discipline of philosophy, taking up literary speech allowed them to put forward the specificity of their experience as women and to escape the totalizing grip of the conventional philosophical quest for an overarching—masculine—universal. "I would . . . encourage a philosophical engagement with this tradition in order to make philosophically relevant and fruitful the insights emerging from it, in order that the silence and absence of African women in and from philosophy may be addressed."[30]

For her part, Bibi Bakare-Yusuf proposes that we adopt an intersectional analytic framework capable of recognizing the *plurality* of sources of domination, whether gender, race, caste, religion, class, sexual orientation, geography, and so on; the interrelation between these variable identities; and their practical effects, which are differentiated according to the context.[31] Concretely, if one can easily accept that seniority may be the dominant form of power somewhere, it is highly improbable that it is the *only* such form. To the contrary, each variable acquires its specific value as a function of the social relationship within which it is deployed and other variables with which it interacts. Concretely, the borders between different vectors of power such as gender and seniority are not airtight and each situation gathers together its own arrangement of small and greater modalities of oppression in a complex web of significations. Only a bottom-up approach, which begins from the complex phenomenological experience of lived injustices and then moves back toward theory, permits us to philosophize about gender as it is incarnated in the *real lives* of African women.

In *Nervous Conditions* (2004), for example, Tsitsi Dangarembga presents an intricate story which establishes a female resistance to masculine privilege, whether traditional or modern, and to the right of seniority with which it is interwoven.[32] Written in the first person, this breathtaking novel retraces the destiny of a determined girl, Tambu, born in a traditional rural milieu. The book opens with this sentence: "I was not sorry when my brother died" because in fact the death of her elder brother Nhamo allows her to realize her own dream of returning to the primary school from which she had been withdrawn.

Encouraged and cared for by her uncle (her father's elder brother) Babamukuru, a man shaped by the modern education he received in England and endowed with important responsibilities in a school run by white missionaries, Tambu dedicates herself to study body and soul. She is bound by friendship with her cousin Nyasha who, back in the country after having been raised in England, is visibly wasting away from an anorexia brought about by the heartrending gap between her hopes for personal emancipation and the authority of patriarchal values upheld by her father. At the end of the novel, although she has just been accepted on scholarship at the country's best school, Tambu's destiny is hanging by a thread, since the family patriarch looks on this advancement with a sour eye. The following excerpt explains the ways in which the intersection of gender and seniority creates a particular experience of oppression:

> "It is not a question of money," he assured me. "Although there would still be a lot of expense on my part, you have your scholarship, so the major financial burden would be lifted. But I feel that even that little money could be better used. For one thing, there is now the small boy at home [still a baby]. [. . .] As you know, he is the only boy in your family, so he must be provided for. As for you [. . .] by the time you have finished your Form Four you will be [. . .] in a position to be married by a decent man and set up a decent home. [. . .] I have observed from my own daughter's behaviour that it is not a good thing for a young girl to associate too much with these white people, to have too much freedom. I have seen that girls who do that do not develop into decent women."[33]

Having lost any idealizations about the precolonial past, the heuristic tool of coloniality permits us to acknowledge, in the figure of Tambu, the detail of iniquities that African women endure at the intersection of gender and race, at the heart of the capitalist world-system. The concept of coloniality claimed by the Latin American decolonial school draws its assumptions from dependency theorists (Samir Amin, Andre Gunder Frank, Immanuel Wallerstein, and others). Since the 1960s, these authors took an interest in the mechanisms by which postcolonial economies remain dependent on foreign financial sources, notably through the instrument of debt. The well-known structural adjustment programs implanted during the 1980s not only provoked a generalized pauperization in Africa but also its feminization.

For example, thanks to the dismantling of public services, women find themselves supporting a growing labor burden, taking on work that they would not previously have done because they no longer have the means to pay for services: the privatization of the distribution of drinkable water means they have to draw water from lakes, many times a day; likewise with the chopping of wood, which replaces the electricity necessary for cooking food. Health and education services being the first affected, women are also the first to be taken out of school; they are less frequently vaccinated, less cared for, give birth in unsafe sanitary conditions; infantile and maternal mortality rates exploded; and so on. Finally, women are more vulnerable on the job market, given their weak access to means of production, such as land and credit.[34]

Paradoxically, the approaches to development oriented by gender have yet to become a priority both for bilateral donors and for multilateral agencies like the IMF and the World Bank: faced with the failure of the initial Women in Development strategy, donor agencies such as Women and Development, and then Gender and Development, outfitted themselves with feminist pretentions over the course of the 1990s. These approaches dilute the feminist question with policies aiming at the transformation of gender relations but in a way that has no real connection to the priorities historically defended by endogenous movements (Lewis 2008) such as the struggle against sexual violence, educational access, family codes reform, inheritance rights, and so on.[35]

The discourses of international feminist solidarity have often reduced the suffering of African women to the oppression exercised by their culture or by men. If these are certainly important problem areas, it is less clear, for example, that the struggle against sexual mutilation, the legalization of abortion, or the recognition of the rights of sexual minorities should be the *priority* of sub-Saharan African women. "The incredible racket organized by feminists, under the pretext of a self-proclaimed solidarity with African women who had to be liberated from the 'barbarism' of their societal practices has created backlashes and led to aftereffects. . . . Definitely, excision must be eradicated along with all other demeaning practices. The women of Africa . . . would have simply liked this solidarity to be more effective on other crucial questions."[36]

In her article, "Why feminist autonomy right now?", Patricia McFadden denounces the diversion of local feminist claims that occurs when development professionals monopolize the question of women.[37] In their role as mediators of the postcolonial State, these experts adopt the ideological frameworks presented as beneficial to the interests of women, although in fact they are serving neoliberal policies that are generally detrimental to such interests. The professionalization of feminism within NGOs and development consulting agencies cannibalizes the grassroots women's movement, sugarcoats the radicality of their struggles, and introduces epistemic distortions. As for the governing elites, they have very quickly understood how their interest is served by exploiting the international community's discourse about gender at the same time that they reaffirm conventional identities on the local level.[38]

A critical analysis of gender in Africa must be able to strip away the ruses of these ideological discourses and bring out the complex network of dominations specifically endured by women. From a methodological point of view, a philosophical discourse about gender in Africa will have no other choice than to draw its prime matter from the stories that women tell about themselves, whether in literature, in social sciences, or within local women's movements and feminist movements.

More research is required to understand the ways in which, over the course of African history and in extremely varied situations, some women acquired material and symbolic power while creating a strong position for themselves in their social organization and political institutions. Depending on the contexts, such knowledge will serve to nourish contemporary strategies of women's resistance.

From a theoretical point of view, to say that gender relations—in other words the social roles assigned according to biological sex—might have been more egalitarian before colonization is still not to say that the notion of gender itself is irrelevant for thinking about African societies of the twenty-first century. In the same way that postcolonial Africa has to come to terms with Africanist premises of an Africa invented by the archives of the colonial library (Mudimbe 1988), some components of gender precolonial representations are also necessarily distorted.[39] For this reason alone, the reactivation of a defeated and partly idealized past could not suffice to counteract in any lasting way the patriarchal privilege drawn from its colonial reorganization, which has been certainly maintained in postcolonial states. A philosophy of gender in Africa must therefore first and foremost get past the social and academic resistance to recognizing the specificity of injustices endured by today's women and borrow concepts which allow us to think about that specificity. In fact, the *tools* of feminism have already been the object of reappropriation by many African militants and other social sciences researchers.

Meanwhile, the political and epistemic domination of the West with respect to gender in Africa is genuine. Interwoven with the maternalist injunctions of Northern feminists and the development policies promoted by funding agencies, the coloniality of gender is equally central in the critical analysis of struggles and challenges which women must take up. A theory that is capable of tackling the complex web of influences that are both external and local, modern and traditional, must simultaneously avoid these two pitfalls: the idealization of customs and the Eurocentric condemnation of culture.

The real lives of African women deserve to be associated with philosophical elaboration.

Translated by Laura Hengehold

NOTES

1. Iman, Ayesha M., Amina Mama, and Fatou Sow, ed., *Sexe, genre et société: engendrer les sciences sociales africaines* (Paris et Dakar: Karthala et CODESRIA, 2004 [1997]); Maréma Touré, "La recherche sur le genre en Afrique : Quelques aspects épistémologiques et culturels." *CODESRIA* (1997): 105–26.
2. Oyèrónkẹ́ Oyěwùmí, *The Invention of Women. Making an African Sense of Western Gender Discourses* (Minneapolis: University of Minnesota Press, 1997).
3. Oyěwùmí, *The Invention of Women*; "Conceptualizing Gender: The Eurocentric Foundations of Feminist Concepts and the Challenge of African Epistemologies." *JENdA: A Journal of Culture and African Women Studies* 2, no. 1 (2002): 1–9.
4. Oyěwùmí, "Conceptualizing Gender," 2.
5. Catherine Coquery-Vidrovitch, *Les Africaines: histoire des femmes d'Afrique noire du XIXe au XXe siècle* (Paris: Éditions Desjonquères, 1994); Odile Georg, "Femmes africaines et politique: les colonisés au féminin en Afrique occidentale." *Clio* 6 (1997): 105–25.
6. Coquery-Vidrovitch, *Les Africaines*.
7. Oyěwùmí, *The Invention of Women*.
8. Oyěwùmí, *The Invention of Women*, 42.
9. Ifi Amadiume, *Male Daughters, Female Husbands: Gender and Sex in an African Society* (London: Zed Publications, 1987); Coquery-Vidrovitch, *Les Africaines*.
10. Bibi Bakare-Yusuf, "Yorubas Don't Do Gender," https://www.codesria.org/IMG/pdf/BAKERE_YUSUF.pdf (2004).
11. Catherine Coquery-Vidrovitch, "The Rise of Francophone African Social Science: From Colonial Knowledge to Knowledge of Africa," in *Out of One, Many Africas: Reconstructing the Study and Meaning of Africa*, ed. William G. Martin and Michael O. West (Urbana and Chicago: University of Illinois Press, 1999): 39–53.
12. Oyěwùmí, "Family Bonds/Conceptual Binds: African Notes on Feminist Epistemologies." *Signs* 25, no. 4 (2000): 1096.
13. Bibi Bakare-Yusuf, "Beyond Determinism: The Phenomenology of African Female Existence." *Feminist Africa* 2 (2003): 8–24; Adrienne Rich, "Disloyal to Civilization: Feminism, Racism and Gynephobia," in *On Lies, Secrets and Silence* (New York: W. W. Norton & Company, 1995 [1979]).
14. María Lugones. "The Coloniality of Gender," in *Globalization and the Decolonial Option*, ed. Walter Mignolo and Arturo Escobar (London: Routledge, 2010): 369–90.

15. Soumaya Mestiri, *Décoloniser le féminisme: une approche transculturelle* (Paris: Vrin, 2016); Hourya Bentouhami-Molino, *Race, culture, identités* (Paris: PUF (Philosophies), 2015).

16. Anibal Quijano, "Coloniality of Power and Eurocentrism in Latin America." *International Sociology* 15, no. 2 (2000): 215–23.

17. Mestiri, *Décoloniser le féminisme*, 97.

18. Iman, Ayesha M., Amina Mama, and Fatou Sow, ed., *Sexe, genre et société.*

19. Anne McClintock, "No Longer in a Future Heaven: Women and Nationalism in South Africa." *Transition* 51 (1995): 104–23; Marnia Lazreg, *The Eloquence of Silence: Algerian Women in Question* (London/New York: Routledge, 1994).

20. Sanya Osha, "Philosophy and Figures of the African Female." *Quest: An African Journal of Philosophy* 20, no. 1–2 (2006): 155–204.

21. Partha Chatterjee, *Nationalist Thought and the Colonial World: A Derivative Discourse?* (London: ZED Books LTD, 1986); cited in Osha, "Philosophy and Figures," 250.

22. Amina Mama, "Challenging Subjects: Gender and Power in African Contexts," Plenary Address, Nordic Africa Institute Conference: 'Beyond Identity: Rethinking Power in Africa', Uppsala, October 4-7th 2001, published in *African Sociological Review / Revue Africaine de Sociologie* 5, no. 2 (2001): 69.

23. Mama, "Challenging Subjects;" Patricia McFadden, "Why Feminist Autonomy Right Now?" *Women In Action* 2 (2004): 65–71.

24. Fatou Sow, "Introduction," in *Sexe, genre et société*, 40.

25. Chielozona Eze, "African Feminism: Resistance or Resentment?" *Quest: An African Journal of Philosophy* 20, no. 1–2 (2006): 97–118.

26. Jean Godefroy Bidima, "Womanism et autoréflexion. Mise en discours et expérience-vécue des féministes africaines." *Afrikanische Frauen und kulturelle Globalisierung / African Women and Cultural Globalization / Femmes africaines et globalisation culturelle*, Bayreuth: Rudiger Köppe Verlag, 8–10 (1998): 109–20.

27. Chimamanda Ngozi Adichie, *Nous sommes tous des féministes* (Paris: Folio:essai, 2014).

28. Pinkie Mekgwe, "Theorizing African Feminism(s): The Colonial Question." *Quest: An African Journal of Philosophy* 20, no. 1–2 (2006): 11–22.

29. Louise Du Toit, "Old Wives' Tales and Philosophical Delusions: On the 'Problem of Women' and African Philosophy." *South African Journal of Philosophy* 27, no. 4 (2008): 413–28.

30. Du Toit, "Old Wives' Tales and Philosophical Delusions," 112.

31. Bakare-Yusuf, "Yorubas Don't Do Gender;" "Beyond Determinism."

32. Tsitsi Dangarembga, *Nervous Conditions*, 2nd ed. (Banbury: Ayebia Clarke Publishing, 2004).

33. Dangarembga, *Nervous Conditions*, 183.

34. ATTAC. *Quand les femmes se heurtent à la mondialisation* (Paris: Mille et une nuits, 2003); Alternatives Sud, *Mouvements de femmes* (Bruxelles: Centre Tricontinental (CETRI); Syllepse, 2015), https://www.cetri.be/IMG/pdf/edr_mvts _femmes_pdf_final.pdf.

35. Desiree Lewis, "Discursive Challenges for African Feminisms." *Quest: An African Journal of Philosophy* 20 (2008): 77–96.
36. Marèma Touré, "La recherche sur le genre en Afrique: Quelques aspects épistémologiques et culturels," *CODESRIA* (1997), 9.
37. McFadden, "Why Feminist Autonomy Right Now?"
38. Mama, "Challenging Subjects."
39. V. Y. Mudimbe, *The Invention of Africa: Gnosis, Philosophy, and the Order of Knowledge.* (Bloomington: Indiana University Press, 1988).

BIBLIOGRAPHY

Adichie, Chimamanda Ngozi. *Nous sommes tous des féministes* (Paris: Folio:essai, 2014).
Alternatives Sud. *Mouvements de femmes* (Bruxelles: Centre Tricontinental (CETRI); Syllepse, 2015).
Amadiume, Ifi. *Male Daughters, Female Husbands: Gender and Sex in an African Society* (London: Zed Publications, 1987).
ATTAC. *Quand les femmes se heurtent à la mondialisation* (Paris: Mille et une nuits, 2003).
Bakare-Yusuf, Bibi. "Beyond Determinism: The Phenomenology of African Female Existence." *Feminist Africa* 2 (2003): 8–24.
———. "Yorubas Don't Do Gender: A Critical Review." https://www.codesria.org/ IMG/pdf/BAKERE_YUSUF.pdf (2004).
Bentouhami-Molino, Hourya. *Race, culture, identités* (Paris: PUF (Philosophies), 2015).
Bidima, Jean Godefroy. "Womanism et autoréflexion. Mise en discours et expérience-vécue des féministes africaines." *Afrikanische Frauen und kulturelle Globalisierung / African Women and Cultural Globalization / Femmes africaines et globalisation culturelle*, Bayreuth: Rudiger Köppe Verlag, 8–10 (1998): 109–20.
Chatterjee, Partha. *Nationalist Thought and the Colonial World: A Derivative Discourse?* (London: ZED Books LTD, 1986).
Coquery-Vidrovitch, Catherine. *Les Africaines: histoire des femmes d'Afrique noire du XIXe au XXe siècle* (Paris: Éditions Desjonquères, 1994).
———. "The Rise of Francophone African Social Science: From Colonial Knowledge to Knowledge of Africa," in *Out of One, Many Africas: Reconstructing the Study and Meaning of Africa*, ed. William G. Martin and Michael O. West (Urbana and Chicago: University of Illinois Press, 1999): 39–53.
Dangarembga, Tsitsi. *Nervous Conditions*, 2nd ed. (Banbury: Ayebia Clarke Publishing, 2004).
Du Toit, Louise. "Old Wives' Tales and Philosophical Delusions: On the 'Problem of Women' and African Philosophy." *South African Journal of Philosophy* 27, no. 4 (2008): 413–28.
Eze, Chielozona. "African Feminism: Resistance or Resentment?" *Quest: An African Journal of Philosophy* 20, no. 1–2 (2006): 97–118.

Georg, Odile. "Femmes africaines et politique: les colonisés au féminin en Afrique occidentale." *Clio* 6 (1997): 105–25.

Iman, Ayesha M., Amina Mama, and Fatou Sow, ed. *Sexe, genre et société: engendrer les sciences sociales africaines* (Paris et Dakar: Karthala et CODESRIA, 2004).

Lazreg, Marnia. *The Eloquence of Silence: Algerian Women in Question* (London/ New York: Routledge, 1994).

Lewis, Desiree. "Discursive Challenges for African Feminisms." *Quest: An African Journal of Philosophy* 20 (2008): 77–96.

Lugones, María. "The Coloniality of Gender." In *Globalization and the Decolonial Option*, ed. Walter Mignolo and Arturo Escobar (London: Routledge, 2010): 369–90.

Mama, Amina, "Challenging Subjects: Gender and Power in African Contexts." Plenary Address, Nordic Africa Institute Conference: 'Beyond Identity: Rethinking Power in Africa', Uppsala, October 4–7th 2001, published in *African Sociological Review / Revue Africaine de Sociologie* 5, no. 2 (2001): 63–73.

McClintock, Anne. "No Longer in a Future Heaven: Women and Nationalism in South Africa." *Transition* 51 (1995): 104–23.

McFadden, Patricia. "Why Feminist Autonomy Right Now?" *Women in Action* 2 (2004): 65–71.

Mekgwe, Pinkie. "Theorizing African Feminism(s): The Colonial Question." *Quest: An African Journal of Philosophy* 20, no. 1–2 (2006): 11–22.

Mestiri, Soumaya. *Décoloniser le féminisme: une approche transculturelle* (Paris: Vrin, 2016).

Mudimbe, V. Y. *The Invention of Africa: Gnosis, Philosophy, and the Order of Knowledge* (Bloomington: Indiana University Press, 1988).

Osha, Sanya. "Philosophy and Figures of the African Female." *Quest: An African Journal of Philosophy* 20, no. 1–2 (2006): 155–204.

Oyěwùmí, Oyèrónkẹ́. *The Invention of Women. Making an African Sense of Western Gender Discourses* (Minneapolis: University of Minnesota Press, 1997).

———. "Family Bonds/Conceptual Binds: African Notes on Feminist Epistemologies." *Signs* 25 (2000): 4.

———. "Conceptualizing Gender: The Eurocentric Foundations of Feminist Concepts and the Challenge of African Epistemologies." *Jenda: A Journal of Culture and African Women Studies* 2, no. 1 (2002): 1–9.

Quijano, Anibal. "Coloniality of Power and Eurocentrism in Latin America." *International Sociology* 15, no. 2 (2000): 215–23.

Rich, Adrienne. "Disloyal to Civilization: Feminism, Racism and Gynephobia," in *On Lies, Secrets and Silence* (New York: W. W. Norton & Company, 1979).

Sow, Fatou. "Introduction," in *Sexe, genre et société: engendrer les sciences sociales africaines*, ed. Ayesha M. Iman, Amina Mama, and Fatou Sow (Paris and Dakar: Karthala and CODESRIA, 2004): 17–47.

Touré, Marèma. "La recherche sur le genre en Afrique : Quelques aspects épisté-mologiques et culturels." *CODESRIA* (1997): 105–26.

Chapter 3

Gender between Kinship and Utopia

Laura Hengehold

In *Deconstruction and the Postcolonial*, Michael Syrotinski observes that the concepts of hybridity, supplementarity, différance, and translation have all been invoked as points of passage between post-structuralism and postcolonial analyses of literature and political events.[1] In his later years, Derrida turned the intellectual resources of deconstruction to the immediate practical task of thinking European identity. This interest was provoked not only by the newly established European Union but also by the challenges of intra-European migration (from Eastern Europe) and intercontinental migration (from Algeria to France, to give one notable example). In texts such as "The Other Heading," "On Hospitality," and "On Cosmopolitanism," Derrida took seriously the demand for a sense of European identity while insisting that any association between this identity and justice in the strongest sense required Europe's boundaries to be perpetually called into question.[2] He grappled with the temptation of every identity to assert itself as a universal and with the impossibility of reconciling universality with specific borders.[3]

Since these essays were written, migratory pressures and their potential consequences for Europe, as well as North America, have only increased. Many immigrants to Europe come from the Middle East and Africa. But international movement within the continent of Africa far exceeds the movement out of Africa.[4] Thus, journalist Alexander Betts, writing in the *Guardian* June 2018, suggests we consider how these countries have addressed their own challenges of migration.[5] To explore how the Derridean concepts of hospitality and the performative might be transformed in such contexts, I focus on the Cameroonian novelist and dramatist Werewere Liking, who was both the recipient and agent of such hospitality in Côte d'Ivoire. I argue that Liking's literary and theatrical work may have the capacity to disrupt hospitality's identification with an understanding of kinship as exchange.

The encounter I stage here between Derrida and Liking is mediated by Romanian feminist and film theorist Anca Parvulescu, whose text *The Traffic in Women's Work* critiques and extends Derrida's ideas where the gender of the migrant is concerned.

Werewere Liking (Eddy Nicole Njock) grew up during the Cameroonian war for independence against France and France's indigenous advocates during the 1950s. After being initiated into both women's and men's secret societies of the Bassa ethnicity, she became a painter and singer.[6] From fear of the Cameroonian government's response to her first book of poetry, she remained abroad after its publication during the 1970s. With anthropologist Marie-José Hourantier, she studied puppetry and oral traditions in Mali, and in 1981 founded the Ki-Yi Villa for the arts in Abidjan, Côte d'Ivoire.[7]

This was during the years of the "Ivoirian Miracle" when cocoa prices were high and labor migration (both internal and international) was welcome in Côte d'Ivoire. However, economic troubles during the 1990s led to a civil war in 2002 when Northerners refused to "return" to their birthtowns and reduce pressure on the land.[8] Liking's Ki-Yi villa eventually expanded into a self-sustaining "village" numbering about fifty people that welcomed refugee and otherwise disenfranchised youth and taught them artistic skills allowing them to perform at a global level.[9] Liking and her sister Nserel, who now run the village, view it as a model for African political and economic self-sufficiency. For many years she resisted dependence on state support, which was scarcely forthcoming, though she does appeal to foreign audiences and tours with her artists. Now she views government funding as a mark of official recognition after many years of civic contribution.[10]

Liking is best known for her chants-romans or song-novels, including *It Shall Be of Jasper and Coral*, *Love-across-a-Hundred-Lives*, and *The Amputated Memory*, but she has also authored and produced numerous plays and performance events best described as mythopoetic ritual theater.[11] Traditional arts in West-Central Africa are sacred and multimedia. Comparisons have often been drawn between the experimental style of her literary and theatrical production and that of writers such as Artaud and Brecht.[12] Nevertheless, her works are loosely based on the specific model of the *mvet* epic of the Beti and Fang, other Cameroonian peoples, a genre that Liking has adapted to include and celebrate female voices.[13] As Katheryn Wright describes, Liking believes African theater "should confront contemporary problems (and propose solutions) in Africa in a form that is based on African symbols, structures, philosophies, and performance techniques rather than on Western conventions. This premise is based on an esthetic need that is itself conditioned by a social need."[14]

In other words, Liking's goal is to renew, combine, and make accessible to audiences from any country some of the powerful narrative forms from specific African cultures that are in danger of being lost as Africans rapidly assimilate to the global consumer market. According to John Conteh-Morgan, this goal arouses some resistance in Cameroon because it is practically a form of blasphemy.[15] But in countries where the postindependence theatrical culture was dominated by French models and accessible only to the upper middle class, she also wants to spread "people theater" allowing poorer and less urbanized audiences to recognize and rework their own experiences.[16]

Love-across-a-Hundred-Lives, for example, retells the story of Sundiata with an emphasis on the hero's mother, who is implicitly related to the women of the 1950s Cameroonian resistance to the French. *Un Touareg* explicitly "weds" a representative of a desert society to one from the forest—groups, moreover, that are often considered "outsiders" in their respective countries. This one performance, as Cheryl Toman points out, incorporates references to over thirty African countries and ten languages.[17]

Much of Liking's creative output is critical of postindependence governments and the international consumer culture to which she sees both men and women reduced. The song-novel *It Shall Be of Jasper and Coral* is narrated by a self-styled "misovire" driven by bitterness toward the men who have failed to build an independent postcolonial Africa as well as the women who benefit from these failures in petty ways. In some works, such as *Love-across-a-Hundred-Lives* and The *Power of Um*, she presents women who demand liberation in order to call both men and women to a higher standard of creativity.

Liking's most recent major work, *The Amputated Memory*, is a semiautobiographical novel about a young woman artist, Halla Njoke, dedicated to her politically and spiritually assertive aunts (three of whom are named Roz) and her grandmother Grand Madja Halla. This book is an effort to repair or compensate for a memory twice amputated: first by government silence on the Cameroonian civil war that accompanied independence from France, a war in which Halla's father fought on the side of the French, and second by family secrets surrounding sexuality and maternity.[18] In these and other works, Liking reinterprets the gist of initiatory rituals and stories in order to transform the meaning of gender and kinship in contemporary Africa. In the process, I argue, she also transforms the meaning of kinship and hospitality in ways that the rest of the world can learn from.

A myth recounted in *It Shall Be of Jasper and Coral* presents the gist of the problem. The Bassa god Hîlombi sent masks to educate and perfect the first humans, but their lesson did not stick. One mask hid and showed himself to a woman, Soo, intending that she would bring his knowledge to humanity, but she was afraid of the feeling of power caused by her newfound understanding and gave it to a man, who immediately appropriated it for himself. In *The Amputated Memory*, Halla's father views himself as a *Lôs*, a rare individual with the right to innovate, attract power to himself, and compete for the labor and loyalty of others. The *Lôs* is a traditional figure in whom acceptance and caution regarding attributes of "modernity" are combined.

One of Liking's goals in *The Amputated Memory* is to present her aunts as female avatars of the *Lôs*, even though the role is traditionally male, thereby innovating in her own right. According to Conteh-Morgan and d'Almeida, Liking distinguishes between two kinds of masks—social masks that are barriers to social responsibility and progress, and religious masks that are gifts of the gods, first to women and then universally: gifts of creativity, self-knowledge, and justice. Not that women's knowledge and power require no study and effort, nor that they are instrumentally justified for what they can bring to men, but they are valuable in and of themselves because they transform both men and women.[19]

In many respects, the European idea of the nation-state was formed on the basis of the idea of belonging as kinship and in resistance to that idea. Citing Vincent Rosivach, for example, anthropologist Peter Geschiere discusses the ancient Greek appeal to notions of "autochthony" to justify the occupation of their territory.[20] The original "lineage" was often an invader or migrant attempting to legitimate its claim to land inhabited by others whose origins were unknown; thus the "autochthone" has a double meaning of nobility and of almost prehuman savagery. The idea of lineage is part of the juridical imaginary of social order as "alliance" described by Foucault in *History of Sexuality; Volume I* and "*Society Must Be Defended*," his lecture course from 1975 to 1976.[21] To summarize schematically, the modern nation-state, which claims sovereignty on behalf of the people rather than the monarch, identifies the excellence of the population with its vitality rather than with its legitimacy or raw power, but it falls back on "blood" when needed—the nation is conceived as an extended kinship group where once the kinship of royalty sufficed.

Is this transition from alliance to biopolitics universal? Is alliance itself universal? The applicability of European ideas of royalty and nationality in other societies has long been questioned. We are just now unraveling the history of colonial efforts to define ethnicities in Africa, sometimes arbitrarily, so as to establish political units that could be "conquered" and assigned rulers representing European interests.[22] Anthropologists such as Marcel Mauss and Lévi-Strauss conceived kinship universally as an exchange between families, in which women were "currency."[23] This reflected their observations of marriage in European societies, as well as the reports from early missionaries and colonial officials in Melanesia, Africa, and South America, who tended to project their expectations about male dominance onto the cultures they encountered (sometimes with encouragement from colonized men). But the meaning of kinship in many parts of West-Central Africa had been evolving on its own prior to colonization.

Cameroonian sociologist Séverin Cécile Abega argued that marriage was not traditionally an "exchange" or "accumulation" of *women* as sexual partners or mothers per se, but an exchange or rather pooling and multiplication of *labor*, including reproductive and care labor, between families whose lineages were then allied politically and economically.[24] Only with the rise of long-distance trade in rare commodities did the value of "tokens" for this alliance become so costly that many men could not afford to marry and wives themselves became "tokens" of fungible wealth rather than commitments to combine labor and political capital. This is the version of "tradition" Liking criticizes when she portrays the character Halla's father promising to give his daughter to a local Swiss landowner in exchange for some cars, and sending her to do housework in his villa until the marriage can be established.

Derrida argues that the structuralist notion of kinship as an exchange of women by men underlies European notions of cosmopolitanism and hospitality. He describes hospitality as willingness to make oneself a hostage, and to offer the wife/hostess or the daughter as a proxy for one's own being-at-home.[25] Hospitality as exchange implies reciprocity, and when no reciprocity is forthcoming or possible, the situation is felt as a violation by the host.[26] Thus, the very idea of hospitality has a gender subtext which, as Anca Parvulescu argues, remains active even when female citizens of Western European nation-states and the new Europe as a whole abandon traditional gender roles and take their place in the market alongside men. On the one hand, the structural role of "wifely" care labor toward children, ailing elders, adult men, and their guests is perpetuated by the very notion of what Derrida calls the "immigrant woman"—in this case, the woman from Eastern Europe who can be included in the biopolitically thriving European community but on unequal legal and economic terms. On the other hand, conservative Europeans invoke the metaphor of hospitality to justify a sentiment of fear or resentment toward those same immigrants who are felt to be taking advantage of "inclusion" and provoking an autoimmune response.[27]

Cosmopolitanism, as explained by Kant, gives strangers the universal right to visit but only for a limited period of time.[28] The EU has continued this tradition in giving political but not economic refugees a right to asylum, and by tying immigration rights closely to traditional forms of kinship, much like the United States. Derrida observes that there is a tension between the need for borders (to have a space within which welcome is meaningful) and the ethical obligation to allow entry; he also questions the porous distinction between political and economic vulnerability, given that political structures shape economic opportunity and are often justified by economic benefits for this or that group. According to Parvulescu, the fear of invasion justifying limits on the "visit" for both Kant and Derrida reveals the suppressed colonial context of Kant's writing: "European guests having acted greedily and violently when welcomed generously by native peoples."[29]

Derrida asks of the Levi-Straussian model: "Are we the heirs to this tradition of hospitality? Up to what point? Where should we place the invariant, if it is one, across this logic and these narratives?"[30] Parvulescu, however, asks whether Lévi-Strauss represents the *only* European tradition of hospitality.[31] She also asks whether Western Europe might not become more "truly" European if it were to seek *welcome* by Eastern Europe rather than demanding that the East conform to its own (Western) model.[32] Reading Derrida with Liking and Parvulescu, my question is whether we might not be able to avoid some of the autoimmune effects of Western ideas about "hospitality" (which is not working so well, particularly in the United States) if we allowed ourselves to be changed by the performance and reality of hospitality modeled by someone like Werewere Liking.

Certainly, the specter and the reality of migration have provoked violent responses in African countries such as South Africa, the Democratic Republic of Congo, Côte d'Ivoire, and Cameroon for reasons that, as Peter Geschiere observes, are similar to those in European countries.[33] In many of these locations, government policies to divide and conquer regions by pitting ethnicities against one another or to build national unity by distributing resources to different regions and/or encouraging internal migration have given rise to perverse effects as people try to claim the national goods, monetary or political, associated with residency in new areas.[34] In the guise of national "autochthony," the nation offered hospitality to all its internally migrating citizens, but the latter were then rejected as "allogenes," when expedient, from the territory where they landed. In Côte d'Ivoire, this invented origin found lacking in the migrants was termed "ivoirité."

Werewere Liking contends that "Côte d'Ivoire is a land of hospitality, a country in which people used to be very open-minded. . . . Everybody came from elsewhere to come here, so that [recent defensiveness] can't last."[35] She also thinks the conflict over borders and identities is an inevitable human reaction—"generally people withdraw into nationalism when they feel threatened." European defensiveness about immigration, she observes, merely repeats the African experience of "invasion" by Northern societies.[36] But she does not associate this phenomenon with the universality of kinship. Rather, such fighting is a symptom of the fact that the West has persuaded Africans that the market is "heaven. Everyone wants to go to heaven!"

A recent article in the *Guardian* also describes positive, creative responses to immigration in countries including Ethiopia, Kenya, and Uganda.[37] The average GDP per capita of Ethiopia, Kenya, and Uganda, for example, "is about 20 times less than Europe's," according to journalist Alexander Betts.

And yet they collectively host about 2.8 million refugees, more than the entire number to arrive in all of Europe's 28 member states during the entire 2015–16 "refugee crisis." Uganda . . . allows refugees the right to work and freedom of movement. It recognized from independence that enabling rural refugees to cultivate under-populated plots of land offered a means to support national development.

Uganda's is the most generous policy, but other countries are opening up, particularly as they realize that new self-reliant enterprises created by immigrants can benefit existing citizens.

This is not to say that the gendered aspect of hospitality has been entirely avoided, for it comes with the international market, far from heaven. In a 2018 report from the UN Conference on Trade and Development (UNCTAD) Jacqueline Andall explored the extent of intra-European migration, including its gender aspects.[38] She finds that while migration has become a rite of masculine passage for youth in some parts of Africa, migration of women is approached more cautiously, with travel bans to countries that have known human rights problems for women.[39] Some of this trade is temporary, while others leads to long-term settlement, and sometimes to "occupy[ing] specific ethnic niches, such as Malian women specializing in selling paintings in Senegal or Togolese women working as domestic workers in a range of African countries."[40]

It is also constrained within models proposed by "kinship" and tradition. Both "departure" and "arrival" governments are attentive to female migrants' experience with care work and concerned about lack of care for family members left behind.[41] But recall that the majority of migration is not even international; it involves movement from the countryside to the city. In Kenya, some survivors of domestic violence have migrated to towns from which men are, at least in principle, banned and other vulnerable women are welcomed.[42] In Côte d'Ivoire, more problematically, the counterpart to the "Eastern girl" whom Parvulescu finds performing the "wifely" roles of sex work or care labor in the newly unified Europe is the "girl from the village" or "little niece" who, under the rubric of "tradition," works as an unpaid servant in the household of her urban relatives or the households of their friends.[43] Although they are not exactly "trafficked," the "little nieces" do not learn marketable or otherwise empowering skills that would enable them to do anything but housework. They are "welcomed" but on suspicious and often humiliating terms.

Liking believes that old cultural and educational forms have enduring value. But she recognizes that it would be futile as well as oppressive to assume and perform these identities as they once were.[44] Across the board, Liking is critical of what kinship and its roles have come to mean. This is why her ritual theater has addressed issues including the treatment of widows and infertile women's rights (or the rights of women with infertile husbands) to recognition for their cultural and political work.[45] It is why her novels and the Ki-Yi Village encourage women's education of all kinds. She wants to know why biological fertility is considered a form of creativity *at odds with* political institution-building and with care work, rather than equally important or compatible with it.

"Signature Event Context" is the essay in which Derrida put forward his reading of the performative.[46] John Austin's speech act theory distinguishes between descriptive or constative speech acts and special performative speech acts, which are valid only in a certain context and include the performer's intentions. The classic example is the wedding declaration: "I pronounce you man and wife." Derrida shows that it is impossible to delimit this context.

> A written sign . . . [is] a mark that remains, which is not exhausted in the present of its inscription, and which can give rise to an iteration both in the absence of and beyond the presence of the empirically determined subject who, in a given context, has emitted or produced it . . . this force of breaking [with its context] is not an accidental predicate, but the very structure of the written.[47]

Performance is always creative in relation to some norm, but in the very act of appealing to or "citing" this norm, it alters the norm, it changes the context—and this "performativity" is not a matter of a performer's intention, for it links him or her with all other readers and actors over time. If a signature were *only* effective when the signer was present and intending to attest to something by writing his or her name, it would *never* be effective. It is for this reason that Judith Butler referred to Derrida (among others) when she wrote that the existence of homophobia proves that straightness is neither an essence nor the effect of a "dutiful" intention but may fail or become "queer" in the very act of being performed and that drag subverts gender conventions in the very act of citing them.[48]

The children anticipated by the *misovire* in Liking's *It Shall Be of Jasper and Coral* will be blue, not black or white, and they will not come from repetition of past cultural forms.[49] In the play *A New Earth*, the masks are given to the children because the available adults have become too corrupt.[50] This is a highly unusual way to invoke and preserve tradition. Moreover, there is a difference of emphasis between Liking's approach to performativity and that put forward by Judith Butler. Butler focused on liberating identities that were suppressed by the conditions for the stability of a given context, even though she knows that such liberation cannot help but change that context. Liking's performance, on the other hand, aims directly at altering the context itself, knowing that this will change its participants.

Some performances go beyond the limits of a given individual's ontological consistency. Nkiru Nzegwu, although she is Igbo and not Bassa, argues that having a child *ontologically changes* a woman who becomes a mother.[51] If the radical material performance of motherhood is a new birth for the adult woman as well as her child, then neither can one understand children as property or passive material to be formed, as so many Westerners do. They are elements of a transformation that affects multiple interacting bodies. In the play that bears her name, the mother-in-law of the character Singue Mura chooses another wife for her husband because, although she has built many institutions in her husband's town, the latter has not given birth to any sons. Interestingly, Singue Mura commits suicide, but the woman who was once known by that name remains alive and at the end of the play, gives birth to *herself* as a different person.

For a certain Western strain of queer feminism, removing women from the context in which they are exchanged by men and making them available as supports and partners for one another is a way to contest the apparent universality of hospitality as traffic in women. By contrast, Parvulescu appeals to the materialist feminism of Alexandra Kollontai, which tried to overturn this economic relationship through "free love."[52] When women are "exchanged," the essential *work* they do to support the boundaries of belonging and to make themselves plausible objects of exchange is concealed. For Werewere Liking, the foundation of hospitality should be neither exchange nor sacrifice, but a different relationship to *work*, work that enlivens rather than work that "uses up" and "wears out" the worker. "You work, but it's the other who decides the price of your goods, who dictates to you what you have to do."[53] Near the start of *The Amputated Memory*, Halla comments that a slave cannot make the connection between work and pleasure, and recalls that her grandmother said "you'll always know whether you are free or not as long as you're able to link work and pleasure."[54]

Neither Parvulescu nor Liking explicitly exclude queer people, but neither do they expect the politics of queer identity (and its aporias) to have the most profoundly liberatory impact on European or African women. Liking does not, like (early) Judith Butler, count on the failure of the norm, but rather on the change in context created by a norm, often called "tradition," that is itself deliberately altered and brought "up-to-date." She does not even consider herself a feminist, for she thinks of feminism in relation to a certain system of national rights, where what concerns her above all is the aesthetics and ethics that might underlie such rights.[55] On the other hand, *Singue Mura* takes up numerous themes most people would consider feminist, and this notion of initiatory performance seems to *welcome* precisely those, whatever their sexual orientation, whose families could never be anything other than "queer," those who have been failed by traditional kinship, and those who see the need for forms of creativity that go beyond commodified labor, care, and childhood.[56] Whatever she is, the *misovire* is not a militant heterosexual.

So, although Liking takes gender for granted in a way that may seem essentialist to many philosophers (for she is not concerned with limit cases), both Liking and Parvulescu seem to think of womanhood in terms of the kind of *labor* associated with gender, labor that escapes a kind of kinship that has become identified with *exchange* rather than the *sacred*. Ideally, it is a labor of creation with the divine rather than merely among humans.[57] "All that I do is from this perspective of a 'medium' in divine creation, and one can only understand my work through the Ki-Yi M'Bock teachings."[58]

The wise man isn't born holy.
Humans are transformed by thought and word,
By actions and realizations,
By time, but by education above all.
What is the mystery, then? Enormous work;
The very mystery of the divine is work.[59]

I hesitate to say that the iterability implicit in initiatory performance is one version of what Werewere Liking calls the sacred partner in creativity.[60] However, Liking does not seem to mind being received by others, so long as that means the host is also transformed by her arrival. We must be alert to the danger of "appropriating" whatever she could contribute to our reflections on global migration without including or combining powers with those she has pledged to teach and protect. There is also the danger, as with so many Western feminists, that an engagement with myth turns out to be wildly conservative or imposes a new orthodoxy. Finally, it goes without saying that I don't want to imply that there is any direct connection between Liking's ideas and the immigration policies of any individual African government! Thinking them together does not mean thinking they are causally or essentially connected.

I also want to caution that Derrida's *performative*, obviously, cannot be reduced to "performance" in the sense of an artistic genre. But I don't think that Liking is just engaging with "performance" as an artistic genre either. It is essential for Europeans and other so-called Westerners like myself (a white American) to acknowledge the ways our invocation of the market and attitudes toward labor are themselves products of creative processes that go beyond our individual intentions. We cannot escape or absolve ourselves of responsibility for whatever we call "sacred" or "mythical" by claiming to be secular. This is why I suggest that societies should try to learn from one another's ways of performing hospitality, and *perhaps imagine kinship on the basis of those welcoming practices rather than the reverse.*

Werewere Liking is an artist who wants to rethink labor, and in our world, rethinking labor is part and parcel of rethinking gender, including its reproductive dimension, in a liberatory way. The conflicts and wars over identity and territory discussed here all arise because there is a scarcity of work in the contemporary world, particularly meaningful and rewarding work. It is no longer clear what children are being educated and trained *to do*, or who might need their labor to be anything but repetition of the same, while care and creation continue to be barely considered work at all. The professor who befriends Halla and her eventual husband in *The Amputated Memory* and invites them to intellectual dinner gatherings expresses this frustration well:

> Does "means" refer only to money? And because my friends spend little, you think they have limited means? How do you evaluate their work, commitment, hospitality, and their creativity? You make me vomit, all of you! What I would like to see happen someday is doing away with money altogether, finding different symbols, different representations of worth![61]

What Liking offers instead of hospitality based on kinship as *exchange* is a notion of hospitality based on work as *performance*—not in the sense of competitive display or production for exchange, but in the sense of transformation, even in ordinary activities. She challenges the twisted way that both tradition and kinship become oppressive rather than liberatory in the false heaven of the market. Work should be welcoming to the worker as well as the audience, and welcoming is not an exchange, but a kind of work. This is a utopian project; "that is to say, [one] freed of all that is blocking our continent today," but a project Werewere Liking thinks is worthy of all newcomers.[62]

NOTES

1. By Homi Bhabha and Robert Young, among others. See Michael Syrotinski, *Deconstruction and the Postcolonial: At the Limits of Theory* (Liverpool: Liverpool University Press, 2007): 2–3.

2. Jacques Derrida, *The Other Heading: Reflections on Today's Europe*, trans. Pascale-Anne Brault and Michael Naas (Bloomington: Indiana University Press, 1992); *On Cosmopolitanism and Forgiveness*, trans. Mark Dooley and Michael Hughes (New York: Routledge, 1997); *Of Hospitality: Anne Dufourmantelle invites Jacques Derrida to respond,* trans. Rachel Bowlby (Stanford: Stanford University Press, 2000). For a critique, see also Marina Antic: "The Balkans and *The Other Heading*: Identity and Identification on the Margins of Europe," *Spacesofidentity* 6, no. 2 (2006), https://doi.org/10.25071/1496-6778.7989.

3. Derrida, *The Other Heading*, 73; *On Cosmopolitanism*, 10–13.

4. UNCTAD [United Nations Conference on Trade and Development], "Patterns and Trends of Migration (Ch. 2)," in *Economic Development in Africa Report 2018: Migration for Structural Transformation* (2018), https://unctad.org/system/files/official-document/edar2018_ch2_en.pdf.

5. Alexander Betts, "What Europe could learn from the way Africa treats refugees," *The Guardian*, June 26, 2018, https://www.theguardian.com/commentisfree/2018/jun/26/europe-learn-africa-refugees-solutions.

6. Michelle Mielly, "Afterword," in Werewere Liking, *The Amputated Memory*, trans. Marjolijn de Jager (New York: The Feminist Press/CUNY Press, 2007): 432.

7. "The teachings of the Ki-Yi M'Bock, those of the Bassa of Cameroon, were, according to my great-aunt, teachings that *respond to a crisis*. . . . The children who live here and who are given this teaching are the stars who, when the time comes, will transmit this knowledge to others." Quoted in Michelle Mielly, "The Aesthetics of Necessity: An Interview with Werewere Liking," *World Literature Today* 77, no. 2 (July–Sep 2003): 55.

8. On Liking's situation during the civil war, see in particular Cheryl Toman, "The Impact of African Feminisms and Performance in Conflict Zones: Werewere Liking in Côte-d'Ivoire and Mali," *Feminist Studies* 41, no. 1 (2015): 72–87; on the civil war and its origins, see Peter Geschiere, *The Perils of Belonging: Autochthony, Citizenship and Exclusion in Africa and Europe* (Chicago: University of Chicago Press, 2009): 2–3.

As Geschiere explains, autochthony was the basis for the French "politique des races" by which ethnic identities were identified and then provided with (supposedly) representative rulers friendly to France (*Perils of Belonging*, 11–12, 14). In Côte d'Ivoire, President Houphouët-Boigny had always presented migrants as crucial to the economy, particularly in the cacao-growing zone. This situation lasted until 1995, when "ivoirité" was increasingly invoked as a justification for opposition to the structural adjustment programs imposed by Houphouët-Boigny's handpicked successor, Alassane Ouattara, as well as a justification for requiring migrants to move back out of areas undergoing economic crisis by politicians fighting against Ouattara (*Perils of Belonging*, 97–98).

9. Cheryl Toman, *Contemporary Matriarchies in Cameroonian Francophone Literature: "On est ensemble"* (Birmingham, AL: Summa Publications, 2008), 84–85; Michelle Mielly, "An Interview with Werewere Liking at the Ki-Yi Village, Abidjan, Côte d'Ivoire, 2 June 2002," *African Postcolonial Literature in the Postcolonial Web*, http://www.postcolonialweb.org/africa/cameroon/liking/2.html.

10. See Amelia Parenteau and Werewere Liking, "An Interview with Werewere Liking of the Theatre Company Village Ki-Yi M'bock," *HowlRound Theatre Commons* 10, Jan. 8, 2018, https://howlround.com/interview-werewere-liking-theatre-company-village-ki-yi-mbock-interview-avec-werewere-liking-du.

11. Liking, *The Amputated Memory; It Shall Be of Jasper and Coral and Love-across-a-Hundred-Lives*, trans. Marjolijn de Jager (Richmond: University of Virginia Press, 2000); with Bomou Mamadou and Binda Ngazolo, *Singue Mura (Considérant que la femme . . .)* (Abidjan: Eyo-Ki-Yi Editions, 1990); *African Ritual Theatre: The Power of Um* and *A New Earth*, trans. Jeanne N. Dingome et al. (San Francisco/

London/Bethesda: International Scholars Publications, 1996); *Un Touareg s'est marié à une pygmée: épopée m'vet pour une Afrique présente* (Carnières, Belgium: Lansman, 1992).

12. Michelle Mielly, "An Interview with Werewere Liking at the Ki-Yi Village."

13. Cheryl Toman, *Contemporary Matriarchies*, 82; Mielly, "An Interview with Werewere Liking."

14. Katheryn Wright, "Werewere Liking: From Chaos to Cosmos," in *World Literature Today* 69, no. 1 (1995): 56–57.

15. John Conteh-Morgan, cited in Toman, *Contemporary Matriarchies,* 83, note 48.

16. Unlike the African restaging of European works as part of colonial cultural policy, popular theater combines traditional ritual, public consciousness-raising, and contemporary artistic techniques. See Gilbert Doho, *People Theater and Grassroots Empowerment in Cameroon,* trans. Marie Lathers (Trenton, NJ and London: Africa World Press, 2006) and Penina Muhando Mlama, *Culture and Development: The Popular Theater Approach in Africa* (Uppsala: Scandinavian Institute of African Studies, 1991).

17. Toman, *Contemporary Matriarchies*, 82.

18. See Mielly's "Afterword" to Liking, *Amputated Memory*, 441–42.

19. John Conteh-Morgan and Irène Assiba D'Almeida, "Introduction;" and Juliana Makuchi Nfah-Abbenyi, "Un-Masking the Mediator: Werewere Liking's Flashes of Light," in *The Original Explosion that Created Worlds: Essays on Werewere Liking's Art and Writings,* ed. John Conteh-Morgan and Irène Assiba d'Almeida (Amsterdam/New York: Rodopi, 2010), 18–19, 63–88.

20. Geschiere, *Perils of Belonging,* 11–12. The historians cited are Rosivach, Detienne, and Loraux.

21. Michel Foucault, *The History of Sexuality: Volume I, An Introduction,* trans. Robert Hurley (New York: Vintage Books, 1990), 146–50; *"Society Must Be Defended": Lectures at the Collège de France, 1975–76,* trans. David Macey, ed. Mauro Bertani and Alessandro Fontana (New York: Picador, 2003), 239–56.

22. See, among others, Geschiere, *Perils of Belonging,* 14–16.

23. Claude Lévi-Strauss, *The Elementary Structures of Kinship,* Revised Edition, trans. James Harle Bell, John Richard Von Sturmer and Rodney Needham (Boston: Beacon Press, 1969), especially chapter 5.

24. Séverin Cécile Abega: *Violences sexuelles et l'Etat au Cameroun* (Paris: Karthala, 2007), Chapter 1.

25. One example is Antigone, who could not mourn her father, Oedipus, because part of his self-exile from Thebes involved forbidding Theseus to tell anywhere where he had been buried; another is the Biblical patriarch Lot, who gave his daughters to men of the town so as to protect his male guests from rape by them (Derrida, *Of Hospitality,* 93–119, 151–55). The problem with deconstructive claims that borders cannot be fully closed is that such claims provoke autoimmune panic, what Derrida calls "police without borders" (*On Cosmopolitanism,* 14). A third Biblical example: the Levite of Judges 19-20, who gave his concubine to strangers when they refused to sleep with his daughters; when the concubine died of wounds sustained during rape,

he cut her into pieces which were sent to the other tribes of Israel, launching a bloody war (*Of Hospitality*, 155).

26. Anca Parvulescu, *The Traffic in Women's Work: East European Migration and the Making of Europe* (Chicago: University of Chicago Press, 2014), 132–34.

27. On autoimmunity, see Jacques Derrida and Giovannna Borradori, "Autoimmunity: Real and Symbolic Suicides," trans. Pascale-Anne Brault and Michael Naas, from *Philosophy in a Time of Terror: Dialogues with Jürgen Habermas and Jacques Derrida,* ed. Giovanna Borradori (University of Chicago Press, 2003), 85–136.

28. Immanuel Kant, "Perpetual Peace," in *Political Writings,* ed. Hans Reiss (Cambridge: Cambridge University Press, 1991), 105–8; cited in Derrida, *On Cosmopolitanism,* 10–13.

29. Parvulescu, *Traffic in Women's Work,* 134.

30. Derrida, *Of Hospitality,* 155; cited in Parvulescu, *Traffic in Women's Work*, 138.

31. Parvulescu, *Traffic in Women's Work,* 137.

32. Parvulescu, *Traffic in Women's Work,* 132.

33. Geschiere, *Perils of Belonging.*

34. Geschiere gives several examples of government projects in the east of Cameroon that provoked mistrust among communities who were forced to compete for resources. These societies, historically very inclusive and fluid, were always ready to accept more people as bodily wealth and to invent kinship relations for whoever happened to reside with them. So while kinship did not necessarily mean closure in the past, this is becoming less true (*Perils of Belonging,* 82–83).

35. Christine Cynn, "If I had a Hundred Arms, I Would Do Many Things: An Interview with Werewere Liking," trans. Maboula Soumahoro and Christine Cynn," in *S&F Online, Barnard Center for Research on Women* 7, no. 2 (2009): clip 9 http://sfonline.barnard.edu/africana/liking01.htm.

36. "I've told you that this business [*ivoirité*], almost all developing peoples have known it at one point or another. . . . Today it's Europe that feels invaded and that is afraid, that rejects everyone and wants to withdraw when it did almost everything to bring people over there, with ropes around their necks, shackles around their feet and all that." Cynn, "If I had a Hundred Arms," clip 10.

37. Betts, "What Europe Could Learn."

38. Jacqueline Andall, "Intra-African Female Labour Migration: Common Issues, Work and Rights," UNCTAD Background Paper No. 1 (May 2018).

39. Andall, "Intra-African Female Labour Migration," 5.

40. Andall, "Intra-African Female Labour Migration," 4.

41. Andall, "Intra-African Female Labour Migration," 8.

42. Julie Bindel, "The village where men are banned," *The Guardian,* Aug 16, 2015, https://www.theguardian.com/global-development/2015/aug/16/village-where-men-are-banned-womens-rights-kenya.

43. Mélanie Jacquemin, "Can the Language of Rights Get Hold of the Complex Realities of Child Domestic Work? The case of young domestic workers in Abidjan, Ivory Coast," *Childhood* 13, no. 3 (2006): 389–406.

44. Mielly, "The Aesthetics of Necessity," 55.

45. See *The Power of Um*, in Liking, *African Ritual Theatre*; and Liking, Mamadou and Ngazolo, *Singue Mura*.

46. Jacques Derrida, "Signature Event Context," in *Margins of Philosophy*, trans. Alan Bass (Chicago: University of Chicago Press, 1982): 307–30.

47. Derrida, "Signature Event Context," 317.

48. Judith Butler, *Gender Trouble: Feminism and the Subversion of Identity* (New York: Routledge, 1990).

49. Liking, *It Shall Be of Jasper and Coral*, 109–13.

50. Liking, *African Ritual Theatre*.

51. Nkiru Uwechia Nzegwu, *Family Matters: Feminist Concepts in African Philosophy of Culture* (Buffalo: SUNY Press, 2006), 51–52.

52. Parvulescu, *Traffic in Women's Work*, 144.

53. Cynn, "If I Had a Hundred Arms," clip 11.

54. Liking, *Amputated Memory*, 31.

55. Cynn, "If I had a Hundred Arms," Clip 15–16.

56. Michelle Mielly, "An Aesthetics of Necessity in the Age of Globalization: Village Ki-Yi as a New Social Movement," in *The Original Explosion that Created Worlds: Essays on Werewere Liking's Art and Writings,* ed. John Conteh-Morgan and Irène Assiba d'Almeida (Amsterdam/New York: Rodopi, 2010), 45; also, in the same volume, Irène Assiba d'Almeida, "La 'misovire' et la critique: La reception des oeuvres de Werewere Liking," 316–17.

57. "If you are in the image of a God who does not resemble you, your own creation cannot resemble yourself. To me, this is quite common sense. So my work consists in really going deep into myself, as a native African, and see what can come out and is human and in which each human can recognize himself without making it impossible for me to recognize myself." Cynn, "If I Had a Hundred Arms," clip 7. Note that she speaks of gods who resemble people and not of fitting people to an external image of the divine, including its gender (she speaks openly of the divine as female). Nor does she claim the ability to enumerate women's "proper" powers in advance.

58. Mielly, "The Aesthetics of Necessity," 56.

59. Liking, *Amputated Memory*, 31.

60. But see Amy Hollywood, "Performativity, Citationality, Ritualization," in *History of Religions* 42, no. 2 (2002): 93–115.

61. Liking, *Amputated Memory*, 396–97.

62. Mielly, "The Aesthetics of Necessity," 52. With many thanks to my colleagues, Cheryl Toman and Gilbert Doho.

BIBLIOGRAPHY

Abega, Séverin Cécile. *Violences sexuelles et l'Etat au Cameroun* (Paris: Karthala, 2007).

Andall, Jacqueline. "Intra-African Female Labour Migration: Common Issues, Work and Rights," UNCTAD Background Paper No. 1 (May 2018).

Antic, Marina. "The Balkans and *The Other Heading*: Identity and Identification on the Margins of Europe." *Spacesofidentity* 6, no. 2 (2006), https://doi.org/10.25071 /1496-6778.7989.

Betts, Alexander. "What Europe could learn from the way Africa treats refugees," *The Guardian*, June 26, 2018, https://www.theguardian.com/commentisfree/2018/ jun/26/europe-learn-africa-refugees-solutions.

Bindel, Julie. "The village where men are banned," *The Guardian*, Aug 16, 2015, https://www.theguardian.com/global-development/2015/aug/16/village-where -men-are-banned-womens-rights-kenya.

Butler, Judith. *Gender Trouble: Feminism and the Subversion of Identity* (New York: Routledge, 1990).

Cynn, Christine. "If I had a Hundred Arms, I Would Do Many Things: An Interview with Werewere Liking," trans. Maboula Soumahoro and Christine Cynn, in *S&F Online, Barnard Center for Research on Women* 7, no. 2 (2009), http://sfonline .barnard.edu/africana/liking01.htm.

d'Almeida, Irène Assiba. "La 'misovire' et la critique: La reception des oeuvres de Werewere Liking," in *The Original Explosion that Created Worlds: Essays on Werewere Liking's Art and Writings,* ed. John Conteh-Morgan and Irène Assiba d'Almeida (Amsterdam/New York: Rodopi, 2010): 301–32.

Derrida, Jacques, "Signature Event Context," in *Margins of Philosophy*, trans. Alan Bass (Chicago: University of Chicago Press, 1982): 309–30.

———. *The Other Heading: Reflections on Today's Europe,* trans. Michael Naas and Pascale-Anne Brault (Bloomington: Indiana University Press, 1992).

———. *On Cosmopolitanism and Forgiveness*, trans. Mark Dooley and Michael Hughes (New York: Routledge, 1997).

———. *Of Hospitality: Anne Dufourmantelle invites Jacques Derrida to respond,* trans. Rachel Bowlby (Stanford: Stanford University Press, 2000).

Jacques Derrida and Giovannna Borradori, "Autoimmunity: Real and Symbolic Suicides," trans. Pascale-Anne Brault and Michael Naas, from *Philosophy in a Time of Terror: Dialogues with Jürgen Habermas and Jacques Derrida,* ed. Giovanna Borradori (University of Chicago Press, 2003): 85–136.

Doho, Gilbert. *People Theater and Grassroots Empowerment in Cameroon,* trans. Marie Lathers (Trenton, NJ and London: Africa World Press, 2006).

Foucault, Michel. *The History of Sexuality: Volume I, An Introduction,* trans. Robert Hurley (New York: Vintage Books, 1990).

———. *"Society Must Be Defended": Lectures at the Collège de France, 1975–76,* trans. David Macey, ed. Mauro Bertani and Alessandro Fontana (New York: Picador, 2003).

Geschiere, Peter. *The Perils of Belonging: Autochthony, Citizenship and Exclusion in Africa and Europe* (Chicago: University of Chicago Press, 2009).

Hollywood, Amy. "Performativity, Citationality, Ritualization," in *History of Religions* 42, no. 2 (2002): 93–115.

Jacquemin, Mélanie. "Can the Language of Rights Get Hold of the Complex Realities of Child Domestic Work? The case of young domestic workers in Abidjan, Ivory Coast," *Childhood* 13, no. 3 (2006): 389–406.

Lévi-Strauss, Claude. *The Elementary Structures of Kinship,* Revised Edition, trans. James Randall Bell, John Richard Von Sturmer and Rodney Needham (Boston: Beacon Press, 1969).

Liking, Werewere. *Un Touareg s'est marié à une pygmée: épopée m'vet pour une Afrique présente* (Carnières, Belgium: Lansman, 1992).

———. *African Ritual Theatre: The Power of Um* and *A New Earth*, trans. Jeanne N. Dingome et al (San Francisco/London/Bethesda: International Scholars Publications, 1996).

———. *It Shall Be of Jasper and Coral* and *Love-Across-a-Hundred-Lives*, trans. Marjolijn de Jager (Richmond: University of Virginia Press, 2000).

———. *The Amputated Memory*, trans. Marjolijn de Jager (New York: The Feminist Press/CUNY Press, 2007).

Liking, Werewere, Bomou Mamadou and Binda Ngazolo. *Singue Mura (Considérant que la femme . . .)* (Abidjan: Eyo-Ki-Yi Editions, 1990).

Mielly, Michelle. "An Interview with Werewere Liking at the Ki-Yi Village, Abidjan, Côte d'Ivoire, 2 June 2002." *African Postcolonial Literature in the Postcolonial Web,* http://www.postcolonialweb.org/africa/cameroon/liking/2.html.

———. "The Aesthetics of Necessity: An Interview with Werewere Liking." *World Literature Today* 77, no. 2 (July–Sep 2003): 52–56.

———. "Afterword," in Werewere Liking, *The Amputated Memory*, trans. Marjolijn de Jager (New York: The Feminist Press/CUNY Press, 2007): 429–45.

———. "An Aesthetics of Necessity in the Age of Globalization: Village Ki-Yi as a New Social Movement," in *The Original Explosion that Created Worlds: Essays on Werewere Liking's Art and Writings,* ed. John Conteh-Morgan and Irène Assiba d'Almeida (Amsterdam/New York: Rodopi, 2010): 29–52.

Mlama, Penina Muhando. *Culture and Development: The Popular Theater Approach in Africa* (Uppsala: Scandinavian Institute of African Studies, 1991).

Nfah-Abbenyi, Juliana Makuchi. "Un-Masking the Mediator: Werewere Liking's Flashes of Light," in *The Original Explosion that Created Worlds: Essays on Werewere Liking's Art and Writings,* ed. John Conteh-Morgan and Irène Assiba d'Almeida (Amsterdam/New York: Rodopi, 2010): 63–88.

Nzegwu, Nkiru Uwechia. *Family Matters: Feminist Concepts in African Philosophy of Culture* (Buffalo: SUNY Press, 2006).

Parvulescu, Anca. *The Traffic in Women's Work: East European Migration and the Making of Europe* (Chicago: University of Chicago Press, 2014).

Parenteau, Amelia and Werewere Liking, "An Interview with Werewere Liking of the Theatre Company Ki-Yi M'bock," *HowlRound Theatre Commons* 10, Jan. 8, 2018, https://howlround.com/interview-werewere-liking-theatre-company-village-ki-yi-mbock-interview-avec-werewere-liking-du.

Syrotinski, Michael. *Deconstruction and the Postcolonial: At the Limits of Theory* (Liverpool: Liverpool University Press, 2007).

Toman, Cheryl. *Contemporary Matriarchies in Cameroonian Francophone Literature: "On est ensemble"* (Birmingham, AL: Summa Publications, 2008).

———. "The Impact of African Feminisms and Performance in Conflict Zones: Werewere Liking in Côte d'Ivoire and Mali," *Feminist Studies* 41, no. 1 (2015): 72–87.

UNCTAD [United Nations Conference on Trade and Development], "Patterns and Trends of Migration (Ch. 2)" in *Economic Development in Africa Report 2018: Migration for Structural Transformation* (2018), https://unctad.org/system/files/official-document/edar2018_ch2_en.pdf.

Wright, Katheryn. "Werewere Liking: From Chaos to Cosmos," in *World Literature Today* 6, no. 1 (1995): 56–62.

Chapter 4

The University, Cognitive Justice, and Human Development

Florence Piron

Today I wish to discuss my ideas and my observations on the potential of African universities to become genuine tools of human and social development, in harmony with African values and forms of knowledge (*savoirs*).[1] Such values and forms of knowledge are precious for the whole world, but sometimes underestimated even in Africa itself. These ideas are the product of many research projects, past and recent, but also result from innumerable conversations with African students and faculty, my doctoral students and others, who talk to me about their life, their dreams, their difficulties, the temptation of the North, extraversion, but also about their love for Africa, its traditions, and their countries.

They also speak to me frequently about their experience of *diglossia*: the state in which two languages coexist in a given territory and, for historical and political reasons, have distinct statuses and social functions, one represented as superior and the other inferior within the population. This diglossia gives my interlocutors a complicated relationship with French, today considered the working language or lingua franca in Francophone Africa. Nevertheless, it is also a colonial language and one that they master more or less well; the language of the elite, of the university, of refined intellectual debates, of power. This overvaluation of French has led individuals and teaching institutions to devalorize the languages said to be local or national, or any "tongues" whatsoever, even though these are maternal languages, inscribed within and structuring culture and its relationship to the world, bearers of collective memory.

In Niger, students have told me that their greatest problem is finding the right words to express their thought in a language that does not come from their childhood, from their primordial relationship to the world, and that they do not dare to speak up in their courses for fear of being mocked by the others

71

for their errors. Students have told me that they were punished in primary school if they used their original language. I then realized that my greatest privilege as a white person was not just the good material conditions in which I live, but that of being able to think in my own language, to use my mastery of subtleties in this language to articulate the complexity of my reasoning process in the best way possible—something that, for example, is more difficult for me in English. This basic cognitive injustice has pushed me to make a commitment, in the open access publishing house I created, to concrete action on behalf of plurilingualism and to encourage authors to translate their abstracts, at least, into their original language or into the language of people with whom they communicate.[2]

FROM THE MULTIVERSITY TO COGNITIVE JUSTICE

Mpambo Multiversity

In Uganda, there exists a private university that employs both colonial languages and maternal languages in its activities. More generally, it teaches both the knowledge coming from Western science or the Western philosophical tradition and traditional knowledges. This school, Mpambo Afrikan Multiversity, incarnates in part (because I do not yet know enough about it) the ideal of cognitive justice animating me.[3]

Originating in reflections of the Indian anthropologist Shiv Visvanathan and reworked by the SOHA network (Science Ouverte en Haïti et en Afrique), the concept of cognitive justice refers to an epistemological, ethical, and political ideal aiming at the liberation and free circulation of socially pertinent forms of knowledge everywhere on the planet, and not simply in the countries of the North.[4] It goes hand in hand with a model of science that practices an inclusive universalism, open to all forms of knowledge and all epistemologies, and not a universalism that claims to be abstract, when in fact the norms on which it is based are American centered and exclude anything differing from themselves.

This ideal is very much opposed to the cognitive injustices that manifest themselves every day in the public space of science, in the North as well as in the global South(s), where the experience of diglossia is extremely important because it inhibits students' and researchers' ability to deploy the full potential of their capacity for apprenticeship or for scholarly research and social action on behalf of the lasting local development of their city or their country. Mpambo Multiversity rightly strives to reinforce its learners' self-confidence and their ability to act by permitting them to use a plurality of languages, which allows them to think and revalorize not just ancestral forms of knowledge, but also the modes of thought and of knowledge creation that come from their own cultures.

Barefoot College

Another very special educational institution is the Barefoot College, founded in India forty years ago. The specialty of this college consists in training older women from villages, not very literate for the most part, to install and maintain solar panels. A few such institutions can now be found around the world.[5] The exceptional feature of this project is that it assumes from the start that quasi-illiterate women have capacities to learn, therefore the preconditions for knowledge on which one can build and thereby lead them to acquire knowledge which is not just technical, modern, practical, evolving, but necessary to the common good, to the management of energy in the villages. The goal is to help women villagers combine local knowledge and experiential knowledge, acquired through experimentation and practice, to help their villages and to gain self-confidence that will ultimately improve their autonomy and social status.

The Models of Jacotot and Von Humboldt

Their wager evokes another, much older model: the one proposed by Joseph Jacotot, the ignorant schoolmaster.[6] Appointed by a Flemish university to teach Greek although he could not speak his students' language, he discovered that the students, motivated, could succeed in deciphering the text with the aid of a bilingual edition. From this, he came to a pedagogical theory that was revolutionary and quickly stifled by the academy, to the effect that all intelligences were equal, and that before all else, the teacher should be a "coach," a guide who must ignite the desire to understand in learners who would then manage for themselves. Here one finds the founding principles of what is today called active pedagogy, deliberately flipped classrooms rendered possible thanks to computerization, and in which more and more universities take an interest today.

Unfortunately for Jacotot, at exactly the same historical moment another Enlightenment philosopher (Wilhelm von Humboldt) invented a concept of the university that "caught on" far better, because it is still, even today, the framework of African universities as well as those in the North. The crisis that Northern universities are currently experiencing, to which I will return below, is clearly linked to the incongruence between this early nineteenth-century model and the conditions of the contemporary world, whether these are the neoliberalism which values competences other than the specialized bodies of

knowledge that were the pride of Humboldtian universities, or the advent of
the digital era which permits many other forms of apprenticeship and research.

Humboldt's model has five characteristics. Most important, it unifies science, which at that time was emerging strongly in tandem with industrial,
capitalist, and colonial development, with the training of elites in law, medi-
cine, and technology which the medieval university had as its specific mission up until that time. Apart from this unification of science and teaching in
a single institution dedicated to training the necessary engineers and techni-
cians for the industrial revolution and the exploitation of the colonial world's
natural resources, Humboldt's utopia preached the holistic and unitary nature
of knowledge, what for my part I would call the "capture of knowledge by
science." Put differently, while there existed and still exists a plurality of
knowledges, both in form and in content, Humboldt decreed that only a single
valid body of knowledge could exist. This is the one proposed by science and
in particular by its positivist epistemology, and which it attached to philosophy, making the latter first and foremost philosophy of knowledge.

The third important idea is the superiority of research over teaching within
the university: teaching serves to transmit knowledge validated by science,
not to create it or to co-construct it. Today, one can see that this hierarchiza-
tion is at the heart of the knowledge regime organizing contemporary science
in the Northern countries (less so in in Africa where the resources of universities are primarily dedicated to teaching).[7] It is also the origin of many difficulties universities have faced when introducing innovation to teaching, for
example, adapting it to social transformations. The fourth idea also imposes
hierarchy on levels of teaching, making "higher" education the summum of
the educational mission, even when literacy and democratization could have
been the most important level. Here yet again, our era does nothing but reinforce this principle, embodied, for example, in differences of social status and
salary between professors at different levels. The final Humboldtian idea is
a paradox that continues to permeate university life: the belief that the university must simultaneously be independent with respect to the state, but also
unavoidably rely upon it for financial support—at least in the case of public
universities, whose mission is reproducing the elites that the state needs.

Thorsten Nybom's article on Humboldt's vision indicates that the latter quite explicitly wanted the university to be an ivory tower, using the
argument from German romanticism that the quest for truth, overvalued in
comparison to the quest for justice or beauty, could only be pursued in a
pure environment, sheltered from the world, in the greatest autonomy, even
though it was financed by the state.[8] (This is what no longer works today in
the Northern countries given the state's disengagement from higher education and its obsession with the profitability of investments and other aspects
of managerial thought). In a very interesting way, according to Nybom, this

argument supposed that university professors had to cut themselves off from the political world, renounce all political functions, all desire for power, to better consecrate themselves to the excellence of their works—which meanwhile were destined to train engineers and other experts for the conquest of the colonial world and industrial omnipotence! This paradox is at the heart of the problems that universities and particularly their research mission face as a result of pressures toward making organizations and businesses socially responsible, a principle often invoked when reflecting on the human and social development of communities.

Positivist Epistemology

In fact, these movements tend to prevent the research university from claiming to want or to be capable of satisfaction with a purely internal mission, that of assuring the progress of knowledge, without concern for the world in which it exists, which finances it and uses it, or which might need this knowledge to solve problems or live according to its values. The pluralist theory of knowledge(s) that I use, on the other hand, considers that scholarly and scientific kinds of knowledge, like all knowledge, but even more so because of their prestige, their symbolic capital and their alliance with the market, participate in the construction of societies and their development. To claim the contrary, that is, to claim that they are mutually independent, is a symptom of what I call positivist epistemology, which is hegemonic and very contagious in the research world.[9] Positivist epistemology seeks to have us believe that knowledge can be separated from society, when the very history of science shows how closely it has been linked with the conquering project of European modernity and colonization. In my view, the university can serve local development in producing knowledge that is relevant to this development and harmonizes with local values and priorities, while simultaneously producing (degreed) citizens who know this knowledge and use it. For this reason, I would like to take a closer look at this epistemological obstacle, which is all more powerful because it is so rarely seen with clarity. I will also show that this obstacle generates instances of cognitive injustice.

The central feature of positivist epistemology is the idea that emotions, feelings, affects, in short everything that refers to identity and personal, local, or cultural life, are obstacles; sources of bias, error, and irrationality, but also of inefficiency and a lack of professionalism. According to this epistemology, which is so clearly linked to the Humboldtian university, all scientific activity must struggle to purify itself of this "human" dimension of life so that studies can advance according to their internal logic and not in response to external demands which could render them "impure," for example, imperatives of development or local problems such as climatic changes experienced

in this or that region. Researchers, but also administrators, are thus inculcated with a feeling of obligation to live a disconnect, an unbinding, a cut, a
separation, indeed a gulf between themselves and the rest of what I call "the
world," which could contaminate the accomplishment of their mission (isn't
this the vocabulary of "solid evidence"?)[10] From this perspective, it is evident that local preoccupations or individuals and groups committed to local
problems must not influence scientific research, since it is entirely oriented
toward the scientific public space and its economy of publication. Above all,
they must not suggest themes for research. Rather, positivist epistemology
asks scientists to take refuge behind their responsibility/task of "advancing
knowledge." In this way, they can overlook the consequences their work
has on the world, which is what I would consider their responsibility/bond
with fellow citizens—something that would lead them, for example, toward
action-research, participatory research, discussion, or debate.[11]

A Different Diglossia

Here I see a different diglossia, the one that sets up an opposition between
ordinary language, which the members of a community speak with one
another, and scholarly language, the only one capable of telling the truth
because it claims to be free from values, points of view, or locality, and is
therefore in a better position to reach the universal. Above all, scholarly
language claims to be mastered only by those with a scholarly training, a
small fraternity or sisterhood, regardless of the discipline. For me this is a
pure language game, a kind of rhetoric! For example, in a scholarly text, the
jargon, as well as the exclusion of the first person "I" and all mention of the
author's social and cultural location is considered an indicator of neutrality
and of scientificity, therefore of credibility and symbolic capital. Once I was
asked to substitute a "we" for my "I" in an article without changing anything
else about the content because that would sound more scholarly! To the contrary, I practice the "I" because I think that it is preferable to show the point
of view from which one speaks, rather than hiding it. Qualitative research
or action-research, particularly in the human and social sciences, has also
adopted the "I."

Beyond these language games, there are beliefs and dogmas to fight against
if scholarly research is to be liberated from this obligation to be neutral and
if it is to be allowed to serve the most urgent collective, social, and environmental problems in a given context. To make research and the university
where it takes place socially responsible in this way requires that researchers and the institutions where they work be recognized as full members of
this shared world and participate in the world by their work, alongside other
citizens, without fear of losing scientificity. A highly innovative mechanism

like the "Science Shop" ["boutique des sciences et des savoirs"] can facilitate this building of connections and collaborations between a university's teacher-researchers and students, and the community and other associations of a region.[12]

What makes the positivist dogma intolerable for me is that I observe in reality to what extent this ideal of purity, separation, and autonomy is a historical sham, a consequential myth, a fiction that generates cognitive injustices. I have mentioned the links between the development of Western science and colonization, which must never be forgotten. Positivist epistemology interprets science as knowledge enabling a natural or cultural object to be controlled by predicting its behavior, thanks to laws that are so abstract they can be called universal. The goal of control and exploitation, or of governmentality, as Foucault would say, is completely integrated into these epistemologies, to which one can oppose other epistemologies much more centered on links between objects of the natural and spiritual world that tend toward harmony, like the thought of *Ubuntu* in Africa, *Buen vivir* in Bolivia and Ecuador, or the indigenous epistemologies of Canada, which give rise to very different methodologies. While the distinctiveness of scientific laws comes above all from their effort to decontextualize knowledge, the epistemologies that I have cited or even the narrative turn in social sciences aims at recontextualizing knowledge by situating it, for example, in the life or the culture of the one who uses it.

American Hegemony and the New Academic "Voluntary Servitude"

The field that one calls social studies of science and technology proposes an analysis of the contemporary regime of knowledge and the sciences, to use Dominique Pestre's expression, showing that science today has almost left the universities, has been separated from its mission of forming society's future elites, and has become progressively sidetracked into a self-driving world-system.[13] This system is centered in the United States around a set of newly created commercial institutions that present themselves as the new world judge of scientificity: the databases which are permitted to decide, on the basis of their indexing system, what is and is not good science, true science, namely, the Web of Science and SCOPUS.[14] These databases are marketing tools developed by publishers whose financial goal is to increase sales of their products.[15]

With the rise of the impact factor—a quantitative index that includes no reflection on the quality of published texts—these databases and the five commercial publishers who profit from this system (Elsevier, Springer Nature, Wiley, Taylor & Francis, and Sage) are the emperors before whom the scientists of the entire world prostrate themselves with a superb voluntary servitude, even though, of course, they protest in private, particularly against the arrogant affirmation that "English is the universal language of science."[16] Even the scientific leaders of Francophone Africa, which in the meantime is at the extreme periphery of this world-system, aspire more than ever to get their journals indexed in this system, although Clarivate Analytics says explicitly that it only accepts a few regional journals from time to time—and the CAMES uses this system in its promotion criteria![17]

Here I note in passing the grave moral crisis which has befallen the knowledge regime as it converts to a knowledge economy and to cognitive capitalism: instances of research fraud, conflicts of interest, and massaged data multiply; databases are on sale to the highest bidder, researchers become entrepreneurs and carelessly mix public subventions and private profits, studies cannot be replicated and remain unsatisfying, even if, at the same time, the jargon of "conclusive data" tries to make them seem otherwise.

The Knowledge World-System: Money and the Dissemination of Knowledge

This scholarly world-system produces many forms of cognitive injustice in the countries of the South. The first and most striking cognitive injustice produced by the system is the inequality of access to scholarly publications depending on where one lives or on one's faculty status. This is what I call closed science, science transformed into a commodity which is inaccessible to those unable to pay, in the North as well as in the South. The epitome is obviously Elsevier which asks $38.95 for access to a PDF of a book review or an article published thirty years ago or which demands astronomical sums from libraries and universities for web services which do not even include printing and mailing costs. This is purely and simply the effect of branding, like the one associated with any "luxury" or "quality" product.

When Cairn.info asks five Euros payable by credit card for a PDF, this might seem more reasonable. But it is a genuine barrier in countries where a student only rarely has a bank account and never a credit card. This is also a much larger sum, proportionate to salary, for university lecturers and researchers from the South than for those of the North. I have seen too many absurd situations of this kind: a professor from Niger publishes an article in a journal in Cairn.info which then requires students from Niger to pay five Euros to read an article talking about Niger. To this hurdle are added the local problems of access to the web, to computers, and even to electricity, but also the lack of what is called digital literacy: students' ability to get maximum benefit from scholarly resources on a web with which they are unfamiliar. The majority of students with whom I work in Africa or in Haiti use their smartphone and their 3G connection to read articles online, necessarily those which are open access. And I can't even start on the fees required of authors, this new and highly successful, but scandalous commercial tactic that the journals justify by referring to their "right to make profits" and that thankfully not all journals practice, whatever some may think.[18]

Injustice in the Generation of Knowledge

To this cognitive injustice in the access to scholarly publications another is added, more complex: a forcible slowing of the capacity to create knowledge relevant to a given country and to circulate it freely on the web, in relative synchrony with the challenges, the needs, the priorities, and the choices of local societies, those that can contribute to human development. In fact, this other form of cognitive injustice is an amalgam of three forms: the difficulty of creating knowledge, that of getting it published and circulated in the North and in the South, and that of creating knowledge which is relevant to the researcher's own country. The difficulty of creating knowledge is linked in the first place to the lack of resources dedicated to research in African universities. Rarely are teachers and researchers given research budgets, the necessary laboratories and infrastructure, or fellowships for doctoral students who, in the Northern countries, are really the ones doing the empirical work. Nor are there many science-oriented policymakers who allocate budgets for the conduct of research on subjects judged to be national priorities. In fact, laboratories often count on their famous partners in the North to finance research, to the point of losing sight of the subjects that were initially marked as priorities—above all if they were never unambiguously delimited. One sees this clearly with the current trend in Northern countries toward research in artificial intelligence, which drains millions, while in Africa, other needs are much higher on the research agenda: climatic change, agroecology, renewable energy sources, healthy urbanization, governmental practice, the preservation of languages, and so on.

But it is not just that these countries have limited resources to create official research programs responding to their priorities. They also perpetuate or cannot escape a situation of extraversion toward the North, which blocks every effort in this direction.[19] It is Northern science which has the money, which does the publishing, and which, moreover, claims to be universal and therefore the "best" (since locality renders knowledge impure and irrational). The ideal in Southern countries is thus to be trained in science by the countries to the North, to adopt without contestation the epistemologies of the North, for example, the way they distinguish the disciplines, and to imitate the science of the North as best they can, despite the cautionary words of Frantz Fanon, Cheikh Anta Diop, Abdou Moumouni Dioffo, Joseph Ki Zerbo, and other pioneers of African research. On returning to Africa, a Congolese researcher who did a thesis on nuclear fission thanks to a Belgian fellowship was regretful because he saw that his outstanding competence had no relevance to his country's needs. This exemplifies the difficulty of creating knowledge, but also the difficulty of putting the knowledge that exists in universities into genuine circulation.

This second difficulty, for example, can be seen in African higher education, in the collections of reading texts which contain European classics far more often than African classics. This situation perpetuates epistemic alienation, the idea that the white outweighs the black and that nothing interesting is being done in African universities. However, quite material considerations also undermine the circulation and the utilization of these African scholarly resources by African universities, namely, the lack of local resources and competences to assure the digitization and high-quality online presentation of these documents, in other words, with the metadata enabling search engines to find the files. In fact, African scholarly production primarily takes the form of theses, mémoires, and research reports, or even articles in departmental publications without great material resources which, until recently, were rarely digitized and tended to sleep on the library shelves, rather than to circulate between universities, and particularly between universities of the South, so as to be available for teaching purposes. For example, I discovered that the Sahel Institute in Maroua (Cameroon) and the department of Geography in Ouagadougou (Burkina Faso) were unaware of one another's work on desertification, while everyone knew French researchers' work on the same subject!

Mistrust of the Digital World

In addition to these very material obstacles, one also finds mistrustful attitudes with respect to the circulation of knowledge online: a mistrust of the digital medium which is thought to be of lower quality than hard copy, a fear (which I find strange) of publishing one's work lest it be stolen, a lack of digital literacy, which means that professors and researchers of a certain age are not aware of the web's potential and the existence of scholarly discourse online, and finally, incomprehension at the idea of open access, which brings visibility, citation, and prestige, while putting it on sale brings very little if not nothing and limits its impact. In short, all this discourages the digitization of theses, mémoires, journals, and thus their availability to classrooms in the North as well as sharing between universities in the South.

But the South alone is not responsible for this situation. The politics behind the indexing of journals by Clarivate shows this in no uncertain terms: it is extremely difficult for Africans to publish on their own in these databases, which are supposed to be universal Science itself, without the help of white colleagues. Still further, studies by unrelated research teams show the existence of a systemic racism in the system of scientific publication. For example, an experiment has revealed that a manuscript is more easily accepted in the scholarly journals of the North when an African author's name is changed to a European name—a phenomenon well known from studies on women in science. The fact that the publishing system of the scientific world should be so difficult to break into does not, to be sure, facilitate the diffusion and the circulation of knowledge done in Africa. The local journals are not valued by this world-system, although they contain the knowledge that the region or country in question needs!

Let us add one more factor that is often combined with these forms of injustice, linked to the difficulty of creating and circulating knowledge between African universities in digital format: the continual expansion of the number of articles in open access among scientists in the North (for reasons that I do not have space to explain here)—one of whose effects is the over-representation of Northern scholarly activity in open access and therefore a potential source of neocolonialism.

CREATING ACCOUNTABILITY

The Task of Governments and Universities

Becoming aware of these injustices, which limit the creation and the free circulation of scholarly knowledge in the service of the priorities of Southern countries and inhibit the decolonization of higher education, is the first step toward making universities increasingly responsible. But it is also a first step toward making demands on the governments of Southern countries which, accustomed to the canonical division according to which science comes from the North and data comes from South, do not always see why it is necessary to invest in science at the national level rather than to let its partners take care of funding. To encourage institutional open access, to resist the commercial economy in knowledge so to move toward a social and solidarity-based economy of knowledge, these are the ways out of such injustices.

Concrete Projects

I have been involved with two very concrete projects to remedy these injustices. The first is a platform of open access African journals accompanied by tools to help with the editing of articles and research projects, called scienceafrique.org. The second, more important, is DICAMES, the pan-African scholarly archive of CAMES which is going to gather together the scholarly production of all universities in the CAMES space.[20] DICAMES will eventually be filled with thousands of theses and articles, enabling teachers and students to improve their lecturing techniques and the content of their courses! Students have told me that professors prevent them from using the web to verify or validate the content of what is being taught, but the use of digital African resources could simultaneously improve the quality and the relevance of students' own work as well as that of professors. However, the material conditions still need to be assembled and some professors will have to accept no longer being the indisputable masters of knowledge in their classrooms which is sometimes very difficult for them.

Here I allude to a last form of cognitive injustice that we have listed in our survey but which goes somewhat beyond the scope of this chapter.[21] We called it the Pedagogy of Humiliation. It refers to those situations where, for all sorts of reasons ranging from incompetence or the feeling of not being properly recognized, which can make the faculty so bitter that they abuse their power and despise students they consider as "ignorant" little siblings, professors do not hesitate to adopt humiliating practices, for example, by not correcting work, by refusing support, by giving zeros for effort, by shaming writers for their errors in French, and so on. It is as if the professor became more valuable compared to the failure of the students! This strange, but well-observed rationalization does not encourage self-confidence and the power to act which are essential to creativity and innovation, above all in the case of women who already face so many obstacles in their university careers, first as students and then as faculty.

CONCLUSION: MULTIVERSITY AND
CONCRETE PROPOSALS

A university is not necessarily the site where elites are reproduced or a school of professional training or an incubator for future citizens. A university is what a society wants it to be. A university/multiversity can be imagined as a site of exchanges and sharing of useful knowledge for sustainable local development and for the common good, a segment of space-time allowing students and the general population to develop their competencies, interests, and horizons. A living situation lending itself to mutual aid and mutual comprehension, spreading into society as a whole.

How might we imagine a just university?

At the level of *teaching*:

• Develop a kind of pedagogy that aims at empowerment, by insisting on each person's capabilities

- Teach by example, using collaboration, teamwork, honesty, punctuality, and care for the common good
- Learn to think together and to live together in society (co-citizenship)
- Use the vast reservoir of available knowledge forms, including but certainly not limited to the sciences: traditional, everyday, experiential, political, cultural, and ethical
- Insist on the right to learn in the language one uses for thinking
- Insist that professors be respected, but also open to dialogue and to the students' knowledge

At the level of *research:*

- Privilege research questions that are relevant for the community, those that have meaning, rather than those that are inspired by external problematics
- Privilege participatory action-research based on communities. These partnerships are open to local preoccupations, mobilize collective intelligence and local knowledge, and assure the transmission of knowledge produced among those acting for local sustainable development
- Disseminate the research thus realized in open access on the web so that it can be used everywhere
- Include a variety of epistemological approaches necessary to the ecology of knowledge

At the level of *service to communities:*

- Create permanent links with regional employers (through a mechanism such as a placement service or coordinating office), public services, or businesses
- Create permanent links with associations which do local development, by means of institutions such as "science shops"
- Create living laboratories and incubators, which can be meeting places bringing together professors, students, and population outside the formal context of teaching to generate ideas and innovation

At the level of *management:*

- Use an approach that favors consultation and participation of all members of a university community to avoid relations of force and conflicts
- Use the web to manage systems: for note taking and management of diplomas and certifications (to combat corruption and incompetence)
- Privilege a kind of harmonious living-together, including the struggle against harassment, humiliation, discrimination, and favor mutual aid rather than competition for resources

- Assure efficient communication, such as updating addresses and sending bulletins.

Is it possible to reinvent a university that reinforces and values a country's women and men, values, cultures, languages, and preoccupations, rather than one that seeks to imitate models which derive from colonial history or aim at entering a world-system dominated by the United States and Great Britain? Yes, it is possible thanks to cognitive justice, but only on condition that we are willing to change our ways of doing things and renounce dogmas which, in the North as in the South, prevent us from advancing toward a pluralist, inclusive science and a multiversity in the service of the common good.

Translated by Laura Hengehold

NOTES

1. This text is the result of presentations made in Niger, Haiti, and Cameroon, based in part on Florence Piron, "Justice et injustice cognitives: de l'épistémologie à la matérialité des savoirs humains," in *Les Classiques des sciences sociales: 25 ans de partage des savoirs dans la francophonie*, ed. Émilie Tremblay et Ricarson Dorcé, Histoire de la bibliothèque numérique/Les Classiques des sciences sociales et réflexions sur son avenir (Quebec: Éditions science et bien commun), 273–87. (https://scienceetbiencommun.pressbooks.pub/classiques25ans/chapter/justice-et-injustice-cognitives/). For the sake of publication, the slides have been omitted as well as the purely oratorical aspects of the text. The subtitles and some references have been added by the editors.

2. https://scienceetbiencommun.pressbooks.pub/.

3. See, for example, this essay by founder Paulo Wangoola, "Mpambo Afrikan Multiversity, Dialogue and Building Bridges across Worldviews, Cultures and Languages," in *Anthropologists, Indigenous Scholars and the Research Endeavour*, ed. Joy Hendry and Laara Fitznor (Routledge, 2012).

4. See Shiv Visvanathan, "La quête de justice cognitive." Dans *Justice cognitive, libre accès et savoirs locaux. Pour une science ouverte juste, au service du développement local durable*. Sous la direction de Florence Piron, Samuel Régulus et Marie Sophie Dibounje Madiba (Québec: Éditions science et bien commun, 2016) https://scienceetbiencommun.pressbooks.pub/justicecognitive1/chapter/en-quete-de-justice-cognitive. SOHA is an action-research project that took place from 2015 to 2017 (see http://projetsoha.org to learn more). Several new research and doctoral projects emerged from it over the course of 2018, as well as the creation of Association pour la promotion de la science ouverte en Haïti et en Afrique and a research group on cognitive justice, open science, and the commons at l'Université Laval (Quebec).

5. More information can be found at https://www.barefootcollege.org/. The Barefoot College model (The Social Work and Research Centre) was founded in Tilonia, India, 1972 by Bunker Roy. It became the subject of the 2012 documentary *Rafea: Solar Mama* by Mona Eldaief and Jehane Noujaim.

6. See Jacques Rancière, *The Ignorant Schoolmaster: Five Lessons in Intellectual Emancipation*, trans. Kristin Ross (Stanford: Stanford University Press, 1991).

7. Dominique Pestre, *À contre-science. Politiques et savoirs es sociétés contemporaines* (Paris: Editions du Seuil, 2013).

8. Thorsten Nybom, "The Humboldt Legacy: Reflections on the Past, Present, and Future of the European University," *Higher Education Policy* 16 (2003): 141–59.

9. See Florence Piron, "L'amoralité du positivism institutionnel: L'épistémologie du lien comme résistance," in Laurence Brière, Mélissa Lieutenant-Gosselin and Florence Piron, eds., *Et si la recherche scientifique ne pouvait pas être neutre?* (Quebec: Éditions science et bien commun, 2019), 145–46.

10. See Achille Joseph Mbembe, "Decolonizing the University: New Directions." *Arts and Humanities in Higher Education* 15, no. 1 (2016): 32–33.https://doi.org/10.1177/1474022215618513.

11. Piron, *Et si la recherche scientifique*.

12. See Florence Piron, "Les boutiques des sciences et des savoirs, au croisement de l'université et développement local durable," in *Justice cognitive, libre accès et savoirs locaux: Pour une science ouverte juste, au service du développement local durable,* ed. Florence Piron, Samuel Regulus, Marie Sophie Dibounje Madiba (Quebec: Éditions science et bien commun, 2016), https://scienceetbiencommun.pressbooks.pub/justicecognitive1/chapter/les-boutiques-des-sciences-et-des-savoirs-au-croisement-entre-universite-et-developpement-local-durable/.

13. Pestre, *À contre-science*, especially chapter 8.

14. See Pablo Kreimer and Adriana Feld, "Sociologie des sciences: divers objets, diverses approches, divers agendas." *Sociologies pratiques* 1 (Supplément) (2014): 137–49. https://doi.org/10.3917/sopr.hs01.0137.

15. Larivière, Vincent, Stefanie Haustein and Philippe Mongeon. "L'oligopole des grands éditeurs savants." *Découvrir. Le magazine de l'Acfas* (2015).

16. Testa, James. "Journal Selection Process in the Web of Science." Clarivate Analytics (Web of Science) (2016). https://clarivate.com/essays/journal-selection-process/.

17. Testa, "Journal Selection Process." CAMES (Conseil Africain et Malgache pour l'enseignement supérieur) is an organization coordinating degree requirements and faculty qualifications between universities in Francophone Africa so that students can reliably acquire transfer credit in different countries and move, if they desire, to European institutions whose requirements and qualifications are now being standardized through the Bologna process.

18. David J. Solomon and Björk Bo-Christer, "Publication Fees in Open Access Publishing: Sources of Funding and Factors Influencing Choice of Journal." *Journal of the American Society for Information Science and Technology* 63, no. 1 (2011): 98–107.

19. Paulin Hountondji, *Endogenous Knowledge: Research Trails* (Dakar: Codesria, 1997).
20. footnote on DICAMES http://savoirs.cames.online.
21. http://projetsoha.org.

BIBLIOGRAPHY

Frésard, Laurent, Christophe Perignon et Anders Wilhelmsson. "The Pernicious Effects of Contaminated Data in Risk Management." SSRN Scholarly Paper ID 1537244 (Rochester, NY: Social Science Research Network, 2011). https://papers.ssrn.com/abstract=1537244.

Kreimer, Pablo and Adriana Feld. "Sociologie des sciences: divers objets, diverses approches, divers agendas." *Sociologies pratiques* 1 (Supplément) (2014): 137–49. https://doi.org/10.3917/sopr.hs01.0137.

Larivière, Vincent, Stefanie Haustein and Philippe Mongeon. "L'oligopole des grands éditeurs savants." *Découvrir. Le magazine de l'Acfas* (2015). http://www.acfas.ca/publications/decouvrir/2015/02/l-oligopole-grands-editeurs-savants.

Mbembe, Achille Joseph. "Decolonizing the University: New Directions." *Arts and Humanities in Higher Education* 15, no. 1 (2016): 29–45. https://doi.org/10.1177/1474022215618513.

Nybom, Thorsten. "The Humboldt Legacy: Reflections on the Past, Present, and Future of the European University." *Higher Education Policy* 16 (2003): 141–59.

Pestre, Dominique. *À contre-science. Politiques et savoirs es sociétés contemporaines* (Paris: Editions du Seuil, 2013).

Piron, Florence. "Justice et injustice cognitives: de l'épistémologie à la matérialité des savoirs humains," in *Les Classiques des sciences sociales: 25 ans de partage des savoirs dans la francophonie*. Edited by Émilie Tremblay et Ricarson Dorcé, Histoire de la bibliothèque numérique/Les Classiques des sciences sociales et réflexions sur son avenir (Quebec: Éditions sciences et bien commun, 2018): 273–87. https://scienceetbiencommun.pressbooks.pub/classiques25ans/chapter/justice-et-injustice-cognitives/.

———. "L'amoralité du positivism institutionnel: L'épistémologie du lien comme résistance," in *Et si la recherche scientifique ne pouvait pas être neutre?* Edited by Laurence Brière, Mélissa Lieutenant-Gosselin and Florence Piron (Quebec: Éditions science et bien commun, 2019): 135–168.

———. "Méditation haïtienne. Répondre à la violence séparatrice de l'épistémologie positiviste par une épistémologie du lien," *Sociologie et sociétés* 49, no. 2 (2017): 33–60. https://corpus.ulaval.ca/jspui/bitstream/20.500.11794/16322/1/Florence%20Piron%20Sociologie%20et%20socie%CC%81te%CC%81s.pdf.

———. "Les boutiques des sciences et des savoirs,au croisement de l'université et développement local durable," in *Justice cognitive, libre accès et savoirs locaux: Pour une science ouverte juste, au service du développement local durable*. Edited by Florence Piron, Samuel Regulus, Marie Sophie Dibounje Madiba (Quebec:

Éditions science et bien commun, 2016). https://scienceetbiencommun.press-books.pub/justicecognitive1/chapter/les-boutiques-des-sciences-et-des-savoirs-au-croisement-entre-universite-et-developpement-local-durable/.

Piron, Florence, Antonin Benoît Diouf, Marie Sophie Dibounje Madiba, Thomas Hervé Mboa Nkoudou, Zoé Aubierge Ouangré, Djossè Roméo Tessy, Hamissou Rhissa Achaffert, Anderson Pierre and Zakari Lire. 2017. "Le libre accès vu d'Afrique francophone subsaharienne." *Revue française des sciences de l'information et de la communication* (11). https://doi.org/10.4000/rfsic.3292.

Rancière, Jacques. *The Ignorant Schoolmaster: Five Lessons in Intellectual Emancipation.* Translated by Kristin Ross (Stanford: Stanford University Press, 1991).

Solomon, David J. and Björk Bo-Christer. "Publication Fees in Open Access Publishing: Sources of Funding and Factors Influencing Choice of Journal." *Journal of the American Society for Information Science and Technology* 63, no. 1 (2011): 98–107. https://doi.org/10.1002/asi.21660.

Testa, James. 2016. "Journal Selection Process in the Web of Science." Clarivate Analytics (Web of Science). https://clarivate.com/essays/journal-selection-process/.

Vessuri, Hebe, Jean-Claude Guédon et Ana María Cetto. "Excellence or Quality? Impact of the Current Competition Regime on Science and Scientific Publishing in Latin America and Its Implications for Development." *Current Sociology* 62, no. 5 (2013): 647–65.

Wangoola, Paolo. "Mpambo Afrikan Multiversity, Dialogue and Building Bridges Across Worldviews, Cultures and Languages," in *Anthropologists, Indigenous Scholars and the Research Endeavour.* Edited by Joy Hendry and Laara Fitznor (Routledge, 2012): 28–43.

Chapter 5

Specters of the Infinitesimal

Posthuman Francophone Worlds

Nick Nesbitt

The world of francophone anti- and postcolonial letters, the world of Toussaint Louverture, Dessalines, and Baron de Vastey, of Aimé and Suzanne Césaire, of Frantz Fanon and Edouard Glissant, of Maryse Condé, René Depestre, and Giselle Pineau, was a world that endured more than two centuries. It is the world of the former slaves described so vividly by CLR James in *The Black Jacobins*; it is the world of Césaire's Negritude, of the black subject "debout et libre," in the famous words of *Cahier d'un retour au pays natal*.[1] It is a world that will no doubt live on in the posthuman condition we are currently entering, as a tenacious survivor. In any case, this anti- and postcolonial world is above all profoundly, and in ways that are only now becoming apparent, humanist. In the 1960s, in the so-called Structuralist and Post-structuralist moments, it seemed obvious what *posthumanism* meant: If Sartre centered his philosophy around a critical refashioning of the Cartesian ego and its *projects*, if actually existing state-Socialisms in the wake of 1917, and the global, revolutionary anticolonial movements inspired by them from China to Algeria, Viet Nam and Cuba, spoke tirelessly of the creation of a "New Man," if all this and more formed twentieth-century "Humanism," it seemed obvious to the generation of the 1960s, readers of Althusser, Foucault, Balibar, and Lacan, what would constitute a true antihumanism, whether it allowed itself to be called structuralist or not. This antihumanism at the time took two main forms: First, a critique of identity, of the subject as self-same, conscious agent producing, as praxis, its world, the subject of Vico's famous *verum est factum* principle that states that only what the subject produces does it truly know. All this would be replaced by Freud via Lacan, the place of the I revealing its absolute constitution and determination by the unconscious, structured like a language.

Second, the antihumanism of the 1960s was a critique of political economy, a return to Marx by thinkers like Althusser, Rancière, and Balibar, a
return that in its looking back to the Marx of *Das Kapital*, violently rejected
the Marxist Humanism of the 1940s and 1950s epitomized not only by Sartre
(who was of course their main target), but by implication at least, the field
of militant, Communist francophone writers: Jacques Roumain, Aimé and
Suzanne Césaire, Jacques Stéphen Alexis, Frantz Fanon, and CLR James, to
name only the most famous.

This Marxist structuralism was an antihumanism insofar as it argued that
our own-most, conscious self-identity, in our actions and our understanding
of their meaning, in our projects, in other words, was precisely the site of the
most fallacious *mis*recognition. As subjects, we are necessarily and inevitably
subjects of ideology. Moreover, we are so precisely in the realm of production, where Hegel's Master and Slave dialectic had told us that the wretched
of the earth could recognize their own freedom to transform the world, and
where, as such, we believed our own identity to be that of the free-subject-able
to-choose, as Sartre constantly reminded readers able to make a decision and
form a project—no matter how constrained and debased our situation, from
plantation slavery in St. Domingue to omnipresent colonial violence in Algeria.
It was precisely here, in the realm of production, that structuralism announced
that this humanism, the humanism of the free and self-conscious subject, had
long ago been revealed by Marx as mere illusion, if we had only cared to listen
rather than becoming lost in humanist daydreams. As Balibar put the matter
with stunning simplicity in his contribution to *Lire le Capital*, "Production is
not the production of things, it is the production and conservation of social relations," in other words, the reproduction of our own bondage to capital.[2]

It seemed clear for many years, until about the year 2000, I would say, that
this logic formed a clear and coherent division between twentieth-century
humanism and the anti-humanism typical of the 1960s, which continued as
something like what has been called French Theory, until around ten or fif-
teen years ago. This conceptual division between humanism and antihumanism, the very foundation of language and identity not only in Francophone
Studies but humanistic inquiry in general of the last fifty years, has suddenly,
I want to propose in what follows, not so much disappeared as become dysfunctional and antiquarian as an explanatory apparatus. Here I would like
to sketch out, in provisional form, the parameters of this division between
francophone humanism and what I would call the properly posthuman, to
distinguish it from the mere antihumanism of the 1960s.

The antihumanism of the 1960s, to anticipate my conclusion, remained
a humanism insofar as it merely sought to enlarge the scope of the human
itself, to encompass the unconscious and ideology, for example, as part of
the human experience, aspects that evaded the conscious dominion of the

subject while nonetheless remaining part of the human experience. While the Freudian and Lacanian critiques of consciousness were undoubtedly crucial and continue to prove crucial to such a project, it is the critique of identity as subject to capital in Marx, that is to say, and in Marx's reception by francophone thinkers such as Césaire, Alexis, and Fanon, that I wish to focus on here. I do so precisely because the era of the posthuman we are now entering constitutes not so much a psychological transformation (though it will surely prove to be that as well) but an epochal revolution in the mode of capitalist production, and consequently of the human subject's place within capitalism itself, for as long as that system persists in its global domination. This age of the inhuman we are now entering, which for decades seemed to be the stuff of science fiction, suddenly fully and brutally displaces humans from the center of social existence in ways totally unsuspected and invisible to the antihumanists of the 1960s like Althusser and Foucault. Insofar as our globalized world has in the last twenty years become generally, if not categorically, subsumed to the logic of capital, subsumed to the requirement that to survive and count as social beings we must valorize value, make a profit, in other words, for whoever owns the capital that employs us, this familiar logic, which appeared to previous generations of Marxists as exploitation, as the exploitation of humans by humans, with machines the mere mediators of this exploitation, this logic has suddenly been overturned. Man is suddenly, as if out of nowhere, no longer at the center of the social world he has created, the world of capital. The implications for our understanding of human identity and the place of language in the articulation of this identity are enormous.

Here I will back up, and recall briefly the familiar parameters of that world of language and identity in the francophone world, a world encapsulated most precisely in Hegel's famous dialectic of the Master and Slave. Hegel's philosophical drama supplied francophone studies in the radical, Marxist humanism of writers such as Césaire, Alexis, Fanon, and even, more ambiguously, Glissant, with its fundamental human drama of freedom. This was the freedom of human against human, each risking their life, each "staking its own life [. . .] in a life and death struggle," writes Hegel, wherein "its whole being has been seized with dread, [. . . and] everything solid and stable has been shaken to its foundations."[3]

Let me propose the opening months of the Haitian Revolution as the moment in which the problem of language and identity in relation to slavery and anticolonialism suddenly becomes visible to a shocked world. The language of the Haitian Revolution in its most radical and compelling formulations encompasses and reconceives concepts such as "esclave," "l'humanité," "liberté," "égalité," "droits de l'homme," "indépendance," and "noir," "blanc," and "mulâtre," to name a few of the obvious candidates (Nesbitt, *Universal Emancipation*). A seemingly simple problem immediately confronts humanity, a problem that draws the problem of language and identity into intimate relation with the politics of colonialism from the very beginning: if these words of the Haitian Revolution are French words, written, as in the famous 1797 letter of Louverture to the French Directory, how are we to know whether their utterance constitutes some sort of Event, in the fullest sense of the word, for peripheral, colonized francophone identity, rather than a mere recapitulation of the same, the same old identities, the same old social relations, the same old politics?

We can counterpose two examples: the first is one of a series of letters from the first months of the revolution in the Spring of 1792, letters written to the local authorities in St. Domingue by the leaders of the slave insurrection Jean-François, Biassou, and Louverture, at a time when they were still siding with the Spanish monarchy, decrying the French Revolution's injustices to the world order. In these infamous exchanges, the nominal leaders of the former slaves sought to assure their own continued freedom and that of a few associates, bartered away in exchange for handing back their followers to the whip of plantation slavery. When I analyzed these letters in my book *Universal Emancipation*, I saw in the appearance and usage of phrases such as "nous avons pris la liberté" and "nous prenons la liberté" as covert, timid announcements of the coming revolution against the world of slavery that would be concretized as the independence of the Haitian nation in 1804.[4] Looking at them again today, I read this language precisely as the negation of the Event of the St. Domingue Revolution, of the destruction of the world of plantation slavery and its replacement by a society founded upon universal human equality. Instead, the writers of these early letters of the Haitian Revolution clearly continued to think within the logic of monarchy, hierarchy, in short, the divinely ordained order of the Ancien Régime.

In contrast, witness Toussaint Louverture's famous declaration of August 1793, in which he announces to his fellow revolutionaries, and, indeed, to the world, his arrival on that stage. This brief statement is so astoundingly brilliant and original: "Je suis Toussaint Louverture."[5] The former slave sheds the name of his master's plantation, Bréda, gives himself the name he desires, constitutes himself, indeed, as autonomous subject, as the world-historical identity that he would become. *Je* is no longer *un autre*, the name of the other, of the slave master's whim. There where the slave was, Toussaint Louverture will be. Toussaint, in choosing the name Louverture, posits himself as Event, as a fracture in the world of the Ancien Régime, and, indeed, in the world of a pre-Jacobin, French Revolution that had no desire whatsoever to move toward the abolition of slavery logically implied by the *Déclaration des droits de l'homme*. Furthermore, Louverture goes on to name the parameters of this intervention that will, by 1804, destroy one world and create another: *liberté* and *égalité*, which, he declares, he wishes to reign sovereign in St.

Domingue. This is the order of an entirely new world, one that denies the legitimacy of hierarchic social structure, of servitude and bondage.

How can these two francophone statements emanating from the same site in the dark heart of colonial plantation slavery deploy identical language with such violently contrasting implications, the one affirming monarchy and a hierarchical ordering of the world, in which masters (among whom the writers wish to be counted) rightfully rule slaves; the other affirming the flat, nonhierarchical structuration of radical egalitarianism as universal emancipation? Clearly, the distinction to be drawn must refer to the conjuncture or structure of relation defining their meaning: in the first, despite being written by black subjects, former slaves, words such as *liberté* are understood to be partial, reserved for a rightful elite, while those of Louverture, only a few years before himself not only a slave, but subsequently a free black slave *owner*, look forward to a society based upon the universal human right to be free from enslavement.

The subsequent writings of Henry Christophe's scribe Baron de Vastey congeal the various contradictions of the humanism of francophone language and identity. The Vastey we find in *Colonial System Unveiled* takes his place as the first postcolonial thinker, the rightful predecessor to Césaire and Fanon.[6] How, in the absence of their explicit exposition, are we to understand Vastey's use of such concepts as *colonialism*, *system*, and *critique* in his critique of postcolonial Haitian identity? How does Vastey articulate his critique of the principal phenomenon at issue in *Colonial System*, namely, violence (both in its colonial and revolutionary variants)?

Vastey's singular intervention into this debate is to describe colonialism as a general system of *acts* of violence, acts for which those human actors are to be held accountable, for perhaps the first time. Vastey's critique of colonialism as a system of acts made by responsible human agents is thus radically *humanist*. To state that colonialism is a system, and even a system of human acts, in the abstract, was doubtless an insight to be gained from a careful reading of a text such as Raynal's *Histoire des deux Indes*. Vastey's reconceptualization of colonialism as a system pushes beyond the encyclopedic, predominantly descriptive articles of Raynal, however, to conceive of this system critically, as generalized acts of *violence*. As a humanist critique of colonial violence, *Colonial System* thus announces the analogous anticolonial humanisms of Césaire, Sartre, and Fanon alike.

Vastey's critique, as the enumeration of these acts of violence, articulates the outlines of a general, ideological system of *human* actions. This system is ideological precisely in the sense that until Vastey, the colonial system, while having its various critics and reformers such as Brissot and *Les Amis des Noirs*, as well as its defenders such as Malouet himself, understood such acts of violence as Vastey describes to be more or less unfortunate side effects of a *necessary* state of affairs (French colonialism as an economic or political necessity). Vastey puts to judgment this unquestioned state of necessity: reaffirming its just end in the independence of Haiti, but also, beyond anything argued before him, calling for the condemnation, by eternal shame if not court of law, of the individuals responsible for this system of general injustice. This in turn indicates the fullest sense of Vastey's critical "unveiling": to reveal precisely what is hidden by empirical "reality" itself, hidden by colonialism understood as the normal, necessary state of France's affairs; to reveal the utter untruth of this system that uniformly covers up, when its proponents are not outright justifying, its attendant forms of violence.

Vastey's *Colonial System* at once urges the destruction of a system of general violence, while offering a positive image of the political system that should rightfully replace it. Vastey's text, despite the clearly inegalitarian nature of Christophe's monarchy, deserves to be considered a fundamental moment in what I have elsewhere described as a Black Jacobin tradition in the Francophone Caribbean world. This tradition, specific to the French context, indicates one of the fundamental singularities of the formation of language and identity in the Francophone world, quite dissimilar to the Anglophone, Hispanophone, and Lusophone colonial contexts.

In this light, it would also be essential to reconsider Aimé Césaire, who was not only the poet of Negritude or the forger of identities among the oppressed "au compass de la souffrance"; but also, and above all (as we have tended to forget, at Césaire's own instigation), the Black Jacobin Césaire, the Césaire who was an enthusiastic Communist (in inclination and affirmation, if not always party affiliation) from his first writings in 1935 until at least 1975, the Césaire for whose own action Robespierre, Grégoire, Louverture, and later Fanon, but also the peripheral militant intellectual Lenin, were constant references, the Césaire who faithfully and regularly recalled the Jacobin and Haitian Black Jacobin revolutions much as Hegel would drink a toast each year to the French Revolution. We could not, I think, speak of language and identity in the francophone world without recalling Césaire.

But in conclusion I shall invoke this world into which I believe we are now suddenly being thrown, this posthuman, inhuman world. It is not the age-old world of the inhumanity of man to man, that we have known and will certainly continue to witness endlessly. The inhuman of which I speak is this sudden condition, like Kant's Copernican turn, proclaimed by many, by Marx, by Nietzsche and Freud, by Althusser and Lacan, all of whom announced the displacement of Man from his universal and ontological centrality. Among all these, however, it is only Marx who foresaw the particular nature of the contemporary displacement of Man we are living through.

While it has been widely acknowledged since Smith, Ricardo, and Marx that capitalism is driven forward most powerfully (and disruptively) by gains in productivity due to the automation of labor and the replacement of human workers by machines, in the past decade this process has entered a new and perhaps decisive phase, in which nearly all types of human labor, including many high-skilled, high-paid employments that were thought impossible to automate only a few years ago (such as the driving of cars, surgery, and university-level teaching), have already or will become automatable in coming decades. The resulting global expulsion of humans from wage-based labor in a world that continues to be subject to capitalism, need it be added, could well be catastrophic (almost certainly for laborers without capital, as well as, potentially, capitalism itself).

Some four hundred pages into the 1858 notebooks by Marx collected as the *Grundrisse*, he distinguishes between the age of tools, which humans use as prostheses to extend their own power over nature, and that of the machine, characteristic of capitalism, in which humans tendentially, according to Marx, become mere appendages of the machine.[7] This aspect of Marx's critique, encompassing the concept of relative surplus value, his labor theory of value, his analysis of machines and their contradictory status in capitalism as exponentially increasing the production of wealth all the while they gradually render humans superfluous to the production process, eliminating value; all of this has tended to be overlooked in the Leninist, production-based Marxian thought of the twentieth century.

Marx's critique of value, of the dynamic, in other words, that impels capitalism to search out ever greater surplus value through the automation of production and the replacement of human by machinic labor, underscores this fundamental, underlying structure of capitalism. This dynamic has only become globally—rather than merely locally, in this or that factory, industry, or even national economy—determinant since the 1970s.

I would define this "posthuman capitalism" as the newly dominant tendency in twenty-first-century capitalism for living labor power to become a mere "infinitesimal, vanishing quantity" in the vast majority of global production processes. This tendency is by no means contradicted by the statistically demonstrable fact that since the 1980s, ever-more people work globally. On the contrary, the two are arguably corollaries of precisely the same tendency. A massive numerical, empirical increase in employment in recent decades is in fact the immediately perceptible form of this tendency, its appearance in everyday lived experience. Contemporary econometric studies reduce employment to a mere statistical variant, while scrupulously avoiding addressing historical changes in the quality (as working conditions, living wage, degree of exploitation, etc.) of that work. While current discussions of automation tend to focus obsessively on the displacement of workers by machines and possible resulting unemployment, this concern arguably obscures a more fundamental contemporary dynamic, in which empirical statistics of global employment actually tend to increase, but the *value* of that labor power decreases (a process perceptible as stagnant or decreasing wages, as worsening working conditions, as an increasing tendency to [super-] exploitation).

We live increasingly in an automated planet of slums, in which the majority of humanity continues to depend for survival on wage labor, even as potentially 85 percent of global production suddenly becomes automated. The underlying, structural form of this tendency occurs as general automation constantly reduces the *value* of labor power to "infinitesimal" levels even as what Marx called the "valorization of value" (i.e., the production and realization of surplus value) remains a general social compulsion. So-called primitive or primary accumulation, in which the essential means of production and reproduction are made available only in the form of market commodities, continues to violently ensure this general dependency upon wage labor for the mass of global humanity. Automation in the centers of global capital constantly devalues the labor power not just of American or German workers in closest proximity, but, most powerfully and destructively, that of a proletarian global South subject to the constant depression of international norms of socially necessary labor time.

This "reduction in value" refers not to a decline in the monetary wage living labor receives in its employment by any specific capital, though this phenomenal form of value (as money) is indeed tendentially reduced in labor's global competition with increasingly automated labor processes. Instead, the reduction of the value of labor power I am indicating refers more fundamentally to the disappearance of the very *capacity of living labor power actually to produce surplus value*. This, in a word, amounts to the disappearance of its essential value to capital, insofar as machines and all other forms of constant capital merely relay but are unable to produce any new value, while at the same time capital continues to demand the constant production and expansion of surplus value as its life blood, forcing, as a general social compulsion, billions of living human laborers to continue to toil or suffer violent marginalization across the planet.[8]

To adequately conceptualize this process will require, therefore, a critique not merely of transhistorical conceptions of labor, but a further critique of the static, transhistorical conceptions of the value-producing power or capacity of living labor that still characterizes many recent and contemporary readings of *Capital* and value-form theory. This capacity, in other words, is not a constant within capitalism that depends merely on the empirical sums of people put to work globally. Instead, it indicates a general power—enabled and enforced in the structuration of society by the valorization imperative—that tendentially diminishes with decreases in socially necessary labor times for the production of commodities, in so far as these decreases are no longer overcome by the introduction of new, compensatory living-labor-intensive production processes. In essence, such a theory would conceptualize, in the theoretically adequate terms of *Capital*, Marx's initial, metaphorical, empirical, and imagistic formulation of what he termed capitalism's "moving contradiction" in the *Grundrisse*'s famous "Fragment on Machines," a conceptualization Marx never arrived at, but one that, I am arguing, remains latent within the overall conceptual logic of *Capital I–III*.

To name the contemporary era "posthuman capitalism," as I am proposing here, is not simply to link a specific notion of the "posthuman" to capitalism and its critique (something notably absent in previous presentations of the so-called posthuman), but, more strongly, to affirm that despite the astonishing transformations of automation, robotics, and AI since 2000 and the enormous possibilities this implies for the invention, transformation, and super-production of use-values for humanity, we nonetheless do in fact still live in capitalism; that, in other words, despite dumbfounding increases in what Adorno and Horkheimer long ago, in the era of high-Fordism, identified as capitalism's regressive negation of "the increase in economic productivity which creates the conditions for a more just world,"[9] humanity remains ever-more subject to the general social compulsion to valorize value; that, moreover, for all its mutations, contemporary late capitalism is in fact still today characterized by the basic structural features and forms that Marx first identified (absolute and relative surplus value, constant and variable capital, formal and real subsumption, and the like), except for the fact that their ordering, predominance, and the existence of countertendencies has suddenly been reconfigured as an unchecked tendency to devalorize the value-producing power of living labor itself.

Reading the Marxist-humanist Caribbean literature of great writers such as Césaire and Alexis today, in this light, one continues to find astonishing ciphers of our possible futures. Césaire's *Cahier* can in this sense be taken not merely as a condemnation of the suffering and underdevelopment of colonial Martinique circa 1939, as it always has been, but as proleptic, pointing forward to our contemporary and near-future context of worlds without work, worlds that nonetheless continue to be subject to the inequities and exclusions of global capitalism, and thus, for those expelled from the world of wage labor, subject to what threatens to become a dystopian hell rather than the paradise of post-capital labor long celebrated by Negri. "Les Antilles qui ont faim, les Antilles grêlées de petite vérole, les Antilles dynamites d'alcool, échouées dans la boue de cette baie, dans la poussière de cette ville sinistrement échouées": to this day do not the opening pages of *Cahier* remain one of the most vivid and powerful descriptions not (only) of a colonial past, but rather of our present, our contemporary, and future world of global slums, starvation, suffering, and exclusion?[10]

In this sense, to read the works of twentieth-century anticolonialism today, and above all those articulated in terms of a supposedly *dépassé* Marxist critique of global political economy, requires not to unveil some "true" meaning long hidden within their depths, but rather, as Althusser undertook to read Marx "symptomatically" in *Lire le Capital*, to formulate today the *questions* that such endlessly suggestive texts answered, and answered richly, fully, and quite explicitly, but whose corresponding question they were unable to formulate.

The problem of a posthuman world in which human labor forms no more than an infinitesimal, vanishing quantity in the production of surplus value, is precisely such a question, one that has only recently become thinkable. The "answer" to this unposed question—"What would a world look like in which, in the face of automated, machinic production, human labor became 'infinitesimal,' but in which capitalism continued to structure social relations?"—I am suggesting, is precisely the world such texts have always laid before our eyes, a world in which the vast majority of humans have become literally superfluous, the wretched of the earth; it is an answer that perhaps finds its most richly dystopian description in Jacques Stéphen Alexis's Marxist novel from 1955, his masterpiece *Compère général soleil*.[11]

I call Alexis's novel Marxist not only because of the author's affiliations with Haitian Communism, nor even because the centrality of the theme of proletarian experience and the possibility of revolution, but because it seems to announce, in its very contradictions, this postrevolutionary, post-proletarian, post-labor, indeed, posthuman world we are now entering, more than half a century after its composition. It is not that the novel is populated with robots and computers doing the labor of humans; rather, the characters in the novel are obsessed with finding work in a world in which it is either brutal and dehumanizing, or simply not available. My point is that *Compère général soleil* presents a sort of dystopian image of the growing global underclass, expelled from capitalism, a world in which not even the sweatshops offer the promise of a wage, for those unable to reeducate or even educate themselves for a world in which they must compete with wageless, tireless workers. We tend to think of the rich Atlantic economies as those hardest hit by deindustrialization; while this was true in the 1980s and 1990s, since 1996, the changes we are suddenly witnessing are global and will increasingly hit the poorest economies the hardest. Alexis's novel describes a world in which people are constantly searching for work, and in which Communism holds out to them the promise of work.

The language of the novel draws our attention repeatedly to concepts such as le peuple, le travail, les usines, and les ouvriers.[12] Primary among the paradoxes structuring its narrative is undoubtedly that between its two central concepts *communisme* and *travail*. The latter is surely the key word of the entire novel, reappearing on something close to every one of its 350 pages. The first example we have of work, however, is not proletarian wage labor in a factory or sweatshop, but the forced prison labor Hilarion is forced to do after he's caught stealing a wallet in the novel's opening pages. This is the labor, Alexis comments "de cette désepérance d'une race de pariahs."[13] While in prison, moreover, Hilarion's life is changed; he is awakened and given a vision, when the Communist militant Roumel promises him "je te trouverai du travail."[14] Indeed, the entire novel is animated by the "promesse d'un travail" that, even in those cases when it does arrive for the novel's characters, proves infinitely poorer, brutish, and exploitative than that image of hope itself.

The promise of what used to be called Third World Communism, embodied in the character Roumel, reveals itself in the novel profoundly and, I would add, tragically, engaged not with the critique of capitalism, but rather with this promise of work. Here is a passage from Roumel's militant speech of commitment and conversion to Hilarion while the two are in prison together:

Je suis communiste, Hilarion, et je suis en prison parce que nous sommes forts, de cette force de jours et des nuits qui vient de leur triomphe inéluctable. Nous ne sommes encore qu'une poignée de communistes dans ce pays, mais dès que nous avons ouvert la bouche, ils ont eu peur. Tu veux savoir ce que nous avons dit? . . . Qu'on respecte celui qui travaille. Qu'on lui donne de quoi vivre avec sa famille. Qu'on lui garantisse du travail. Qu'il ait le droit de défendre ce travail. [. . .] Et puisque ce pays ne vaut que par ses travailleurs, qu'ils prennent la direction des affaires, dans l'avenir qu'une nouvelle république naisse, où il n'y ait place que pour les travailleurs.[15]

In all this, in the entire novel, not a word about capitalism as a system, as a structure that obligates all of us subject to it to valorize value, about the ways those who possess nothing but their labor power to sell are forced to hand over their surplus as surplus profit to the capitalist. Instead, not only in Haiti, but, one might add, in revolutionary anticolonial communism throughout much of the twentieth century, only the promise of recuperatory modernization, catching up with the rich North Atlantic Joneses. This promise, which made some sense in the twentieth century for those Fanon called the wretched of the earth, today stands revealed as a specious and impossible dream in a world in which billions labor in miserable conditions, but in which that living human labor, in competition with ever-more powerful robotic and computerized workers, becomes a literally *infinitesimal* component of value. Human labor is fast becoming, that is to say, a quantum still greater than zero, but phenomenologically imperceptible.

Through the twentieth century, as globalization unfolded under what Lenin called the logic of imperialism, the modernization hoped for by Jacques Stéphen Alexis's novel was able to effectively transform societies, and the global project of actually existing Socialism effectively brought some measure of egalitarian distribution to the process. Today this logic suddenly no longer holds, but at the same time, perhaps paradoxically, I think that a return to Marx is as crucial as it ever was for understanding these dynamics. Not the Marx of the revolutionary proletariat. This quite simply because in the contemporary context of total automation, utter precarity of employment, and the internal distribution of inequalities (as in the familiar distinction between tenured and hourly contractual academic laborers), living labor, whether proletarian or elite, has become utterly replaceable. Above all, it is now in fact becoming tendentially superfluous, all as ever-more humans, in aggregate, work their fingers to the bone to eke out a life at margin of subsistence: Arendt and Agamben's mere-life as the universal tendency of capitalist automation.

The global underclass that is a result of these processes finds, I am arguing, a powerful and visionary representation in a novel of Haitian exploitation such as *Compère général soleil*. In a world without work, without proletarian factory labor, what's left are what's known throughout the francophone Caribbean as *les djobs*, the scraping of a living from whatever is at hand in an impoverished land, returning home at night with a few gourdes from the market by buying cheap and selling a bit more dearly. This is the petit commerce that Hilarion's wife Claire-Heureuse undertakes for the survival of their fragile family unit, the precarity of which is revealed when the Artibonite river floods and commerce is destroyed for all those lacking the capital to hoard goods in anticipation of their coming scarcity. Claire-Heureuse and Hilarion's shop is ruined, and they leave to work in the killing fields of the Dominican Republic, where, in the novel's culmination, Trujillo's infamous 1937 massacre of migrant Haitian workers leads to the novel's own despondent conclusion.

As the few workers able to escape the slaughter set out, hunted like animals, for the promise of safety at the Haitian border, the promise of Roumel's communism of the masses, of the solidarity of the exploited and the revolutionary power of proletarian struggle, stands revealed in its impotence before the violence of capital, in this case the relative riches of Dominican plantation owners, the military, and all those whipped up in genocidal fury against the vulnerability of Haitian laborers. Tracked like animals, dispersed, molecular, these workers are subject to a horrendous vulnerability that is the opposite of the collective, voluntarist image of revolutionary spontaneity so dear to thinkers like CLR James and Alexis himself:

Leur groupe s'était renforcé de ceux qui avait réussi à s'enfuir des balles. Ils avançaient, à demi marchant, à demi rampant dans les frondaisons ruisselantes des cannaies. Au moindre bruit, on s'aplatissait au sol et on épiait. Parfois ce n'était que de fausses alertes, d'autres fois, de nouveaux venus dont le regard s'allumait d'un mince éclat d'espérance, à la vue d'autres rescapés. La masse du groupe leur semblait une chance prodigieuse d'avoir la vie sauve. Ils s'y agglutinaient avec précipitation comme cherchant à disparaître dans sa collectivité. Puis le groupe se remettait en marche, comme une prudente cohorte de fourmis, lentement, dans une progression hésitante, tâtonnante, évitant les chemins, les sentiers, l'oreille aux aguets.[16]

Like that of Alexis's own tragic end, *Compère général soleil* unflinchingly tells the story of this failure; not the failure of Marxism, but rather, one might say, the failure of twentieth-century revolutionary anticolonialism to be Marxist enough, to go beyond grasping at the promises of compensatory modernization, of work at any price, and to bring an end to the value form itself that continues to structure global capitalism today. The paradoxes of the posthuman age we are rapidly entering make themselves felt at every level of society, everywhere in the world that capitalism has in fact subsumed work under the compulsion to valorize value, to make a profit for somebody somewhere, no matter how infinitesimal, undercompensated, exploitative, and fleeting that work may be. As capitalism enters into new forms of crisis in the age of posthuman labor and compensatory financialization, Alexis's visionary, despondent fiction *Compère général soleil* shows us, from the bottom of global society, a dystopian image of that possible future, a future that can perhaps only be avoided if the very idea of what it means to struggle for social justice can be reconstructed, transformed into the struggle to create a world in which the obligation to work and make a profit for another is longer the be-all and end-all of social existence. Following Marx's visionary critique of capitalist modernity and its culmination in the horror and unfulfilled promise of human life liberated into the hell of a work-free capitalist world, we might do worse than to propose a common horizon for the universal struggle for social justice in this century, not as Lenin's electrification plus soviets, but instead as the formula: total automation and post-humanization of work plus universal equality.

NOTES

1. C.L.R. James, *The Black Jacobins: Toussaint Louverture and the San Domingo Revolution* (New York: Vintage, 1963); Aimé Césaire, *Cahier d'un retour au pays natal* (Paris: Présence Africaine, 1956).

2. Louis Althusser, et al. *Reading Capital: The Complete Edition* (New York: Verso, 2017), 302.

3. G.W.F. Hegel, *The Phenomenology of Spirit* (Oxford: Oxford University Press, 1977), 115, 117.

4. Nick Nesbitt, *Universal Emancipation: The Haitian Revolution and the Radical Enlightenment* (Charlottesville: University of Virginia Press, 2008).

5. Nesbitt, Nick, ed., *Toussaint Louverture* (New York: Verso 2008).

6. Baron de Vastey, *The Colonial System Unveiled,* ed. Chris Bongie (Liverpool: Liverpool University Press, 2016).

7. Karl Marx, *Grundrisse: Foundations of the Critique of Political Economy (Rough Draft)*, trans. Martin Nicolaus (London: Penguin, 1973).

8. Thanks to Max Tomba for suggesting this essential clarification of my argument.

9. Theodor Adorno and Max Horkheimer. *The Dialectic of Enlightenment: Philosophical Fragments* (Stanford: Stanford University Press, 2002), xvi.

10. Césaire, *Cahier,* 8.

11. Jacques Stéphen Alexis, *Compère Général Soleil* (Paris: Éditions Gallimard, 1955).

12. Alexis, *Compère,* 208.

13. Alexis, *Compère,* 46.

14. Alexis, *Compère,* 50.

15. Alexis, *Compère,* 68.

16. "Their group gained reinforcements from those who had managed to flee the bullets. They advanced, half walking, half crawling, through the wet foliage. At the slightest sound, they flattened themselves on the ground and kept watch. Sometimes it was only a false alarm, other times, newcomers joined them, their gaze illuminated by a sliver of hope at the sight of those who had managed to escape. Their combined forces seemed to them a prodigious promise of life. They stuck together determinately, as though to disappear in the collective. Then the group began again to walk, like a prudent quora of ants, slowly; they walked with hesitation, feeling their way, avoiding the roads and paths, their eyes attentive to possible ambush." Alexis, *Compère,* 314.

BIBLIOGRAPHY

Adorno, Theodor and Max Horkheimer. *The Dialectic of Enlightenment: Philosophical Fragments* (Stanford: Stanford University Press, 2002).

Alexis, Jacques Stéphen. *Compère Général Soleil* (Paris: Éditions Gallimard, 1955).

Althusser, Louis, et al. *Reading Capital: The Complete Edition* (New York: Verso, 2017).

Césaire, Aimé. *La tragédie du roi Christophe* (Paris: Présence Africaine, 1963).

———. *Aimé Césaire: Écrits politiques, Vols. I-V.* (Paris: Nouvelles éditions Jean-Michel Place, 2016–2018).

————. *Cahier d'un retour au pays natal* (Paris: Présence Africaine, 1956).

————. *Poésie, théâtre, essais et discours*, ed. A. James Arnold (Paris: CNRS éditions, 2014).

Césaire, Suzanne. *Le grand camouflage: Écrits de dissidence (1941–1945)*, ed. Daniel Maximin (Paris: Seuil, 2009).

Hegel, G.W.F. *The Phenomenology of Spirit* (Oxford: Oxford University Press, 1977).

James, C.L.R. *The Black Jacobins: Toussaint Louverture and the San Domingo Revolution* (New York: Vintage, 1963).

Kurz, Robert. "The Crisis of Exchange Value: Science as Productivity, Productive Labor, and Capitalist Reproduction," in *Marxism and the Critique of Value,* ed. Neil Larsen, Mathias Nilges, Josh Robinson, and Nicholas Brown (Chicago: MCM Press, 2014).

————. *The Substance of Capital* (London: Chronos, 2016).

Marx, Karl. *Capital: A Critique of Political Economy, Volume One,* trans. by Ben Fowkes. (London: Penguin, 1976).

————. *Grundrisse: Foundations of the Critique of Political Economy (Rough Draft),* trans. by Martin Nicolaus (London: Penguin, 1973).

Nesbitt, Nick. *Voicing Memory: History and Subjectivity in French Caribbean Literature* (Charlottesville: University of Virginia Press, 2003).

————. *Universal Emancipation: The Haitian Revolution and the Radical Enlightenment* (Charlottesville: University of Virginia Press, 2008).

————, ed. *Toussaint Louverture* (New York: Verso, 2008).

Postone, Moishe. *Time, Labour, and Social Domination: A Reinterpretation of Marx's Critical Theory* (Cambridge: Cambridge University Press, 1993).

Trouillot, Michel-Rolph. *Haiti, State Against Nation: The Origins and Legacy of Duvalierism* (New York: Monthly Review Press, 1990).

Vastey, Baron de. *The Colonial System Unveiled,* ed. Chris Bongie (Liverpool: Liverpool University Press, 2016).

Wood, Ellen Meiksins. *The Origin of Capitalism: A Longer View* (London and New York: Verso, [1999] 2002).

Chapter 6

Anthropocenes and New African Discourses

"Dwelling in the World" with Poetry and Criticism

Jean Godefroy Bidima

Mounana, located in Gabon, is one of the zones in Central Africa that currently has an elevated rate of radioactivity.[1] The Gabonese, the regional plants that they eat, the water that they drink, the brush animals, the birds and fish which try to make a living in the air and water, all share, with fear and gasping breath, this heavy heritage that seems to have been left behind by French companies who mined uranium here. This is a *first* example of *humanity's action on nature and life following industrialization.* In Nigeria, in Ogoniland, oil extraction thanks to the combined efforts of the Nigerian federal state and foreign firms has polluted the soil, the vegetation, and the fauna. Thus biodiversity is attacked in the name of industrialization.[2] This is a *second* example of *humanity's action on nature and life following industrialization.* In Abidjan, Côte d'Ivoire, there have been outcries over the dumping of radioactive waste, which endangered the country's populations.[3] Fingers were pointed at foreign nuclear powers which, taking advantage simultaneously of African elites' cupidity and the weakness of Southern states, shook off their burdensome nuclear waste. Here, a *third* example of *humanity's action on (and against) nature and life as a result of bad government.*

Peasants practicing nonindustrialized agriculture in African countries, particularly in the Congo basin where there is a significant forest, cause *deforestation* as they slash and burn before planting in the stubble. The burning of forests therefore has a major impact on the flora and fauna and also on biodiversity. We must set aside the argument that this sort of action on nature results from African traditions which must be preserved. The brush-fires involved lead to deforestation and the destabilization of biodiversity.

In its aggression against the forest, traditional agriculture is helped along by the foreign countries which have been cutting precious wood there since the colonial period.[4] A *fourth* example of *humanity's action on nature and life by means of African traditional techniques and the timber industry.*

In 1986, at Lake Nyos in the west of Cameroon, a gas of volcanic origin emerged from the earth and killed every living thing around: livestock, plants, and human beings. There are concerns that the same situation may result from the Nyiragongo volcano which is active in the eastern Democratic Republic of Congo on the border with Rwanda.[5] Here we see a *first* example of *nature's action against nature* and life. A volcano does not result from humanity's destruction of biodiversity. Lake Chad, which feeds four States in the region of the Sahel (Cameroon, Chad, Nigeria, and Niger), is drying further and further—just as the Sahara did long ago, and this is not something for which humans are responsible. This is a *second* example of *action on nature by nature itself*, which has its own capacity to self-destruct.

These examples allow us to frame an investigation of what is happening in the Anthropocene. The frame is composed of destructive human actions toward nature as well as the destruction of nature by means of its own processes. The question of the Anthropocene in Africa and of the environment in general must be posed not in reductionist terms but in boundary-crossing terms and in the form of a puzzle. The African philosophers who have for some time now developed an interest in questions of the environment and the preservation of our common dwelling place, the earth, could benefit from this crosswise approach. In fact, the question of the Anthropocene, which implies that of the environment, must be approached in a transversal and intensive manner. We must find the overlap between what *humanity can do* and *what humanity wants to do with* and *to* nature. We must also superimpose the geographical pessimisms professed by environmentalists over their eschatologies and juxtapose strategies of anthropocentrism with new conceptions of biocentrism.

In this contribution, our objective is to reformulate the philosophical question of the Anthropocene and the environment in Africa by examining reductive discourses which turn on the idea of an apocalypse or *collapsology* (look out for the end of the world), economic considerations which turn on analogies with banking (one must conserve, invest in biodiversity), political preoccupations (the question of climate justice), public health (what new diseases are emerging from this situation?), spirituality (the relationship between humans and nonhumans), and epistemology (the opposition between holistic and analytic approaches). Our goal is to reconsider this question in light of African philosophy, starting (I) from an *analysis of the obstacles that emerge when one wants to address the Anthropocene/environment in Africa*. Following this (II), we will examine the *anthropological and political ambiguities* implicit in certain philosophical options relative to their current "biopolitical" orientations.

And finally (III), we will analyze the new *politics of the relationships between human subjects and their environment* in present-day Africa.

OBSTACLES TO AN AFRICAN PHILO(ECO)SOPHY

The question posed here is one of knowing what the conditions of possibility for an "ecosophy" in Africa might be. To be more explicit, why have African philosophical discourses paid so little attention to ecological problems over the course of the last fifty years? Above all, what obstacles have emerged to an African philosophical orientation that would take into account ecology and questions surrounding the Anthropocene? This reticence can be explained by five barriers.

1. Current African Philosophies Are Dominated by a Narrow Anthropocentrism

Humanity, the philosophizing Subject who has overthrown the tribal gods and the ancestors, is at the center of these philosophies. Are we talking about a *crisis?* It is evident that humanity's crisis is a crisis of *Muntu* and not of nature, although *Muntu*—who is neither a pure spirit reasoning through syllogisms, nor a being who can survive without breathing potentially polluted air, nor an entity whose context is purely historical to the exclusion of geography and climate—is constituted by nature. Is it a matter of the *transmission of traditions?* This great theme, which runs through the African treatises of philosophical anthropology, addresses only the *transmission of material and spiritual heritage* between generations of human beings. And when one thinks of nature, it is alienated under an instrumental form with the notion of individual or communitarian property. To be sure, among the anthropologists and philosophers of African law one finds the notion of the bond, but when these African philosophies speak of crisis resulting from the "rupture of bonds," they are immediately thinking of the *social bond.*[6] The "social," meanwhile, is reduced to living beings and to the departed *ancestors.* Introducing philosophies of the social contract has not helped these African philosophies to escape a narrow anthropocentrism either. With a vague notion of obligation vis-à-vis one's human contemporaries and predecessors (ancestors), obligation becomes an intercommunitarian and intergenerational affair. But one has no obligations vis-à-vis the nature which precedes one's appearance in the world and that which will be left when one quits the world. The contract was not established with nature, as Michel Serres wishes, but with humans.[7] Often, any contract with chthonic forces is suspected of being superstition and magic.

Within this framework, discussion centers on the rupture of the social contract that violent states maintain between citizens and the political body and
the criticism of broken commercial contracts between subjects. The object/
nature is that *against which* we make the contract and is not considered a
party to the contract. Obviously, nature is not consciously able to enter into
the obligations of a signatory. Within narrow anthropocentrism, the notion
of *collective harmony (vivre-ensemble)* which several philosophies of solidarity in Africa have taken as their theme is reduced to a circle involving
the subject, the community, the state, and ancestrality/religiosity. But from
the perspective that interests us, "collective harmony" implies transactions
between humans (past, present, and future) as well as nonhumans. The "collective harmony" of this narrow anthropocentrism has been an obstacle to
any solid reflection on the environment in the work of African philosophers.

2. The Subject-Object Division

The philosophical reflection undertaken by Africans in the twentieth century,
which began by posing the problem of colonization using the vocabulary and
the grammatical categories of European languages, failed to pose the question of the Anthropocene. Aristotle's table of categories, which presented
being in its many senses, starting from the abstraction of being as substance
and ending with its possible categories of predication, was highly esteemed.[8]
Democritus, Epicurus, Leucippus, or Spinoza excepted, certain Western
philosophies have led thinkers to consider Nature from a passive standpoint
on the basis of dualisms such as soul/body, the *cogito*/extension, or activity/
passivity. With the soul and body, we accompany Plato; Descartes welcomes
us to the world of the *cogito* and extension; and with activity and passivity,
we find ourselves among the phenomenologists with the Subject aiming
intentionally at its object. This Subject/Object division has authorized the
human domination of nature. A reflection from Horkheimer is illuminating:

> The human being, in the process of his emancipation, shares the fate of the rest
> of his world. Domination of nature involves domination of man. Each subject
> not only has to take part in the subjugation of external nature, human and
> nonhuman, but in order to do so must subjugate nature in himself. Domination
> becomes "internalized" for domination's sake. What is usually indicated as a
> goal—the happiness of the individual, health, and wealth—gains its significance
> exclusively from its functional potentiality.[9]

This functionalist consideration of the object/nature does not allow a philosophy of the environment to be elaborated. For nature is reduced to a set of
functions, rather than being the multiform expression of life.

3. The Inability to Think Life: Critiques of Ethnophilosophy, Great Obstacles

The debate over ethnophilosophy with which the philosophical scene in Africa was occupied centered the attention of African philosophers on the definition of philosophy and not on the reality and the environment surrounding them. This debate affected only the methods of philosophy and not the reality in whose name philosophy claimed to speak. The crisis of African humanity (*Muntu*) turned around ideological superstructures (its philosophy, its feelings, its rhetorical circles, and its ruses of transmission) rather than material infrastructures. It remained an academic debate with pedagogical, political, cultural, economic, and anthropological consequences. On the pedagogical plane, the ethnophilosophical question became a formula for the authentification of genuine African philosophers. One could not enter African philosophy except through this door, which separated members of the real philosophical homeland from the ethnophilosophers. One discriminated, distinguished, sorted out, invented a "discursive policy" [*police*] (in Foucault's sense) and after many years these comprised a list of rules for the internal control of African philosophical discourses.[10]

In this game, inspection procedures were formalized along with a horizon identifying those who would be in the "Church" (the holy African Philosophy) and the "heretics" (the ethnophilosophers) who would be cast outside and who, perverse like all heretics, masked themselves using philosophy. The missionaries were suspected of disguising themselves as philosophers, of hiding an evangelizing agenda behind their backs (Father Tempels, the Belgian missionary in the Congo, was a scapegoat in this category), and were cast out from the field of African philosophy. Nor was the ethnologist welcome any longer; though disguised as a researcher, he was really just another link in the chain of colonial authority. Certain aspects of African culture were no longer welcome in African philosophy. While the aphorisms of Pascal, Nietzsche, Adorno, Wittgenstein, or La Bruyère were still accepted as philosophical, the "crusade" with its rational shield and arrows of analytic precision fought against ethnophilosophy by declaring that its proverbs and sayings could not be philosophy.

Discredited and shameful, but ironic nonetheless, ethnophilosophy sought help to gain admission to the great ball of concepts. It proposed that every philosophy is the daughter of its "ethnos" and that every philosophy is "ethnophilosophy" in some place or other. This was somewhat convincing to the anti-ethnophilosophical "crusaders" who transformed this flagging and sterile debate into a criterion of philosophical promotion. In this debate, which should have been about the rightful question of how to define philosophy, the latter became a self-referential discourse which only spoke about small problems concerning the definitions of words, logical arguments, and political quibbles. Philosophy was no longer a reflection on the world, but on the words being used in philosophy. In the quarrel over ethnophilosophy, African philosophers succeeded in excluding reflection about experience of the world, or rather in reducing the experience of philosophy to a question of definition and not an observation of the reality of the Cosmos, as did the Greeks and pre-Socratics.

What exactly was the problem with ethnophilosophy? The grievances were many. Just a reminder: its *method* is not that of philosophy, which remains the practice of a solitary being and not the prerogative of an anonymous thought valid for all members of the community. Its *epistemology* is pernicious because it resists the sacred dichotomies of subject and object, myth and reason, individual and collective, nature and culture. Rather, its approach is holistic: the subject, the object, the "between" linking subject and object, actual living beings (human, animals, plants), nonliving beings (ancestors), and the "soon to be born" form a single chain across which circulates vital force. The ethnophilosophical project was characterized as a political strategy for converting Africans to colonial forms of logic. But where the critics of ethnophilosophy did fail was in exorcising the question of vitalism.

Father Tempels, who studied the Baluba and who was so fervently criticized by later African philosophers, reactivated the alliance between the Luba and vital force. This implies relationships between humans and nonhumans, humans and nature. In his study of Bantu psychology, Tempels demonstrated the bond between *Muntu* (the generic expression of African humanity) and his or her natural environment, which involve all the forces of life:

> Just as with Bantu ontology, which resists the European concept of the individu-
> ated thing existing in its own right and isolated from other things, Bantu psy-
> chology cannot conceive the human being as an individual, a force existing only
> on its own outside of its ontological relationships with other living being(s), out-
> side of its own relation with the animate and inanimate forces that surround it.[11]

What Tempels wants to emphasize—and what was criticized as the promotion of animism—was the interconnection of multiple modalities of life via the reciprocal "co-birth" (*co-naissance*) between the subject and nature. The subject and nature are linked by the *stratum of life*, and the critique of "vitalism" by anti-ethnophilosophies has prevented a clear understanding of Nature in Africa.

4. A Certain "Autarchic" Conception of History: When History Is Blind to Nature/Life

How have African philosophers conceived of African history? Not as the history of concepts and other philosophemes they resurrected or invented, but as that which implies the history of life and living beings? An acceptable African history was constituted around a desire to show that Africans, too, had a relationship to time and to memory. What it tells are the stories of great empires and kingdoms (Mali, Monomotapa, Ethiopia, etc.), emperors (Sundiata Keita in latter-day Mali, Chaka Zulu in South Africa), slave traders (Tippu Tip in eastern Africa), internal conquests (Usman Dan Fodio in latter-day Nigeria), achievements in art and material culture (Sao art and ceramics in Chad, the fortresses of Monomotapa in Zimbabwe in architecture, textile arts and weaving in West Africa).[12] Because they were overshadowed by multiple factors (enslavements, colonizations, externally oriented university epistemologies, populist Afrocentrisms) these constitute the reality of that history. These are sketched out as "sites of memory" in the framework of the revalorization of African nation-states. *The methodological concerns* in this way of writing African history are problems of diachrony and synchrony, writing and orality, great African personalities and the denunciation of Eurocentrisms that have infiltrated the writing of this history, and the extraction of a genuine object of study from the intrigues of the colonial narrative of history. *This history is founded on the greatness of Africa.* The writing of this history evaluates centers of knowledge diffusion such as Timbuktu.[13] In this excessively anthropocentric way of conceiving history, we see Fernand Braudel's theme of the *longue durée* recycled, but this duration is assumed to be the time of man. *What is forgotten: nature as life.*

We need a history of nature in Africa. Put differently, the history of Africa cannot be incomprehensible except when it involves the events, characters, and material culture given to us by art and archeology. We also need a history of nature, its concept and its articulations in the variety of African imaginaries, its representations in art, the role of natural elements in African historical events. What role has geography played in the emergence of episodes in African history? What has been the role of wind in conquests, wars, resistances? What role have the seasons, famines, and plagues played in the fall of African empires? How has geology (e.g., volcanos) structured the movements of populations and their struggles to occupy a given land? History must concern itself with these aspects of nature, which bring us back to phenomena of movement and life. Nietzsche reminds us:

These are the services history is capable of performing for life; every man and every nation requires, in accordance with its goals, energies, and needs, a certain kind of knowledge of the past, now in the form of monumental, now of antiquarian, now of critical history: but it does not require it as a host of pure thinkers who only look on at life, of knowledge-thirsty individuals whom knowledge alone will satisfy and to whom the accumulation of knowledge is itself the goal, but always and only for the ends of life and thus also under the domination and

supreme direction of these ends . . . this is the natural relation of an age, a culture, a nation with its history.[14]

The new wave of "decolonization" of philosophy in Africa pays very little
attention to problems linked to university politics, to gender, to the juridical
question of the form of the State, to cognitive justice, and no attention to the
implicit presuppositions which structure the form of their critical thought.
Will "decolonization" go so far as the deconstruction of dualisms such
as nature/culture, objective/subjective, subject/object, perceiver/perceived?
The ontology of this "decolonial" thought has yet to be formulated. For the
moment we have only its politics and its epistemologies. Ontology forces us
to define being and its derivatives and from there, to pose the question of the
environment or of the Anthropocene.

On what conditions was an African eco(philo)sphy possible? The conditions for the formulation of such a philosophy were potentially present in the
fields of African philosophical discussions, but they were stifled (a) by the
dichotomies (such as subject/object, nature/culture, activity/passivity) that it
inherited from certain Western philosophies which it believed demarcated
the field as such; (b) by the rejection of a *biocentric* conception of reason,
to the advantage of the very worn out conception of anthropocentric reason
(which is what explains the war that was carried out against animism and
ethnophilosophy); (c) finally, by a narrowed *conception of history* which
occupied itself uniquely with *Muntu* and its greater or lesser crises rather
than with nature, which is a subject acting in a *biocentric* conception of
history.

DISCOURSES AND PRACTICES: NOTES ON THE
QUESTION OF THE ANTHROPOCENE IN AFRICA

The question of the Anthropocene has become a new trend/fashion with
its own promoters, miracle workers, and subchapters such as ethics of the
earth and animist ethics—for a humanity which has become tired of itself
and which, without resolving the problems on the table, often takes refuge
in discourses of fear or of economic production which engenders new fears
of its own. Must the expression "Anthropocene" be treated as Wittgenstein
recommended certain others be treated: "one must sometimes withdraw an
expression from the language and send it off to be cleaned—before returning
it to circulation once again"?[15]

This question of the Anthropocene involves us in reflection on *what is happening to us* and *what we do with what happens*. As Fréderic Neyrat puts it
so well, the Anthropocene is

an ideological hybrid. In the word Anthropocene, we find *Anthropos*, in other words, we humans, we the species that specializes in chemical calculations. After all, *what happens to us*, and what we endure, is it really anything but what we do, and bring about? Yes, we have to protect ourselves—but we are at once the danger and the solution, a *pharmakon* all by ourselves, to revisit this Greek term which means both poison and that which can cure us.[16]

When discourse on the Anthropocene is exported into debates in African philosophy, the question becomes one of showing how it has come to shelter certain other discourses in its idiom.

1. Apocalyptic Discourse/Collapsology (the End of the World Approach)

When one poses the question of the environment and of the Anthropocene in Africa, one must pay attention to the kinds of discourse that accompany this question from various angles. The first kind of discourse is that of the Apocalypse. The environmental question is presented in terms of fear or dread regarding what has happened or what is going to happen.[17] Anxiety about what might happen can also have an inhibiting function with respect to action. It is a kind of disorientation which could lead one to take up a science of "collapsology":

> This is the complete object of collapsology, which we define here as the trans-disciplinary exercise of how to study the fall of our industrial civilization, and of that which might come afterward, relying on the two cognitive modes of reason and intuition, as well as on recognized scientific works. However, it will only constitute a small help in the process of interior transition that each person is henceforth led to undertake.[18]

Faced with this talk of apocalypse, some believe that discourse of or about the Anthropocene is a vast effort to make humankind feel guilty. A discourse in which Man becomes the party most responsible for the irreversible natural changes taking place in the biosphere. This responsible Man must expiate his grave error by conforming to rules and laws which are there to save him. Any constraint placed on such laws would be an act of betrayal. From this perspective, the mission of ecological discourses, starting with environmentalism and including deep ecology, is often to *cause fear*, and by means of that fear, to elicit confessions as one might before a tribunal. The confession that Man must make is that of having broken his alliances with nature and with the gods, of having considered the human subject as a being of mastery and action, of having scorned the vitality found among nonhumans and of having fabricated an ethics lacking in compassion toward animals and plants, and finally of having alienated the life that is found in them and in nature. Here we will enumerate those philosophies—the list is just indicative—which surreptitiously sustain such fear/warning.

a) The Legacy of Hans Jonas: "The Heuristics of Fear"

Jonas, having been a soldier and thus very attuned to the fragility of life during wartime, had a conception of life into which dangers were integrated. Jonas's *Principle of Responsibility*, which is a distant response to the optimism of Ernst Bloch's *Principle of Hope*, put the question of the bond between humanity and nature and between Man and life at the center of reflection.[19] Jonas critiques the over-technicization of nature as well as technological rationality and its dangers. He critiques the instrumental conception of nature, and in this respect he follows the same thread as members of the Frankfurt School, whose Freudian and Marxist presuppositions he did not share.

Jonas elaborated an ethics that would no longer be based on humanity but on life. To this end, his conception of responsibility is turned toward the future and on the fragility of both beings and of nature. The major problem is to take steps based on the fear that nature might be annihilated by human action. From the same perspective, animals and plants lose their instrumental status and become objects of human responsibility: "Only the living being, in the structure of its need and in its threatened character—and in principle every living being—can be the object of such a responsibility."[20] In this non-anthropocentric ethics, fear must play a fundamental warning and awakening role:

> The research presented here finds its place in this void (which is at the same time the void of today's relativism regarding values). What can play the role of compass? The very anticipation of menace! It is only in the first glimmers of the thunderstorm approaching us from the future, in the dawn of its planetary increase and in the depth of its human stakes, that we can discover the ethical principles which allow new obligations corresponding to new forms of power to be deduced. . . . This I call the "heuristics of fear." Only the premonition of humanity's deformation provides us with the concept of humanity which will allow us to guard against it.[21]

Discourses on the Anthropocene involve this "heuristics of fear" of which Jonas speaks. The question of the Anthropocene suggests the irreversible deformation of both nature and humanity. Jonas poses this question of irreversibility in a Western world for which nature is disenchanted. But when one introduces this problematic of the Anthropocene in Africa, where nature is not yet disenchanted, how should one manage religious fears of (and regarding) nature and technological menace? It is also worth noting that this fear of catastrophes in the West has led to phenomena of surveillance in public spheres.

The other side of the fear that most often accompanies the question of the Anthropocene is energy security with respect to the various considerations involved in climate change. Politics and meteorology are no longer just connected with migrations and the organization of conquests and wars, but henceforth are marked with the seal of anxiety and fear. Why? Because climate change is irreversible and its contours escape us and remain unknown to us, which means we are subject to the fear that can surge up from transactions with the unknown:

> The functioning of the Earth's system is extremely complex. We are only just beginning to understand the grand mechanisms at work here, and many elements still escape us. This is very well illustrated by climate change; as we begin to change the functioning of the biosphere's systems, the multiplication of complications is accompanied by uncertainties and menaces.[22]

How can we be effective in this period of the Anthropocene, when the *Anthropos* in question does not know and continues to be ignorant of the secret mechanisms of the biosphere and is encouraged in this lack of awareness by the organization of economic production? Depending on the circumstances, the fear engendered by this situation can be either beneficial or damaging. The great historian of fears, Jean Delumeau, assures us that "fear is ambiguous. Inherent in our nature, it is an essential fortification, a guarantee against perils, an indispensible reflex allowing the organism to provisionally escape death. . . . But, if it goes past a manageable dose, it becomes pathological and creates blockages."[23] As for the fear on behalf of future generations to whom a dangerous and polluted world will be handed down—a fear related to a noble hope, "the intergenerational concern for others"? This fear is usually only the expression of a *pretext* for having failed to accomplish what we ought to have done here and now to render the world "habitable," not just in the sense of greenery and well-oxygenated spaces but in the sense of justice. Wittgenstein, lucid, warns us that "when someone prophesizes that the coming generation will take on such or such problems and resolve them, most of the time this is just a wishful dream, by which he excuses himself for not having accomplished what he ought to have accomplished."[24]

The question of climate change, which is included in present and future risks, is always a constellation charged with anxiety, seconded by fear, and followed by the "imagination of the unimaginable." A secret report of the Pentagon on the subject of climate change presents this conjugation of fear, anxiety, and catastrophe.[25] The report expresses this relationship from the outset: "The goal of this report is to imagine the unimaginable—to push back the frontiers of present research on climate changes in order to better understand their consequences for the national security of the United States."[26]

To give a critical evaluation of discourses on the Anthropocene and on climate change, a relationship must be introduced between *geology* (the Anthropocene concerns an irreversible geological modification), *geography* (climate and its changes), *law* (who is the subject of law?), and *theology* (who has sinned, and how can they be brought to redemption?)—something that is rarely done within the framework of African philosophies.[27]

b) The Warnings of Ulrich Beck: Thinking with Risks

Ulrich Beck, who is concerned about risk management, posed this fundamental question, which has oriented his own attitudes toward risks: "Must one be worried? Up to what point? Where does the border between justified worry, inhibiting anxiety, and hysteria lie? And who will tell us? Can scientists who issue contradictory opinions at one and the same time be trusted with this mission? . . . Must we believe politicians and the media?"[28] This worry is one that has a relationship with space and time. From the spatial point of view, Beck believes, we are currently dealing with the phenomenon of globalization and its interconnection of the local and global. The consequence of this globalization is what he calls "cosmopolitization." In fact, Beck holds that our conception of society has often followed what he qualifies as a national perspective: "society is not just comprised as a national, territorial society organized and delimited by States. When social actors adhere to this belief, I speak of a 'national perspective.'"[29] With the cosmopolitical perspective, which conceives of politics in a way that accounts not only for the interaction between international actors but also for the development of new communication technologies, risks and dangers become the great preoccupation from which fears emerge. One will only, from this perspective, be able to think the question of the environment and of the Anthropocene by putting the notion of risk at the center of reflection.

The first risk is that countries undergoing development will experience precarization in ways that could lead to irreversible damages. Beck contends that

at the very moment when people in the West enjoy a decade of peace and opulence . . . a growing number of countries are sinking into debt, unemployment, deterioration of social and health services . . . the World Bank, an instrument in the hands of the G7, has encouraged countries to sign contracts with private groups . . . the great international organizations have pocketed the benefits while the states who . . . were already poor have had to take on their risks.[30]

Injustice is among the risks and one cannot pose the question of the Anthropocene without keeping in mind the fear engendered by the risks humanity is running. Beck, who is preoccupied by food security and its risks and puts the security of peoples before that of capital, has theorized regarding what he calls "a universalism of threats independent of their place of origin: in practice, all human beings are linked by the food chains. They cross borders. The degree of acidity in the air does not just attack sculptures and artworks, it has also worn away . . . modern customs boundaries."[31] This philosophy of risk accompanies Beck's reflection on "ecological expropria-tion," which is in fact "a social and economic expropriation coupled with the continuity of juridical property."[32]

2. Economic Discourse: "Let Us Preserve and Conserve the Resources of Life and Nature"

The discourse on the preservation of nature takes on economic accents. From this perspective, nature is not an energy, a mobility, a flux whose multiple concretizations and organizations have a single common point that we call life; to the contrary, nature is considered as a set of resources. This conception of nature as resource divides the latter into several types of resources (human, energy, etc.). Beneath this ranking of nature's com-ponents in light of human interests is hidden an implicit philosophy which sketches out the world in terms of pure instrumentalities and which has "Management" as its creed. The conservation of nature and environmental ethics is dressed in the syntax of the market and of administration. The preservation of nature is "Management," the ethics of the Earth is a form of "management."

> Management is a form of knowledge—the nameless knowledge of power which is descending over the planet. It announces the reign of administration. "Management" is today a word without a homeland that wants to say every-thing. It is a very old word, with both French and English origins: a hybrid child of the European tradition. It reminds us of the house, the family, and household implements but also of something to do with ceremonies or the way that horses are drawn up. . . . Management is a tool comparable to the army . . . it pulls individuals along according to the logic of four functions in which the military project was once summed up: organize, coordinate, command, control.[33]

Preoccupations around the notion of "sustainable development" set the managerial logic of the biosphere to music. In fact, this concept comes from bureaucrats and managers who legislate over nature as a resource:

> The concept of sustainable development as it is used today has been defined . . . by the world commission on the environment and development (CMED), presided over by Madame Gro Harlem Bruntland, who gave her name to the Commission's report. The definition is the following: "a form of development which satisfies the needs of the present generation while preserving for future generations the possibility of satisfying their own."[34]

The spirit and terminology of management are translated quite well by an expert panel declaration on the risks linked to the climate question. In 1992, many Nobel Prize winners highlighted the importance of this issue: "If we want to avoid the greatest human miseries, it is imperative that we make a profound change in our management of the Earth and the life that it contains."[35] In their declaration, the words "management of the Earth and of life" figure strongly, which brings us back to our observation that life and nature are being conceptualized using the model of "management." As the "conservation of the environment" is an economic concept opposed to the waste of resources, we are still in the ethics of "Management":

> A single concept, conservation, organized both a new kind of law for the natural world and the Progressives' approach to government and social life. It began as a theory of natural-resource management and returned again and again to that touchstone. . . . Two statutes, the 1897 "organic act" of the U.S. Forest Service (creating the service and setting out its structure) and the 1916 counterpart for the National Parks Service, expressed conservation ideas very concretely. Both laws reserved land for federal management, land that would otherwise have been on track to become private property.[36]

In addition to the model of managerial thought, questions relating to the Anthropocene extend to everything involving technology.

There are often religious accents in this trend toward the conservation of nature. Man is only God's gardener in the Judeo-Christian vision. Man and woman, as well as animals, are situated within a garden whose sole owner is God. To transform this nature would be presumptuous, but to destroy and above all to pollute what does not belong to you would be a genuine sacrilege. What is in play here is God's sovereignty over the earth and the Garden. "God is cast in the role of Creator and 'supreme landlord' in the Pentateuch. The land owes its existence to him, and he creates its inhabitants, continually monitoring and supervising their behavior. He allocates land to people: Adam is placed in Eden (Gen 2:8) Canaan is promised to the Israelites (Gen 15, 16–21) . . . to the Edomites (Deut 2:5) and Moabites (Deut 2:9)."[37]

Man, tenant and gardener, must take care of what does not belong to him. We might link the question of care here to that of service. To put oneself at the service of nature in order to praise it in itself renders it divine. But transgression must have a *punishment* at the end of which there will be *redemption*. Punishment is incarnate in the form of *pollution taxes* that must be paid. Debates over pollution taxes are a hot topic. The Hague Declaration on the Environment of March 11, 1989, with the slogan "The Planet is Our Country," already encouraged an awareness of states and sanctions. The "eco-tax" was born and immediately smothered by interest groups and the power of states. In the United States, decision-makers were drawn into debates:

> Other environmental laws set their own unattainable goals. The Clean Water Act required that by 1983 all United States waterways should be clean enough for fishing and swimming, and that by 1985 all water pollution should have come to an end. . . . Indignantly rejecting an amendment that would have added a pollution tax to the Clean Water Act, Senator Howard Baker of Tennessee warned that economic incentives blurred the line between moral obligations and economic convenience.[38]

This *fiscal punishment*, with its points of resistance, finds itself confronted by another kind of discourse which has the mystique of "discourses on salvation and redemption after the profanation of the Nature-goddess," namely, *"ecological restoration."* The United Nations had already suggested a definition at the Rio conference: "States must cooperate in a spirit of global partnership, to conserve, protect, and restore the health and the integrity of the Earth's ecosystem."[39] In the United States, the *Society for Ecological Restoration* was constituted, among whose goals we find the maintenance of an ecosystem's health. This maintenance has taken many fashionable forms, only one of which concerns us here: the *Wilderness.* "The Wilderness Approach, whose goal is the return to a pre-human nature separated from culture, notably including agriculture, was founded on the intrinsic value of nature. This approach essentially originated in the United States."[40] To return to a "prehuman Nature" brings us back to the Garden of Eden and the religious fantasy of a return to "God's work in the Creation." The philosophical dress of this trend hides the stakes of an overlooked theological discourse.

The reason for exploring these trends which accompany discourses about the Anthropocene was to issue an alert for African philosophies, which are in the process of being overwhelmed by the many variants of these current fashions (the question of global warming, the Anthropocene, etc.). They need to know that, behind the screen of political and scientific discourses, other forces are at work: (a) the internationalization of moral panic; (b) the concealment of determining economic factors which are being shored up by interest groups, since the Anthropocene is also the consequence of a certain organization of techno-science and the management of the nation-state; and (c) an implicit theology which slides in beneath the rationalizations given by some Western philosophers who believe erroneously that their ecological paradigms are disenchanted.[41] Theology and the market are tenacious and often hide behind the juridical montages responding to the Anthropocene.

SUBJECTS AND THEIR RELATIONSHIPS: THE ENVIRONMENT'S NEEDS

1) Preserve Life/the Living Being, but Which Life? "Biophilia and Biocracy"

The question of the environment, fears regarding the destiny of the Earth, our common dwelling, fantasies of general loss, the phobia that natural elements will take revenge by means of cataclysms, and lamentations with respect to the suffering of nature's animal life present the framework of an edifice that one might call "biophilia." In the name of life, we must preserve nature both present and future for the inheritance of the generations to come. Life thus becomes a *quasi transcendental* referent in political movements and ethical considerations. However, there remains a question as to what we mean by life when we speak of saving, preserving, modifying, and often of improving the living being. *Post*-humanist, environmental, and *trans*-humanist debates, polemics regarding stem cells, and the challenge of genetic modifications to foods and organisms allow us to draw two types of conclusions following the words of Edgar Morin: "What is life? . . . The question endlessly escapes us and yet endlessly returns."[42]

(1) The question of life must be approached in a modest way, precisely because it escapes us every time. (2) Notions of complexity and organization must be integrated into the knowledge of life, because the latter is not a matter "simply of the knowledge of life. It is at the same time the knowledge of the knowledge of life."[43] For the discourses on the promotion of life in Africa to make sense, what would be necessary, among other things, is not just to evaluate the consequences of the environmental policies of politically and economically dominated African countries, but also to insist on the fact that "the much-proclaimed preservation of life" functions to enable the imposition of a Western vision centered on life. Before defending the rights of life

in the biosphere, we might need to explore what different peoples think of as life.

The defenders of life, whom we characterize as "biocrats" in the Western world, have a vision of life that is often reductive. They could be classified using a distinction between *active and passive biocrats* rather than according to epistemological-political categories (utilitarian, pragmatist, etc.). The "active biocrats" can be found among champions of the defense of animal life, the world of plants, and everything considered as the nonhuman world. Their backdrop is the physicochemical paradigm. Their ontologies are founded on the question of the reciprocity and distribution of life. We are equals by virtue of this reality of life. It is a question of not killing this life that we, humans, share with other beings who populate the biosphere. What unfolds beginning from this ethical consideration will be a relation to the *Umwelt* dominated by biocentrism.

But in this conception of life as priority, one often forgets the *discontinuist* presupposition which has theoretically framed this notion of life in the West. The historian of biology André Pichot reminds us of the two conceptions of life that have followed biologists and anthropologists in the Western history of thought about life.

There have never really been more than two great conceptions of life, two great types of biology, that of Aristotle (which endured above all in the form which Galen gave to it) and that of Descartes . . . for Descartes, everything is brought down to mechanics (extended substance) and to psychology (thinking substance): there is no place for a life which would not take after one domain or the other, biology being conceived on the model of mechanist physics. . . . For Aristotle, on the contrary, it is physics which is conceived completely as a biology.[44]

Pichot studies the steps of the discontinuity, which he describes as follows:

Apart from the temporality of the description of a living being, the most remarkable consequence of the disjunction of evolution is the resulting "gap" which it introduces between the being and its milieu: if the first living entity at time zero of its life was in perfect physico-chemical unity with the pre-biotic environment . . . today's living beings are no longer in such a continuity with their environment.[45]

In this perspective, mechanism, biology, and psychology seem to be levers by which this notion of life is often approached. In speaking about the living being in Africa, however, it would probably be useful to depart from this "scientific" notion of life, not to preach a return to irrationalism, but to show that, on the plane of symbolic effectiveness, we have to exit the physicochemical paradigm (a positivist conception of life) and adopt the paradigm of the *complexity* which surrounds this notion of life. Only this complexity is capable of doing justice to various aspects of life in Africa on the hermeneutical and practical plane.

But, in the conception of life which is put forward by the dominant discourses in the West—and which is disseminated as the discourse of salvation in Africa—one very rarely takes into consideration the social constructions of other cultures regarding the notion of life, which is a *socially constructed* (physicochemical) *fact*. The demand for "respect toward life" and the apparent unilateralness and necessity of the claim that the lives of humans, plants, and animals must be respected insidiously promotes the physicochemical paradigm. This paradigm has neglected two very essential notions: the social construction of living phenomena and a nonlinear conception of history. In leaving behind the physicochemical paradigm and coming closer to the phenomenon of life in a different fashion, one would have to add to the *linear history of nature* (which appeals to the physical phenomena symbolizing life: the history of climates, species, plants, polluting events) its *sedimentary history*. This would examine the various phenomena and metaphors connected with life.

The psychoanalyst Pierre Legendre defines this sedimentary history as one constituting us as speaking beings: "we are constructed on a certain ground of discourse, on the sediments of discourse, of speech."[46] In this sedimentary history of life, the associations of words such as life, vital force, vital energies, and so on might be studied in African languages. A "theology of life" could also analyze the relationships between life and that which is transcendent: African cosmologies could show where the phenomenon of life appears in African cosmogonies, an "aesthetics" of life would pay attention to life as *expression* and, finally, one could analyze the relations between life and the question of destiny in African eschatologies (if they exist). One could also multiply agrarian imaginaries, by studying the place of plants in the economy of dreams, and even deepen this exploration by integrating the relations between life and beings that are no longer living. What is the place of the "not yet" (the unborn) or of "ancestral memories" in tales, myths, and systems of caregiving in Africa? These approaches would thus form the architecture of a *sedimentary history* of life, which can only be formulated as a *constellation* involving the complexity of discourses and imaginaries around life.

The "passive biocrats," for their part, want to reestablish an alliance between diverse aspects of life that has been broken. They love animals, write books on the countryside, adore greenery, and make laws to ensure that the irresponsible people who violate these alliances will be punished. The fight against an anthropocentric ethics, the opening to the nonhuman living world, and an exaggerated conception of the biosphere, all compounded by a re-enchantment of the life of Man and of nature indicate a *very narrow conception of the notion of life.* The relationship they draw between humanity and nature, which often takes on metaphors linked to the Earth Mother, the Earth as nourishing, and the terrestrial envelope, presupposes a conception of the living being which is still an incarnation of the physicochemical paradigm.

What is forgotten in this is that life in Africa goes beyond the physico-chemical. There are two phenomena linked to this orientation: *social death* and the life of *those who no longer live in the physicochemical modality.* In the case of a great offense to the equilibrium of the community (parricide, fratricide, matricide, the poisoner or the sorcerer), the offender was often definitively banished from his or her community, which no longer considered him or her as alive. For such a community, the wrongdoer is dead and will not return to the kingdom of the ancestors. Although living, some part of this individual is considered nonliving. Here, *life is not a physicochemical reality, but a social construction.* The second phenomenon is belief in the existence of "ancestors." An ancestor who is "consulted" so that oracles can be received from him or her is well and truly alive in the imaginary of those who "consult" him. Life beyond the grave is for certain communities more than a physicochemical life; it is the plenitude of life. Here it is not a question of believing or not believing in it; for those who adhere to a certain system of reference, this life beyond is a genuine life. The various "ethics of the earth" which want to honor the life of humans and nonhumans must revise their narrow conceptions of life, and when one judges that life is in danger from multiple ecological risks, one must also extend this fear to the life of ancestors.

Amnesia regarding the memory of the ancestors, memory which partially structures certain African societies most of the time, is a genuine ecological risk. The ecological risks concern "those who are living" in our *Oikos* (house). *Oikos* means both *house* and *patrimony* depending on the case. In Africa, the ecological question can no longer be posed as it is done in the bourgeois and positivist discourses on the Anthropocene in the West (limited to the interests of beings populating the biosphere), but only by integrating all those who enter into the "*Oikos,*" the house and the patrimony. The past history and memory of peoples live in the forests, cities, suburbs, and what one must save from air and water pollution, from climate change, must be considered as taking part in *ecology,* this way the human has of inhabiting its "Earth-house planet" and its "patrimony, material and intellectual, past and present."

2) "Dwell in the World": But Which World?

On the horizon of current African preoccupations we see the approach of this idea, which has been formulated as a slogan: "Dwell in the World" ["*Habiter le monde*"]. African thinkers who write, live, and reflect today have several challenges to take up:

a) On the one hand, to build national or continental cultures which support their fragile states, and on the other, to be mindful of the world's cosmopolitanism and the circulation of humans and goods which this involves.
b) To resist using "local" practices and ideas (what they call *indigenous knowledge*) but also to achieve power within the realm of the "global."
c) To hold onto and perpetuate local traditions, while asking how the evaluation of action and the memory of humanity can be integrated into them using digital means.

This framework offers several options for dwelling with(in) the world.

"Dwelling in the World" Means Decolonizing It

What should we make of intellectual "decolonization" using epistemologies said to be "Southern"? The politico-epistemological label employed in this context implies a "decolonization that is concerned with forms of knowledge" imposed by various colonizing processes and patriarchal systems. Such is the definition of decolonization given by Boaventura de Souza Santos, who represents this option for the Third World well. He continues:

> In this chapter . . . I discuss what I call the second degree of separation between the epistemologies of the South and the epistemologies of the North, beginning with two major problems. The first is how to decolonize knowledge and the methodologies by which it is produced. . . . The second is how to develop postabyssal, hybrid concepts and theories. . . . As a matter of fact, decolonizing the social sciences makes little sense if it does not involve depatriarchalizing and decommodifying them as well.[47]

The Program of "Epistemologies of the South"

Indigenous forms of knowledge and their advancement also give us another way of dwelling in the world. Indigenous forms of knowledge have been celebrated and encouraged in Africa. Here we are thinking of the technological inheritance, the pharmacopeia of traditional medicines, and the codification of communication paradigms, for example, in drumming and the achievements of the textile arts. The colonial and postcolonial devalorization of these forms of knowledge by colonization and the industries that supported it has been denounced. In this case, we are assured by the advocates of a justice without borders, the decolonization of knowledge consists in bringing the epistemologies of the South back into current usage so that justice can be done to them and so that all can be invested in the common good of humanity.

The first observation is that the epistemologies of the South must also be studied in a critical manner. The *decolonial* must also be *integral*. The knowledges of the South (indigenous forms of knowledge) which have been hitherto sidelined also have their own relation with power which was not necessarily patriarchal and colonial. The *distinction* between what was done and not done followed certain rules, but who made these up? Who drew the *limit* between what belongs to techniques of rationality and what belongs to the irrational? Who, in these Southern cultures and societies, *had the right to know?* Was the opposition between the rational and the irrational even relevant in such systems? In cases where these forms of knowledge from the South integrated women or were even produced by women, did this automatically imply that the knowledge had been decolonized? Does de Souza Santos know that women sometimes had a status higher than certain men in caste societies such as Senegal and Mali?

The second observation, which concerns the relation to nature, has to do with agriculture. Writers like Mongo Beti—in the good conscience of criticizing colonialism—have shown how the colonial imposition of export crops, such as cacao, coffee, and rubber, gave rise to a heteronomous relationship between Africans and nature.[48] What this critique of alienation from nature and from the African environment due to colonization lacks, however, is a critique of indigenous forms of knowledge. Nor does Hountondji give this critique in his "indigenous knowledge." One remains satisfied with the attitude of opposition to Northern epistemology and to its truth, political economy, while forgetting to carry out a reversal of this critique so that indigenous knowledge can also have its moment of truth. One example of indigenous knowledge that is neither colonial, nor patriarchal, nor linked to state-supported or post-colonial industry is *slash and burn agriculture* as practiced in Central Africa (Cameroon, Gabon, Equatorial Guinea, Central African Republic, or northern Republic of Congo). This farming technique uses land cleared by burning part of the forest or the brush. The result is deforestation and the impoverishment of the soil. This is a traditional practice of the South that must also be critiqued.

CONCLUSION

"Dwelling in the World": A Composition of Spaces

Where Do We Live?

Geographers, architects, and urbanists respond to the Anthropocene with plans for urbanization (improvement of green spaces, housing, recreation areas, and commercial spaces). In Africa, the bureaucracy of the postcolonial state responds with a portmanteau term which certain ministers even hold as a title: "Land-use Planning" [*aménagement du territoire*]. What this leaves out is a study of places. What does it mean to inhabit a place, to find a place, to plan for a place's use?

How can we "inhabit the world"? Heidegger gives us a response that Africans may find interesting. Dwelling is not simply the purview of geography or ecology in an environmentalist form, but a relation that is established with poetry in the ontological sense of the term.

Heidegger begins by criticizing the geographical-instrumental approach to the notion of dwelling: "Our dwelling is harassed by the housing shortage. Even if that were not so, our dwelling today is harassed by work, made insecure by the hunt for gain and success, bewitched by the entertainment and recreation industry."[49] Then, he identifies dwelling and "building"; one can only truly inhabit by building; "Poetry is what really lets us dwell. But through what do we attain to a dwelling place? Through building. Poetic creation, which lets us dwell, is a kind of building."[50] Finally, he considers that dwelling in and with the world means recovering the meaning of care, of restraint [*ménagement*] (which would overturn modern management!) toward all beings: "to dwell, to be set at peace, means to remain at peace within the free, the preserve, the free sphere that safeguards each thing in its nature. *The fundamental character of dwelling is this sparing and preserving.*"[51] What this Heideggerian analysis inspired by the poet Hölderlin teaches us is that being restrained and taking care are the true attitudes involved in dwelling as an action.

When Africans today speak of the Anthropocene, they have to "dwell in the world," but with poetry and critique. With poetry, in other words, by privileging creation in the noble sense of the word: *re-creation of the self, restraint toward Alterity* (which cannot be reduced to the community of living beings and their biospheres alone, either), and *revision of the institutions and paradigms* which structure the various schools of ecologies. We should also add, because poetry is at stake, a strophe which will concern the "mental pollution of peoples": what are the (internal and external) *polluting agents* plaguing the mentality of a people at a given moment of its enduring? And what are the agents *polluting the lucidity and the dynamism of peoples?* If one were to identify them, would the United Nations have to rewrite its charter to include the mental pollution of peoples? Or, in the same spirit as taxes on carbon pollution in the atmosphere, might one suggest a "pollution tax" on the "noocene" among peoples?

A genuine poetry/creation is critique, which is to say an act that sets statements and practices at a distance. We critique capitalism by way of the "Capitalocene," in order to shed some light on this new fetish the

"Anthropocene" has turned into.[52] For example, we recall the contradictions of the "love for nature" with its reversal of the medal of "indifference" toward the humans who live there, what Malcolm Ferdinand admirably named "reforestation without the world (the peasants of Haiti)," we rewrite the "manifestos," we denounce "environmental racism," but what is often forgotten is the "critique of fine feelings" with respect to nature, climate change, greenery, the torments inflicted on the biosphere, the ethics of alliance between the human and the nonhumans and the concern for "original peoples." The fine sentiment par excellence being what Boltanski calls "suffering at a distance"— one that fails to bring denunciation and action together. The one who denounces evil

> finds a bargain on the price of action . . . it is a commitment in words only, which costs nothing and which soothes the spectator's worries, without in any way reducing the suffering of those who are unfortunate. . . . Above all, denunciation is considered to be genuine engagement . . . akin to a moral attitude . . . if one can show that it represents a cost or a risk for the one who performs it.[53]

Denunciation—by African philosophers and international bureaucracy—of what is happening in Darfur, in the eastern Congo, on Lake Chad, in the mines of Mozambique and South Africa, the sale of entire forests to Western and Asian companies, this denunciation is therefore agreeable, because the one who denounces *suffers*, but *at a distance*.

What narratives do we tell about all this? The questions of the Anthropocene and of the environment in Africa also turn around stories. What is the validity of economic, theological, political, and diplomatic narratives which center on and discreetly structure this question of the Anthropocene? And why did African philosophers take an interest in it so abruptly?[54] How does this narrative, with its multiple metamorphoses and alongside the question of the digital, become a dominant account which, varying with the circumstances, structures the *anxieties* of a world fatigued at its own proclamations, the *euphorias of peoples* deprived of the promise of happiness and security, the *food aid programs* which never successfully nourish the planet, and the *industrial hyperexploitation of nature* which acts so powerfully on the climate, the sharing of waters, the habitat, and migrations? Simone de Beauvoir, disillusioned, said that

> men do not totally believe what they say, and this is what allows them to leap without any embarrassment from one plane of truth to another: in fact, they are never really situated on any such plane . . . but one does not believe in either the truth of gloomy horizons or in the propaganda films, nor in that of proverbs and

disenchanted commonplaces. . . . They know very well that their thoughts are neither gratuitous nor completely sincere, they do not aim at the universal, they are circumstantial thoughts ordered by practical ends: if one pretends to take them at their word, they get irritated.[55]

With the theme of the Anthropocene so present, we wish that the wisdom of nations would prove Beauvoir wrong, in putting action to words and without irritation.

Translated by Laura Hengehold

NOTES

1. Read Jean-Kevin Aimé Tsiba, "La malédiction des ressources minérales. Mounana, d'un village potentiellement riche à une ville fantôme," *Revue canadienne de géographie tropicale/Canadian journal of tropical geography* 4, no. 2 (2017): 65–79. Online December 31, 2017. http://laurentienne.ca/rcgt "The other terrible phenomenon is the radioactive pollution. This goes back to studies done by the laboratory of the Commision de Recherche et d'Information Indépendente sur la Radioactivité (CRIIRAD), Médecin du Monde, the association SHERPA, NGOs . . . stating that radioactivity is omnipresent at Mounana. The reason suggested is the bad management of mining waste and the less than adequate restoration of several sites selected for reasons that were not revealed. The CRIIRAD (2007) affirms that the information presented by AREVA concerning the environmental and health impact of its activities at Mounana absolutely failed to recognize the reality." Read also S. Y. L. Mouandza, A. B. Moubissi, P. E. Abiama, T. B. Ekogo, G. H. Ben Bolie, *Study of Natural Radioactivity to Assess of Radiation Hazards From Soil Samples Collected From Mounana in South-east of Gabon*, International Journal of Radiation Research 16, no. 4 (2018): 443–453.
2. Tombari Bodo and Lekpa David, "Kingdom: The Petroleum Exploitation and Pollution in Ogoni, Rivers State, Nigeria: The Community Perspective (Report)," *European Scientific Journal* 14, no. 32 (Nov 15, 2018): 197. Global public opinion still remembers the condemnation and execution of Ogoni activist Ken Saro Wiwa.
3. A ship from Europe just dumped waste off the coast of Abidjan, causing deaths and illnesses. See K. van Wingerde, "The Limits of Environmental Regulation in a Globalized Economy: Lessons from the Probo Koala Case," in *The Routledge Handbook of White-Collar and Corporate Crime in Europe*, ed. J. van Erp, W. Huisman, and G. Vande Walle (London: Routledge, 2015), 260–275.
4. Arnaud Labrousse and François Xavier Verschave, *Les pillards de la forêt. Exploitations criminelles en Afrique* (Paris: Agone, 2002). This book is an excellent handbook that must be read by African philosophers. It shows how the exploitation and annihilation of the primary forest is carried out in francophone African counties, thereby causing irreversible environmental change.

5. "The sudden catastrophic release of gas from Lake Nyos on 21 August 1986 caused the deaths of at least 1700 people in the northwest area of Cameroon. . . . Because of the previous incident at Lake Monoun, and the many unanswered associated questions, a more extensive and timely evaluation of the Lake Nyos event was immediately initiated, and a diversified, ten-member scientific team consisting of forensic pathologists, geologists, water chemists, environmental engineers, a limnologist, and a clinical physician was organized and sent on short notice to Cameroon." US Department of the Interior, "Lake Nyos." *US Geological Survey*, 21 August 1986, 1–4 [1 and 4, really]. https://pubs.usgs.gov/of/1987/0097/report.pdf.

6. Read Stanislas Meloné, "La parenté et la terre dans les stratégies du développement, l'expérience camerounaise (études critiques)" (Paris/Yaoundé: Klincksieck/ Université Fédérale du Cameroun, 1972), 21; Kéba Mbaye, "Les régimes des terres au Sénégal," in *Le Droit de la Terre en Afrique (au Sud du Sahara)*, Etudes préparées à la requête de l'Unesco (Paris: Maisonneuve et Larose, 1971), 137 and following. Even if Meloné and Keba Mbaye distance themselves from it with this notion of juridical pluralism, their reasoning remains in the tradition of contract philosophies.

7. Michel Serres, *The Natural Contract*, trans. Elizabeth MacArthur and William Paulson (Ann Arbor: University of Michigan Press, 1995).

8. See the work of Rwandan philosopher Alexis Kagame, *La philosophie bantu comparé* (Paris: Présence Africaine, 1976). He sets out to describe an African ontology, taking inspiration from the Greek language in Aristotle's time.

9. Max Horkheimer, *Eclipse of Reason* (New York: Continuum, 2004), 64.

10. See Michel Foucault, *L'ordre du discours* (Paris: Gallimard, 1972), 37.

11. Placide Tempels, *La philosophie bantoue*, 2nd edition (Paris: Présence Africaine, 1961), 70.

12. On Zimbabwe, see Baba Ibrahima Kake, "Evocations historiques: un grand empire de l'Afrique orientale: le Monomotapa," *Présence Africaine*, Nouvelle série 53 (1er trimestre 1965), 208–214.

13. Read this very illuminating work regarding the whole imaginary that has surrounded the construction of the symbolic site of Timbuktu: Simona Corlan-Ioan, *Invention de Tombouctou. Histoire des récits occidentaux sur la ville pendant les XIXème-XXe siècle* (Paris: L'Harmattan, 2014).

14. Friedrich Nietzsche, *Untimely Meditations,* 77.

15. Ludwig Wittgenstein, *Remarques mêlées,* trans. Gérard Granel (Paris: Flammarion, 2002), 100.

16. Fréderic Neyrat, *La part inconstructible de la terre* (Paris: Editions du Seuil, 2016), 69.

17. Normal fear is distinguished by these traits: "A normal fear is an alarm efficiently calibrated in its activation, as in its regulation. In its activation, the alarm of fear is only triggered intelligently, in the face of a genuine danger, and not in the presence of the possibility or the memory of a danger," in André Christophe, *La psychologie de la peur* (Paris: Odile Jacob, 2004), 12, i-book.

18. Pablo Servigne, *Comment tout peut s'effondrer: Petit manuel de collapsologie à l'usage des générations présentes* (Paris: Editions du Seuil, 2015), iBooks, 350.

19. On the relationship between Ernst Bloch and Hans Jonas, read the excellent analysis of Arno Münster, *Principe Responsabilité ou Principe Espérance? Hans Jonas, Ernst Bloch, Günther Anders* (Lormont: Editions du Bord de l'Eau, 2010).

20. Hans Jonas, *Le principe responsabilité: une éthique pour la civilisation technologique*, trans. J. Greisch (Paris: Cerf, 1992), 140–141.

21. Jonas, *Le principe responsabilité*, 7.

22. Michel Bourban, *Penser la justice climatique* (Paris: PUF, 2018), 225.

23. Jean Delumeau, *La peur en Occident* (Paris: Fayard, 1978), 23.

24. Wittgenstein, *Remarques mêlées*, 81.

25. Peter Schwartz and Doug Randall, *Rapport secret du Pentagone sur le changement climatique*, trans. Arnaud Pouillot (Paris: Editions Allia, 2006).

26. Schwartz and Randall, *Rapport secret du Pentagone*, 7.

27. David Millet, *Anthropocène, The Age of Man*, Edited by Dr, Julia Buss (CreateSpace, a DBA of On- demand Publishing, LLc, Edition 2, 2015).

28. Ulrich Beck, *Qu'est-ce que le cosmopolitisme?*, trans. Aurelie Duthoo (Paris: Alto/Aubier, 2006), 70–71.

29. Beck, *Qu'est-ce que le cosmopolitisme?*, 51.

30. Ulrich Beck, *Pouvoir et contre-pouvoir à l'heure de la mondialisation*, trans. Aurelie Duthoo (Paris: Flammarion, 2003), 75.

31. Ulrich Beck, *La société du risque*, trans. Laure Bernardi (Paris: Flammarion, 2006), 66.

32. Beck, *La société du risque*, 70.

33. Pierre Legendre, *Dominium Mundi. L'empire du Management* (Paris: Mille et Une Nuits, 2007), 42.

34. Michel Trommetter and Jean Weber, "Développement durable et changements globaux: le développement durable l'est-il encore pour longtemps," in *Biodiversité et changements globaux. Enjeux de la société et défis pour la recherché*, ed. Bernard Barbeault, Bernard Chevassus-au-Louis, and Anne Teyssèdre (Paris: ADPF-ministère des Affaires Etrangères, 2004), 137.

35. Union of Concerned Scientists, "World Scientists' Warning to Humanity," (1992), cited by Catherine Larrère, in "L'écologie politique existe-t-elle?" *Esprit* 441 no. 1/2 (Jan/Feb 2018): 120.

36. Jedediah Purdy, *After Nature: A Politics for the Anthropocene* (Cambridge: Harvard University Press, 2015), 162.

37. J. McKeaon, "Land, Fertility, Famine," in *Dictionary of the Old Testament, Pentateuch*, ed. Desmond Alexander and David W. Baker (Leicester, England: InterVarsity Press, 2002), 487.

38. Purdy, *After Nature*, 213–214.

39. United Nations, "Rio Declaration on Environment and Development, Principle 7, 1992." Cited by Marion Waller in *Artefacts Naturels. Nature, réparation, responsabilité* (Paris: Editions de l'Eclat, 2016), 56.

40. United Nations, "Rio Declaration," 61.

41. Here we are thinking of the work by Charles Birch and John B. Cobb, Jr. *The Liberation of Life: From the Cell to the Community* (Cambridge: Cambridge University Press, 1981).

42. Edgar Morin, *La méthode*, I (Paris: Editions du Seuil, 2008), 550.

43. Morin, *La methode,* 551.

44. André Pichot, *Histoire de la notion de vie* (Paris: Gallimard, 1993), 7–8.

45. Pichot, *Histoire de la notion de vie*, 945.

46. Pierre Legendre, *Vues éparses. Entretiens radiophoniques avec Philippe Petit* (Paris: Mille et une nuits, 2019), 115.

47. Boaventura de Souza Santos, *The End of the Cognitive Empire. The Coming Age of the Epistemologies of the South* (Durham: Duke University Press, 2018), 108.

48. See Mongo Beti [Eza Boto], *Ville cruelle* (Paris: Presence Africaine, 1971).

49. Martin Heidegger, ". . . Poetically Man Dwells . . ." in *Poetry, Language, Thought*, trans. Albert Hofstadter (New York: Harper and Row, 1971), 213.

50. Heidegger, "Poetically Man Dwells," 215.

51. Martin Heidegger, "Building Dwelling Thinking," in *Poetry, Language, Thought*, trans. Albert Hofstadter (New York: Harper and Row, 1971), 149.

52. Armel Campagne, *Le Capitalocène. Aux racines historiques du dérèglement climatique* (Paris: Editions Divergences, 2017), 89–100; Daniel Cunha, "The Anthropocene as Fetishism," *Mediations* 28, no. 2 (2015): 65–77; Malcom Ferdinand, *Une écologie décoloniale. Penser l'écologie depuis le monde Caribéen* (Paris: Editions du Seuil, 2019), 155–165; Katherine Gibson, Deborah Bird Rose and Ruth Fincher, eds., *Manifesto for Living in the Anthropocene* (New York: Punctum Books, 2015); Razmig Keucheyan, *La Nature est un champ de bataille. Essai d'écologie politique* (Paris: La Découverte, 2018), 21–56.

53. Luc Boltanski, *La souffrance à distance. Morale humanitaire, médias et politique* (Paris: Métailié, 1993), 108.

54. On this subject, see Jean-Godefroy Bidima, "La Nature en Afrique: Trajets et Projets," in *Africa e Mediterraneo* (Bologna) 53 (Dec. 2005), 28–37.

55. Simone de Beauvoir, *L'existentialisme et la sagesse des nations* (Paris: Gallimard, 2008), 26–27.

BIBLIOGRAPHY

Beck, Ulrich. *Pouvoir et contre-pouvoir à l'heure de la mondialisation.* Translated by Aurelie Duthoo (Paris: Flammarion, 2003).

———. *Qu'est-ce que le cosmopolitisme?* Translated by Aurelie Duthoo (Paris: Alto/Aubier, 2006).

———. *La société du risque.* Translated by Laure Bernardi (Paris: Flammarion, 2006).

Beti, Mongo [Eza Boto]. *Ville cruelle* (Paris: Presence Africaine, 1971).

Bidima, Jean-Godefroy. "La Nature en Afrique: Trajets et Projets." *Africa e Mediterraneo* (Bologna) 53 (Dec. 2005): 28–37.

Birch, Charles, and John B. Cobb, Jr. *The Liberation of Life: From the Cell to the Community* (Cambridge: Cambridge University Press, 1981).

Bodo, Tombari, and Lekpa David. "Kingdom: The Petroleum Exploitation and Pollution in Ogoni, Rivers State, Nigeria: The Community Perspective (Report)." *European Scientific Journal* 14, no. 32 (Nov 15, 2018).

Boltanski, Luc. *La souffrance à distance. Morale humanitaire, médias et politique* (Paris: Métailié, 1993).

Bourban, Michel. *Penser la justice climatique* (Paris: PUF, 2018).

Campagne, Armel. *Le Capitalocène. Aux racines historiques du dérèglement climatique* (Paris: Editions Divergences, 2017).

Christophe, André. *La psychologie de la peur* (Paris: Odile Jacob, 2004).

Commission de Recherche et d'Information Indépendente sur la Radioactivité (CRIIRAD) 2007.

Corlan-Ioan, Simona. *Invention de Tombouctou. Histoire des récits occidentaux sur la ville pendant les XIXème-XXe siècle* (Paris: L'Harmattan, 2014).

Cunha, Daniel. "The Anthropocene as Fetichism." *Mediations* 28, no. 2 (2015).

De Beauvoir, Simone. *L'existentialisme et la sagesse des nations* (Paris: Gallimard, 2008).

Delumeau, Jean. *La peur en Occident* (Paris: Fayard, 1978).

Ferdinand, Malcom. *Une écologie décoloniale. Penser l'écologie depuis le monde Caribéen* (Paris: Editions du Seuil, 2019).

Foucault, Michel. *L'ordre du discours* (Paris: Gallimard, 1972).

Gibson, Katherine, Deborah Bird Rose, and Ruth Fincher, eds., *Manifesto for Living in the Anthropocene* (New York: Punctum Books, 2015).

Heidegger, Martin. "Building Dwelling Thinking," in *Poetry, Language, Thought.* Translated by Albert Hofstadter (New York: Harper and Row, 1971).

———. ". . . Poetically Man Dwells . . . ," in *Poetry, Language, Thought.* Translated by Albert Hofstadter (New York: Harper and Row, 1971).

Horkheimer, Max. *Eclipse of Reason* (New York: Continuum, 2004).

Jonas, Hans. *Le principe responsabilité: une éthique pour la civilisation technologique.* Translated by J. Greisch (Paris: Cerf, 1992).

Kagame, Alexis. *La philosophie bantu comparée* (Paris: Présence Africaine, 1976).

Kake, Baba Ibrahima. "Evocations historiques: un grand empire de l'Afrique orientale: le Monomotapa." *Présence Africaine*, Nouvelle série 53 (1er trimestre 1965): 208–214.

Keucheyan, Razmig. *La Nature est un champ de bataille. Essai d'écologie politique* (Paris: La Découverte, 2018).

Labrousse, Arnaud and François Xavier Verschave. *Les pillards de la forêt. Exploitations criminelles en Afrique* (Paris: Agone, 2002).

Larrère, Catherine. "L'écologie politique existe-t-elle?" *Esprit* 144 no. 1/2 (Jan/Feb 2018): 119–29.

Legendre, Pierre. *Dominium Mundi. L'empire du Management* (Paris: Mille et Une Nuits, 2007).

———. *Vues éparses. Entretiens radiophoniques avec Philippe Petit* (Paris: Mille et une nuits, 2019).

Mbaye, Kéba. "Les régimes des terres au Sénégal," in *Le droit de la Terre en Afrique (au Sud du Sahara) Études préparées à la requête de l'Unesco* (Paris: Maisonneuve et Larose, 1971).

McKeaon, J. "Land, Fertility, Famine." in *Dictionary of the Old Testament, Pentateuch.* Edited by Desmond Alexander and David W. Baker (Leicester, England: InterVarsity Press, 2002).

Meloné, Stanislas. "La parenté et la terre dans les strategies du développement, l'expérience camerounaise (études critiques)" (Paris/Yaoundé: Klincksieck/ Université Fédérale du Cameroun, 1972).

Millet, David. *Anthropocène. The Age of Man,* Edited by Dr. Julia Buss (CreateSpace, a DBA of On-demand Publishing, LLC, Edition 2, 2015).

Morin, Edgar. *La méthode,* I (Paris: Editions du Seuil, 2008).

Mouandza, S. Y. L., A. B. Moubissi, P. E. Abiama, T. B. Ekogo, and G. H. Ben Bolie, "Study of Natural Radioactivity to Assess of Radiation Hazards from Soil Samples Collected from Mounana in South-east of Gabon." *International Journal of Radiation Research* 16, no. 4 (2018): 443–453.

Münster, Arno. *Principe Responsabilité ou Principe Espérance? Hans Jonas, Ernst Bloch, Günther Anders* (Lormont: Editions du Bord de l'Eau, 2010).

Neyrat, Fréderic. *La part inconstructible de la terre* (Paris: Editions du Seuil, 2016).

Nietzsche, Friedrich. *Untimely Meditations.* Translated by R. J. Hollingdale (Cambridge: Cambridge University Press, 1983).

Pichot, André. *Histoire de la notion de vie* (Paris: Gallimard, 1993).

Purdy, Jedediah. *After Nature: A Politics for the Anthropocene* (Cambridge: Harvard University Press, 2015).

Santos, Boaventura de Souza. *The End of the Cognitive Empire. The Coming Age of the Epistemologies of the South* (Durham: Duke University Press, 2018).

Serres, Michel. *The Natural Contract.* Translated by Elizabeth MacArthur and William Paulson (Ann Arbor: University of Michigan Press, 1995).

Servigne, Pablo. *Comment tout peut s'effondrer: Petit manuel de collapsologie à l'usage des générations présentes* (Paris: Editions du Seuil, 2015).

Tempels, Placide. *La philosophie bantoue.* (Paris: Présence Africaine, 2e edition, 1961).

Trommetter, Michel, and Jean Weber, "Développement durable et changements globaux: le développement durable l'est-il encore pour longtemps," in *Biodiversité et changements globaux. Enjeux de la société et d'fis pour la recherché.* Edited by Bernard Barbeault, Bernard Chevassus-au-Louis, and Anne Teyssèdre (Paris: ADPF-ministère des Affaires Etrangères, 2004).

Tsiba, Jean-Kevin Aimé. "La malédiction des ressources minérales. Mounana, d'un village potentiellement riche à une ville fantôme." *Revue canadienne de géographie tropicale/Canadian journal of tropical geography* 4, no. 2 (2017): 65–79. Online December 31, 2017. http://laurentienne.ca/rcgt.

US Department of Interior. "Lake Nyos." *US Geological Survey*, 21 August 1986. https://pubs.usgs.gov/of/1987/0097/report.pdf.

Van Wingerde, K. "The Limits of Environmental Regulation in a Globalized Economy: Lessons from the Probo Koala Case," in *The Routledge Handbook of White-Collar and Corporate Crime in Europe.* Edited by J. van Erp, W. Huisman and G. Vande Walle (London: Routledge, 2015): 260–275.

Waller, Marion. *Artefacts Naturels. Nature, réparation, responsabilité* (Paris: Editions de l'Eclat, 2016).

Wittgenstein, Ludwig. *Remarques mêlées.* Translated by Gérard Granel (Paris: Flammarion, 2002).

Chapter 7

Rethinking the Living World in Light of African Philosophy

Toward an Animist Humanism

Séverine Kodjo-Grandvaux

In the middle of the 2010s a slogan appeared in France, both in the militant public sphere and in a small part of the academic world: minds must be decolonized. Since then, many articles, works generated by African or Afropean philosophers, and intellectual and/or cultural meetings in Europe or in Africa have invited the world to consider the heavy historical, epistemic, and epistemological heritage of asymmetrical North/South relations, prisoners of a colonial and imperial politics put in place some five centuries earlier.[1] A politics that had—or might have, according to the point of view—overshadowed the establishment of African independence. This discourse's theoretical and conceptual references are drawn from the Latin American decolonial movement, relying on the work of Enrique Dussel (reader of Paulin Hountondji and Fabien Eboussi Boulaga), Walter Mignolo, Ramon Grosfoguel, and Anibal Quijano. They represent the next stage in the long process of a decolonization of knowledge and mentalities—undertaken by many thinkers such as Frantz Fanon, Cheikh Anta Diop, Kwasi Wiredu, Ngugi Wa Thiong'o, Henry Odera Oruka, V. Y. Mudimbe, Stanislas Adotevi, or Fabien Eboussi Boulaga—necessary to give political independence its full meaning.

Already in 1977, in *La Crise du Muntu*, Fabien Eboussi Boulaga noted that decolonization had happened in several stages. The first consisted in "recuperating colonial power without changing either the form or the content, by acting as if its organization was merely functional, destined to respond to the universal needs of man in general."[2] To interrogate this political, social, and epistemic heritage becomes an imperative for anyone who wants to be able to determine how "to be by and for oneself, in the articulation of having and doing, according to an order that excludes violence and arbitrariness."[3]

Because, as Stanislas Adotevi confirms, decolonization, this "agreed upon disagreement," is nothing but the transfer of domination from one power to another, without substantially modifying the nature of this power or the social relations on which it rests.[4] And this all the more so since the colonial system did not withdraw without first "being assured that spokespeople were in place who were friendly to its ideas and its interests. Decolonization, in short, is the theoretical ruse that permits imperialism, in a succession of distracting moves, to arrive at its goal: the universal repossession of minds and of people."[5]

This is the reason why some sixty years later, intellectuals such as Felwine Sarr, Achille Mbembe, Francoise Vergès, Nadia Yala Kisukidi, and Hourya Benthouhami, participating in the Ateliers de la Pensée organized since 2016 at Dakar, repeatedly specified that although independence was a formal transfer of power, a historical event with a date, it did not necessarily result in a movement to deconstruct that same colonial power that has contaminated minds, knowledge, and ways of being-in-the-world. It is therefore important to finish this process of decolonization, for, according to the distinction made by Latin American thinkers of the decolonial movement, coloniality—constitutive of Modernity—cannot be reduced to colonization. It has survived colonization, pursuing the imperialist domination of Western economies under other forms that prevent all real independence.[6]

Without reviewing this injunction to decolonize minds in detail, I would nevertheless like to recall several of its key principles.[7] Epistemic decolonization is not a systematic rejection of everything whose nature would be Western. A work of deconstruction, it explores the history of concepts and forms of knowledge to pull out their cultural and ideological presuppositions, interrogate them, and decide how far a Western epistemic approach will or will not be relevant for reading African realities. It works toward a reappropriation of discourse about the self and a revalorization of theoretical and practical forms of knowledge discredited by the colonial enterprise in order to assure its domination. It is a matter of repairing "epistemic injustices linked to colonialism" which survive "when the concepts and the categories thanks to which a people understands itself and understands its universe are replaced or affected by the colonizer's concepts and categories."[8] These injustices are examples of what Gayatri Chakravorty Spivak describes as "epistemic violence."[9] All the same, it is not a matter of rehabilitating, on principle, everything that has been harmed by the modern colonial epistemicide, but of simply being capable of deciding what is good for oneself without systematic recourse to either the former master's tools or to his representations.[10] This is what makes Achille Mbembe and Felwine Sarr say that

> those who, for a long time, have been caught in the snares of the other's conquering gaze, find themselves at a unique moment to regenerate the project

of a critical thought that would not rest content with lamenting and taunting. Trusting in its own speech and comfortable with the archives of all humanity, such a thought would be capable of looking forward, of truly creating, and in so doing, opening new paths which are up to meeting the challenges of our time.[11]

These are challenges that involve Africa, certainly, but also all of humanity, since it is a question of thinking "the planetary condition."[12] And here is the second interesting aspect of this decolonial movement: it does not think about Africa in isolation. Rather, it inscribes Africa in a dynamic inviting the West to see itself with clear eyes, in order to rethink its own being-in-the-world and its way of living in the world. Perhaps this is the fundamental contribution made by this form of critical thought, which is now developing in European societies at the start of the twenty-first century. It demands that the West realize that, in Aimé Césaire's words, "colonization tries to *decivilize* the colonizer"[13] and that as a result, the West would do well to finally carry out its own autocritique if it wants to renew its connection to its own humanity.

Henceforth, the imperative to decolonize minds and knowledge does not just affect Africa but is also addressed to the West, so that the latter might shed its old colonial garb. So that it might stop considering itself the only source of knowledge and begin to learn from those that it considers subaltern. So that it might decenter itself in order to better return to itself. And so that its way of being-in-the-world might be passing through [*la traversée*], as Jean Godefroy Bidima invites us to do. A thought of mediation and of translation, the philosophy of *la traversée* tries to articulate "the pluralities from which a determinate history is made,"[14] and hopes to be "a perpetually open gap that refuses identitarian, neurotic, and ligitious withdrawal as much as it resists dissolution in a cloying universalism."[15] It mistrusts "lazy dualisms"[16] and encourages us to work our way into processes that are in motion, to effect detours and to open ourselves to the world in order to express ourselves.

Henceforth, passing through the world's experiences teaches philosophers where they are coming from and who they are. It is an invitation to enter into relation, to wander from place to place, and to inhabit the pathway. To create as a nomad philosopher, apart from all exoticism. From such a perspective, to *think by way of* African philosophies—and by extension by way of all those who have been rendered subaltern, whether they are South American, from the Pacific, or Asian—enables us to think Western being-in-the-world and the limits of the Western way of living in the world against the grain. It means encountering the world, others, and the self in an opening which is an entry into resonance. A willingness to accept the promises of the unexpected and of the balanced relationship which refuses to imprison the other in relations of domination, asymmetry, or bonds that stifle more than they liberate. A circulation between different worlds that permits escape from oneself. A projection of self into the world which, through an echoing motion, returns me to a self that has been transformed by the experience of the world.

This resonant praxis is properly speaking an *echology*.[17] To cross African philosophies, thereby to learn from them, means to better understand how the West has been able to close itself off to other forms of knowledge and put in place an epistemic coloniality. It means to grasp how and under what conditions the West was led to consider itself the "point zero" of knowledge, by which I mean, "the absolute epistemic beginning. . . . To situate oneself at point zero means to have the power to establish a certain way of looking at the natural and social world, recognized as legitimate and validated by the State."[18] And it also means thinking collectively about how a world into which other worlds are folded might be invented, about how to make the universal into something other than a homogenizing particular "hovering over" [*surplomber*], and instead a "lateral" universal[19] "rich with all the particulars,"[20] which is to say, a pluriversal.

We will not understand the contemporary world without a detour through History and the history of ideas. The first wave of colonization, built on enslavement and the slave trade, was contemporaneous with a foundational epistemic renewal of Western modernity, the Galileo-Cartesian revolution. In locating universal reason in man, and no longer in God, Descartes posited the primacy of the *cogito*, on which he constructed the myth of a dematerialized universal reason, with neither flesh nor sexuality, neither gender nor class, neither race nor language, having neither history nor culture, rootless. This led to the fabrication of a singular universal "from above" [*de surplomb*] in whose name the "civilizing mission" of nineteenth- and twentieth-century colonization would be justified. This universal was widely challenged starting in the 1950s by philosophers engaged in the debate over the existence of an African philosophy but also by subaltern, postcolonial, and decolonial studies.[21]

In fact, everything that refers to the body—and therefore to sociohistorical situation—was expelled from the *res cogitans*. Matter, *res extensa*, became something measurable, quantifiable, exploitable, to which nature, henceforth transformed into a resource, was reduced. Descartes enjoins (European) man to become the "master and owner of nature." This is a pattern in the colonial enterprise, which is first and foremost a territorial conquest. The *Précis de legislation colonial* of Louis Rolland and Pierre Lampué is one example of a manual establishing a right if not a duty "to economically improve the countries which are insufficiently so and, above all, to raise individuals belonging to a lower degree of civilization."[22] It is a matter of appropriating lands in order to make them profitable, in a direct line from the Cartesian imperative to dominate the living world; i.e., all living beings. In other words, what one defines as natural resources, including those aspects of humanity identified with nature: women, savages, slaves.[23]

The nature/culture separation[24] that, in modernity, only the West imposes, allows humanity to be split in two: one part which refers to civilization (culture) and the other which remains in the state of nature, toward which Western man feels a right—that of exploiting—and a duty—that of civilizing. This right to dominate one part of humanity, henceforth transformed into an Other of lesser value, into a life whose loss one does not mourn,[25] rests on the reduction of this sub-humanity to its energetic force alone, from which profit can be drawn. Men, women, children of sub-Saharan Africa were vegetalized as "ebony wood" cut from their roots and piled in the holds of ships for transportation to the other side of the Atlantic. On the plantations, the ebony wood became an animal listed beside the master's other livestock. A working animal who cut sugar cane. A stud animal whose couplings were organized— the men were forced to rape the women[26]—to reproduce the species and the master's goods. From the state of nature to civilization a line of "progress" was drawn, that of a Westernization of the world dressed in the clothing of a triumphant universalism.

This will to dominate and control the living world as a whole, which is to say both nature and subalternized humanity, led in a single movement to genocides, ecocides, and epistemicides. It also led to a substantial modification of the geological era. In fact, colonial conquests reduced certain peoples to nothing, causing different ways of inhabiting the world and of being-in-the-world to disappear along with them. The conquest of the Americas was built on the massacre and genocide of first nations. With these peoples, what disappeared were modes of life, knowledge, and know-how along with their environment. In the Caribbean, the creation of plantations required massive deforestation. The "colonial way of dwelling"[27] rests on the massacre of populations, the destruction of biodiversity, the extinction of certain animal and plant species, the erosion of soil, entraining ecological disasters which continue even today. The plantations were among the first examples of intensive monoculture, which contributed to the development of a limitless economy of exploitation and extraction of the planet's soil and subsoil wealth. An economy bringing geological dysregulation in its wake, which has led to the Anthropocene—to such a point that the British geographers Simon Lewis and Mark Maslin consider the start of the Anthropocene to be the European conquest of the Americas. "This major historical event, dramatic for the Amerindian people and foundational for a capitalist world-economy, has left its mark in the geography of our planet,"[28] but also in its geology.

The end of the slave trade and the abolition of enslavement displaced plantations from the Americas to Africa, where they introduced this colonial way of dwelling, in which domination of nature was linked to the domination of

subalternized humanity. If we look closely, this colonial being-in-the-world
has not disappeared with the independence of African states. The populations of the global South and those of the less privileged zones in Northern
countries are the first victims of climatic warming or ecological catastrophes:
one reason why the notion of "environmental racism" was developed in the
United States during the 1970s. This is unquestionably one of the great challenges of the twenty-first century: dismantling the colonial way of dwelling
and (re)thinking our relation to the totality of the living world.

What makes epistemes that do not separate Nature and Culture unique is
that they think of humans as fully integrated into the living world, and even
beyond, in a great whole. According to Abdoulaye Élimane Kane, in many
African ecologies, the cosmos is "considered as a great ordered, harmonious
living being: a whole of which man, paradoxically, is an emanation, a part, a
living being among others, and, at the same time, the archetype which serves
as a measure for everything, the cosmos, space-time, social organization, the
conception and use of numbers, the profane and the sacred, etc."[29] Why is the
human the measure of everything? So that humanity alone can be

> responsible for disorder in the world; because the world deteriorates—whether
> man is or is not the direct cause—the ritual of the world's "repair" constitutes
> one of the most significant acts symbolizing its awareness of this responsibility:
> to repair, to reestablish order involves the essence of political power as much
> as the meaning of number and generally of humanity's relationship to nature.[30]

In central and southern Africa, the notion of Ubuntu, a kind of social *cogito*
that is usually translated by "I am because we are," proposes that relation is
primary and thereby commits us to a relational ethic and ontology. According
to Mogobe Ramose, not only does Ubuntu oblige us to recognize the humanity of others and to behave humanely toward them but it also sketches out
an ecophilosophy resting on the interaction between all entities within the
universe.[31] Henry Odera Oruka and Calestous Juma have likewise argued for
this idea of an "ecophilosophical approach which recognizes the totality of
(spatial, temporal, spiritual and other) interlinkages in nature" because "there
is a need for a shift towards a new epistemological outlook in which humankind is viewed as part of a complex and systematic totality of nature."[32] This
ecocentric conception of nature is distinguished from the Western one, which
is anthropocentric. Odera Oruka and Juma continue by calling us to "adopt a
holistic outlook in which everything is related to everything else. This inter-
relatedness requires a corresponding philosophical approach that looks at
nature in its totality and from which an ethics can be derived reflecting this
outlook," a "parental earth ethics" which obliges us to take care of the living
world as a whole.[33] This would also be a philosophical approach that provides

the outline for taking care of nature and being committed to oppose social inequalities, as well as advocate for a better redistribution of wealth.

There is no longer any reason to differentiate nature from culture. What is relevant is to think them together and perhaps to abandon the concept of nature for "what I call, in a Glissantian spirit, the living-whole [*tout-vivant*], which connects everything that moves, beats, pulses, vibrates, and resonates in an intrinsic and inextricable way. But also everything produced by this interaction and these connected entities, whether the atmosphere created by the respiration of plants and animals or the one that we habitually identify with the order of culture, which is nothing other than the activity of living beings."[34] All matter being energy, the living-whole is properly speaking the vibrating-whole. From now on, how to dwell in the world while vibrating with the living-whole is one of the preoccupations of the abovementioned echology. To decide to enter into resonance is to want to transform ecology, etymologically "*logos* of the house, of the home, the interior," into an echology that brings one outside of oneself. By dwelling fully in the world we can then make a world with all of humanity and the whole of living beings. This requires us to rethink and to expand lines of filiation, to enlarge communities, and to go beyond an anthropocentric humanism. To integrate diversity in itself so as to construct an "in-common" which conjugates the universal in the plural eases the other's pain, privileges qualitative relationships, and permits us to sketch a good life in which everyone can develop their joyful potentials. Not to mention, fully realize themselves.

The majority of African ecologies say the same thing as the astrophysicists: we are all children of the universe. The Earth is born from the death of megastars whose explosion permitted the formation of gold, silver, magnesium, mercury, silicon, sulfur, platinum, uranium, carbon, and so on. The same chemical elements are found in all living beings. There is a material and ontological continuity between the Earth and the universe, which is to say, between the living-whole, the human, the animal, the vegetal, the mineral, and the cosmos. Our chemical matter is the memory of massive stars that burst asunder. Certainly, we live within the universe, but we also carry the universe within us. We are the universe. Everything that exists is traversed by a single energetic reality, a single cosmic breath. Our intimate bond with the universe and the living-whole, it seems to me, invites us to opt for a thought at a large scale and to enlarge our genealogies; to rethink the notions of belonging, alterity and similarity, the other, the foreign and the foreigner, the interior and the exterior; to enlarge our community to the totality of the living, to rethink what makes a community from a political and ethical point of view.

By integrating the living-whole into the human community and, inversely, by settling the human into the heart of the living-whole, animist philosophies recognize that the world beyond the human is not deprived of sense and that it exists through nonhuman thoughts—and therefore through thinking selves that exist beyond the human. But in the end, one can deduce the same from an attentive reading of scientific works, to the extent that some of them have demonstrated that plants are capable of assimilating information, making decisions in light of that information, and adopting a suitable form of behavior to solve a problem. Although (for the most part) they possess no brain, they are covered with molecules identical to those responsible for neuronal activity in the brain which render possible any communication. They are endowed with memory and know how to react to a past trauma. In Japan, plants and trees give off electrical signals several days before an earthquake and some of them change their behavior in order to survive. Scientists understand better and better how trees communicate among themselves, between different species but also with their environment. Some fruit trees emit olfactory messages that invite bees to come gather nectar, which enables them to be reproduced through pollination. Others, in southern Africa, act in the same way to warn their fellow trees of the arrival of foraging goats. The forewarned trees then modify the composition of their leaves so that they become more toxic. Communication can be olfactive, chemical, but also electrical, mediated by special nerve cells at the extremities of their roots. The American anthropologist Deborah Bird Rose, who lived with the Yarralui and Lingara, aboriginal communities in Australia, remarks that

> where humanistic existentialism found humanity isolated in the face of the cosmos, new understandings of life's connectivity tell us that in fact we are not alone. We are in a world of intersubjectivity—a world in which sentient subjects face each other. The Danish biologist Jesper Hoffmeyer takes the understanding of intersubjectivity to a glorious extreme. He contends that all that exists is based entirely on communication. The universe, he says, is a semiosphere. Subjectivity is necessary to life, and indeed is necessary to the whole cosmos. "Life is based entirely on semiosis, on sign operations." Hoffmeyer restores connectivity through an examination of semiotic processes that work across scales from cosmos, to Earth, to living systems, and to individuals.[35]

But how are we to pay attention to the world's different thoughts and consider "the relational ecology of selves which constitutes the cosmos" in order to enlarge its universe of signification?[36]

Philosophy would gain from giving itself a (new) cosmology, a relational cosmology of the living-whole which allows the organic, symbolic, spiritual, and semiotic bond between the human and the nonhuman to speak and finishes by no longer granting this distinction any importance. Such a cosmophilosophy would therefore be a thought going beyond humanism; going beyond, not to denounce the inefficacy or inefficiency of humanism, but to underscore its incompleteness. Neither man nor the human can be the measure of all things on their own.

In the second half of the twentieth century, African philosophy was constructed and defined in opposition to African cosmologies, including animism. At the same time, animism can be reconciled with the transcendence of modern humanism and provide the outline for a humanism that might be described as animist. Of what would this animist humanism consist? A relational ethics that commits human beings in their environment to the living-whole, enjoining them to devote attention and care to everything that is animate and inviting them to Ubuntu and other African ecologies that do not forget that to be acting is always to be interacting. Being human is not so much a state of being as an ethics, a relational and liberatory praxis that allows for full self-realization and tends toward a being-more, for oneself but also for those with whom we are engaged.

This animist humanism would be inscribed in a cosmology of continuous emergence, in which to realize one's humanity comes down to assisting in the deployment of vital force, such as it was conceived in the Bantu philosophy dear to Tempels and the vitalist philosophy of Léopold Sédar Senghor.[37] For Souleymane Bachir Diagne, the latter is

> the effect of an encounter between an ontology of forces underlying the religions of different African lands and, we might say, their common denominator, and the Bergsonian thought of the *élan vital*. This philosophy validates the following principles: 1) to be is to be a life force; 2) whatever reinforces the force of being is good; 3) whatever undoes the force (*déforce*, a neologism of Senghor's), or sucks away its vital substance like a vampire, is bad; 4) All force tends naturally to be *more force*, or in other terms, the destination of being is to become *more being*.[38]

To be human, to realize one's humanity, is thus also to tend toward surplus-being, to reinforce all life and write oneself into the *élan vital*. This is the starting point from which an ethics of relation which reinforces the *élan vital* that animates us and traverses nature can be sketched out. An ethics that would thereby permit us to realize ourselves fully in the development and the growth of our full potentialities, which is to say in self-realization. An ethics that supposes moreover that the human being and culture can be reintegrated with the plenitude of the living. This animist humanism demands not only that nature be preserved but that we participate in its regeneration. The care taken for all living things becomes one of the essential elements in the realization of our humanity and commits us to giving rights to everything that thinks as a self. Such a *care* ethic mobilizes thoughtfulness, vigilance, and consideration. Its gaze is a regard, a form of respect. An intensity of attention, which makes a strong case for all life, and that one finds, for example, in the systems of South America, Australia, India, or even in Australia which give a juridical status to certain natural elements that thereby possess rights—the right to deploy their vital force—and which assign duties to humans in return—a duty to respect and to preserve.[39] Such systems are the juridical translation of indigenous visions of the cosmos, for example, that of the Caledonians, in which the separation of Nature and Culture does not exist.

In fact, in New Caledonia, the 2016 environmental code of the province of the Loyalty Islands province recognizes that "the natural environment is indissociable from the locally applicable cultural practices and customary rules" (Art. 110-1), and that "each person has the right to live in an ecologically healthy and balanced environment, preserving places and landscapes, in accord with the rhythm and harmony of nature. Every person has the solemn duty to preserve and to improve the environment for present and future generations" (Art. 110-2).

It also recognizes that

> the principle of life which signifies that man belongs to the natural environment surrounding him and conceives of his identity in the elements of that natural environment is the founding principle of Kanak society. In order to take this conception of life and Kanak social organization into account, certain elements of Nature may be recognized as having a juridical personality endowed with rights proper to them, subject to the legislative provisions and rules in force. (Art. 110-3)

This is how a colonized culture has been able to play with the modern language of the law to defend its own universe of meanings. Moreover, it has opened the path to a possible expansion of the beneficiaries of law and politics, including the natural elements, future generations, and finally the ancestors. Animist humanism therefore inaugurates a social relation—not between subject and object—but between the human and nature and enlarges the very idea of community to the totality of the living-whole. The distinction between inhabited and uninhabited lands (*érème* and *écoumène*) would be erased. The human being could only realize him or herself in cooperation with the living world, which is what many African, but also Amerindian, Aboriginal, or Asian philosophies teach. At bottom, the extension of the sphere of rights to nature is an animist translation of the idea that the right to a healthy environment is one of the most fundamental human rights. If we think about this correctly, this means the right to a good life, a full and complete life.

To render humanity human is thus a matter of making its being-in-the-world a surplus-being, a being tending toward the accomplishment of life, which is always and necessarily a good life, a better way of living. A better way of living is not living in frantic accumulation, in an always-having-more which leads to the insatiable exploitation of terrestrial resources. Rather it means assuring that each person has access to vitality (*avoir-vital*) and a decent life which allows him or her to enrich his or her being-in-the-world and to expand spiritually. We thus propose animist humanism as an ethics of relation which allows one to be fully a self and not self-dispossessed, and which writes us into the movement of life and self-fashioning. It is also, as previously stated, an ethics that enlarges the semiosphere in which humanity is registered within the whole of living beings and inviting us to listen to the latter. What do the flowers, the mountains, the birds, the rivers, the plains, and the deserts say? What does the wind whisper to us? What do odors suggest and colors murmur? How can we develop a relationship of feeling to the world which allows us to live our bodies and our senses fully? Or rethink sensation and feeling, as we are invited to do by Eboussi Boulaga, for whom "the elimination of feeling was the first condition imposed on Muntu as the cost of his accession to reason or to claim philosophy for himself, a neuter self which would no longer be someone, a living being"?[40]

Now, to be in the world is before all else to be in the domain of feeling. This is the reason Eboussi Boulaga says that

> feeling [*sentir*] is the human body in the form of a primordial comprehension of the world. Man is not a self incidentally, or progressively, in steps. He is himself from the start in being at home among things and others, in the world's actuality. Feeling is the correspondence with this presence. We must say more. Feeling signifies the mutual belonging of man and the world prior to all discourse, all accommodation to norms.[41]

And he adds, "Thanks to the body's capacity to feel, man is not alone in the world, but the world is in him. He is the world. To speak of feeling is to perceive man as one with the world."[42] This is how one could also read the embracing reason [*raison-étreinte*] dear to Senghor, the idea that provoked the flow of so much ink when he wrote the widely denounced alexandrine: "emotion is Black as reason is Greek."[43] Embracing reason, which embraces the world and settles us at the heart of the object, makes intuition the very faculty by which the indivisible whole is grasped and by which we ourselves are inserted in the very movement of that which is presented to us. It is thus, as Souleymane Bachir Diagne analyzes, that which leads us to the heart of life and allows us to know the world vitally, to enter into resonance with it while feeling its rhythm.[44] The latter being "the vital element par excellence,"[45] "the architecture of being, the internal dynamism which gives it form, the system of waves that it puts out at the call of Others, the pure expression of vital

Force. Rhythm; that is the vibratory shock, the force which, across meaning, grasps us at the root of being."[46]

It is the beating of life and that which singularizes each being. To live is then to place oneself at the center of emotion, which comes from the Latin *ex-movere*, in other words that which is moved and sets in movement—and to grasp the real by its invisible aspect, its breath. It is to listen to and understand with. In wakefulness, just as we are taught, particularly by animist philosophies. It is to resonate and to be in resonance. To vibrate with. To give oneself over to this world that we welcome within us—not to put at a distance but to cling, to beat as one with others and with the universe. From this point on, to know the world is to be wakeful and to fully inhabit presence. Thus, we can reintegrate the plenitude of the living-whole, be born and reborn with the living-whole, and sketch a poetics which will let us resonate with the songs of the cosmos.

Translated by Laura Hengehold

NOTES

1. For example, see Norman Ajari, *La Dignité ou la mort. Éthique et politique de la race* (Paris: La Découverte/Les empêcheurs de penser en rond, 2019); Hourya Bentouhami-Molino, *Race, cultures, identités. Une approche féministe et postcoloniale* (Paris: Presses Universitaires de France, 2015); Seloua Luste Boulbina, *Les Miroirs vagabonds ou la décolonisation des savoirs (art, littérature, philosophie)* (Paris: Les Presses du réel, 2018); Nadia Yala Kisukidi, "Décoloniser la philosophie ou de la philosophie comme objet anthropologique," in "Pensée contemporaine et pratiques sociales en Afrique: penser le mouvement," *Présence Africaine* 192 (2015): 83–98; and, to a great extent, the contributions assembled in *Écrire l'Afrique-Monde*, ed. Achille Mbembe and Felwine Sarr (Dakar/Paris: Jimsaan/Philippe Rey, 2017); Felwine Sarr, *Afrotopia* (Paris: Philippe Rey, 2016), and others.

2. Fabien Eboussi Boulaga, *La Crise du Muntu. Authenticité africaine et philosophie* (Paris: Présence Africaine, 1977), 90.

3. Eboussi Boulaga, *La Crise du Muntu*, 15.

4. Stanislas Spero Adotevi, *Négritude et négrologues* (Paris: Union générale d'éditions, 1992); 2nd edition (Bègles: Le Castor Astral, 1998), 153.

5. Adotevi, *Négritude et négrologues*, 166.

6. In particular, see Santiago Castro-Gómez & Ramón Grosfoguel, ed., *El giro decolonial. Reflexiones para una diversidad epistémica más allá del capitalismo global* (Bogotá: Siglo del Hombre Editions, 2007).

7. For a detailed analysis of the kind of conceptual and mental decolonization pursued by African philosophers and intellectuals since the 1950s, see Séverine Kodjo-Grandvaux, *Philosophies africaines* (Paris: Présence Africaine, 2013).

8. Rajeev Bhargava, "Pour en finir avec l'injustice épistémique du colonialisme," in *Socio* (2013), 3.

9. In particular, see Gayatri Chakravorty Spivak, *Les Subalternes peuvent-elles parler?*, trans. Jérôme Vidal (Paris: Éditions Amsterdam, 2020).

10. In particular, see Felwine Sarr, *Afrotopia*.

11. Mbembe and Sarr, "Pour un nouveau siècle," in *Écrire l'Afrique-Monde*, 7.

12. See Achille Mbembe and Felwine Sarr, eds., *Politique des Temps. Imaginer les devenirs africains* (Dakar/Paris: Jimsaan/Philippe Rey, 2019).

13. Aimé Césaire, *Discours sur le colonialisme* (Paris: Présence Africaine, 1955), 11.

14. Jean Godefroy Bidima, "L'ethnopsychiatrie et ses revers: dire la fragilité de l'Autre," in *Diogène* 189 (Printemps, 2000), 12.

15. Jean Godefroy Bidima, *L'Art négro-africain,* "Que sais-je?" no. 3226 (Paris: Presses Universitaires de France, 1997), 108.

16. Jean Godefroy Bidima, *La Philosophie négro-africaine,* "Que sais-je?" no. 2985 (Paris: Presses Universitaires de France, 1995), 124.

17. On echology as an ethics of resonance, see Séverine Kodjo-Grandvaux, *Devenir vivants* (Paris: Éditions Philippe Rey, 2021).

18. Santagio Castro-Gómez, *La hybris del punto cera. Ciencia, raza e illustración en la Nueva Granada (1750–1816)* (Bogotá: Instituto Pensar, Universidad Javeriana, 2007).

19. Maurice Merleau-Ponty, *Éloge de la philosophie* (Paris: Gallimard, 1953), for the two citations.

20. Aimé Césaire, *Lettre à Maurice Thorez* (Paris: Présence Africaine, 1956), 15.

21. For texts taking up this problematic since the middle of the 2010s, see in particular Souleymane Bachir Diagne, "Pour un universel vraiment universel," in Mbembe and Sarr, eds., *Écrire l'Afrique Monde,* 71–78; Jean Godefroy Bidima, "La Traversée des mondes," in *Esprit* (janvier-février 2020), https://esprit.presse.fr/article/jean-godefroy-bidima/la-traversee-des-mondes-42503.

22. Louis Rolland and Pierre Lampué, *Précis de législation coloniale (colonies, Algérie, protectorats, pays sous mandat)* (Paris: Dalloz, 1931), 6.

23. On the question of women, see in particular Carolyn Merchant, *The Death of Nature. Women, Ecology and the Scientific Revolution* (San Francisco: HarperOne, 1980).

24. See Philippe Descola, *Par-delà nature et culture* (Paris: Gallimard/Folio essais, 2005).

25. Judith Butler, *Ce qui fait une vie. Essai sur la violence, la guerre et le deuil*, trans. Joëlle Marelli (Paris: La Découverte/"Zones," 2010).

26. See Françoise Vergès, *Le Ventre des femmes. Capitalisme, racialisation, féminisme* (Paris: Albin Michel, 2017).

27. Malcom Ferdinand, *Une écologie décoloniale* (Paris: Seuil/"Anthropocène," 2019).

28. Christophe Bonneuil and Jean-Baptiste Fressoz, *L'Événement anthropocène. La Terre, l'histoire et nous* (Paris: Seuil/"Anthropocène," 2013), 30.

29. Abdoulaye Élimane Kane, *Penser l'humain. La part africaine* (Paris: L'Harmattan, 2015), 10.

30. Kane, *Penser l'humain,* 11.

31. See Mogobe Ramose, *African Philosophy Through Ubuntu* (Harare: Mond Books, 1999).

32. Henry Odera Oruka and Calestous Juma, "Ecophilosophy and Parental Earth Ethics (On the Complex Web of Being)," in Henry Odera Oruka, ed., *Philosophy, Humanity and Ecology. Philosophy of Nature and Environmental Ethics* (Nairobi: ACTS Press/AAS, 1994) 115, for both citations (my translation).

33. Oruka and Juma, "Ecophilosophy and Parental Earth Ethics," 117.

34. Kodjo-Grandvaux, *Devenir vivants*, 13.

35. Deborah Bird Rose, *Wild Dog Dreaming: Love and Extinction* (Richmond: University of Virginia Press, 2012), 49.

36. Eduardo Kohn, *Comment pensent les forêts. Vers une anthropologie au-delà de l'humain*, trans. Grégory Delaplace (Zones sensibles, 2017), 42.

37. Placide Tempels, *La Philosophie bantoue* (Paris: Présence Africaine, 1949).

38. Souleymane Bachir Diagne, *Bergson postcolonial. L'élan vital dans la pensée de Léopold Sédar Sengor et de Mohamed Iqbal* (Paris: CNRS Éditions, 2011), 47–48.

39. See Valérie Cabanes, *Homo natura. En harmonie avec le vivant* (Paris: Buchet/Chastel/"Dans le vif," 2017).

40. Eboussi Boulaga, *La Crise du Muntu*, 211.

41. Eboussi Boulaga, *La Crise du Muntu*, 211.

42. Eboussi Boulaga, *La Crise du Muntu*, 211.

43. Léopold Sédar Senghor, "Ce que l'homme noir apporte," in *L'Homme de couleur* (Paris: Éditions Cardinale Verdier et al., 1939), 295, reprinted in *Liberté I: négritude et humanisme* (Paris: Seuil, 1964), 24.

44. Diagne, *Bergson postcolonial*.

45. Senghor, *Liberté I,* 35.

46. Senghor, *Liberté I,* 211.

BIBLIOGRAPHY

Adotevi, Stanislas Spero. *Négritude et négrologues* (Paris: Union générale d'éditions, 1992); 2nd edition (Bègles: Le Castor Astral, 1998).

Ajari, Norman. *La Dignité ou la mort. Éthique et politique de la race* (Paris: La Découverte/Les empêcheurs de penser en rond, 2019).

Bhargava, Rajeev. "Pour en finir avec l'injustice épistémique du colonialisme," in *Socio* (2013), 3.

Bentouhami-Molino, Hourya. *Race, cultures, identités. Une approche féministe et postcoloniale* (Paris: Presses Universitaires de France, 2015).

Bidima, Jean Godefroy. *L'Art négro-africain,* "Que sais-je?" no. 3226 (Paris: Presses Universitaires de France, 1997).

———. *La Philosophie négro-africaine*, "Que sais-je?" no. 2985 (Paris: Presses Universitaires de France, 1995).

———. "L'ethnopsychiatrie et ses revers: dire la fragilité de l'Autre," in *Diogène* 189 (Printemps, 2000).

———. "La Traversée des mondes," in *Esprit* (janvier-février 2020), https://esprit .presse.fr/article/jean-godefroy-bidima/la-traversee-des-mondes-42503.

Bonneuil, Christophe and Jean-Baptiste Fressoz, *L'Événement anthropocène. La Terre, l'histoire et nous* (Paris: Seuil/"Anthropocène," 2013).

Butler, Judith. *Ce qui fait une vie. Essai sur la violence, la guerre et le deuil*, trans. Joëlle Marelli (Paris: La Découverte/"Zones," 2010).

Cabanes, Valérie. *Homo natura. En harmonie avec le vivant* (Paris: Buchet/ Chastel/"Dans le vif," 2017).

Castro-Gómez, Santiago, *La hybris del punto cera. Ciencia, raza e illustración en la Nueva Granada (1750–1816)* (Bogotá: Instituto Pensar, Universidad Javeriana, 2007).

——— and Ramón Grosfoguel, eds., *El giro decolonial. Reflexiones para una diversidad epistémica más allá del capitalismo global* (Bogotá: Siglo del Hombre Editions, 2007).

Césaire, Aimé. *Discours sur le colonialisme* (Paris: Présence Africaine, 1955).

———. *Lettre à Maurice Thorez* (Paris: Présence Africaine, 1956).

Philippe Descola, *Par-delà nature et culture* (Paris: Gallimard, «Folio essais», 2005).

Diagne, Souleymane Bachir. *Bergson postcolonial. L'élan vital dans la pensée de Léopold Sédar Senghor et de Mohamed Iqbal* (Paris: CNRS éditions, 2011).

———. "Pour un universel vraiment universel," in Mbembe and Sarr, eds., *Écrire l'Afrique Monde,* 71–78.

Eboussi Boulaga, Fabien. *La Crise du Muntu. Authenticité africaine et philosophie* (Paris: Présence Africaine, 1977).

Ferdinand, Malcom. *Une écologie décoloniale* (Paris: Seuil, «Anthropocène», 2019).

Kane, Abdoulaye Élimane. *Penser l'humain. La part africaine* (Paris: L'Harmattan, 2015).

Kisukidi, Nadia Yala. "Décoloniser la philosophie ou de la philosophie comme objet anthropologique," in "Pensée contemporaine et pratiques sociales en Afrique: penser le mouvement." *Présence Africaine* 192 (2015): 83–98.

Kodjo-Grandvaux, Séverine. *Philosophies africaines* (Paris: Présence Africaine, 2013).

———. *Devenir vivants* (Paris: Ed. Philippe Rey, 2021).

Kohn, Eduardo. *Comment pensent les forêts. Vers une anthropologie au-delà de l'humain,* trans. Grégory Delaplace (Zones sensibles, 2017).

Luste Boulbina, Seloua. *Les Miroirs vagabonds ou la décolonisation des savoirs (art, littérature, philosophie)* (Paris: Les Presses du réel, 2018).

Mbembe, Achille et Felwine Sarr, eds., *Écrire l'Afrique-Monde* (Dakar/Paris: Jimsaan/Philippe Rey, 2017).

———. *Politique des Temps. Imaginer les devenirs africains* (Dakar/Paris: Jimsaan/ Philippe Rey, 2017).

Merchant, Carolyn. *The Death of Nature. Women, Ecology and the Scientific Revolution* (San Francisco: HarperOne, 1980).

Merleau-Ponty, Maurice. *Éloge de la philosophie* (Paris: Gallimard, 1953).

Oruka, Henry Odera and Calestous Juma, "Ecophilosophy and Parental Earth Ethics (On the Complex Web of Being)," in Henry Odera Oruka, ed., *Philosophy, Humanity and Ecology. Philosophy of Nature and Environmental Ethics* (Nairobi: ACTS Press/AAS, 1994).

Ramose, Mogobe. *African Philosophy Through Ubuntu* (Harare: Mond Books, 1999).

Rolland, Louis and Pierre Lampué, *Précis de législation coloniale (colonies, Algérie, protectorats, pays sous mandat)* (Paris: Dalloz, 1931).

Rose, Deborah Bird. *Wild Dog Dreaming: Love and Extinction* (Richmond: University of Virginia Press, 2012).

Sarr, Felwine. *Afrotopia* (Paris: Philippe Rey, 2016).

Senghor, Léopold Sédar. *Liberté I: négritude et humanisme* (Paris: Seuil, 1964).

Spivak, Gayatri Chakravorty. *Les Subalternes peuvent-elles parler?*, trans. Jérôme Vidal (Paris: Éditions Amsterdam, 2020).

Tempels, Placide. *La Philosophie bantoue* (Paris: Présence Africaine, 1949).

Vergès, Françoise. *Le Ventre des femmes. Capitalisme, racialisation, féminisme* (Paris: Albin Michel, 2017).

Chapter 8

From Muntu to Moun

An African Ethicalization of Caribbean Discourse

Hanétha Vété-Congolo

Beyond the physical seizure, mutilation and neutralization of their bodies, meant to materialize their status as objects, the slaving project also sought to impose metaphysical enslavement on Africans in order to ensure that their subjection was irreversible. By metaphysical enslavement, I mean the condition brought about when people whose sense of discernment and free thinking allowing them to recognize truth, reality, and themselves as human persons find those abstract capacities neutralized by domineering precepts and percepts that convince them that their self and existence are untrue, unreal, and nonhuman. Given the emphasis on physicality when approaching issues related to enslaved Africans in America, hence a perception holding them as "a-metaphysical," I am interested in understanding how, thanks to the work of the mind, the enslaved Africans counterpointed the enslaving party's project of establishing a system of values for the Caribbean, a project preventing the edification of the human person and especially, the human person who failed to conform to their perspective of racial superiority. It is also in understanding the type of achievement produced by the work of the mind of enslaved Africans within the plantation logic that one can fully capture the magnitude of the ordeal the said enslaved Africans faced, the extent of their accomplishment, and the meaning of the latter for today's world where ill notions and practices of humanity still attempt assaults on the integrity of humankind and its humanity.

The linguistic depression endured by Africans in the American plantation is largely overlooked but remains a critical parameter to consider when examining plantation facts and their consequences on today's world—especially on the offspring of those having endured enslavement. How, in the context of dehumanizing speech, does one arrive at what I term "Pawòl,"[1] a critical Caribbean discourse assuming ethics and aesthetics? In what language and with what philosophical parameters substantiating this language did Africans derive a system of thoughts and speech disengaging from the plantation precepts? Because, in the French colonies, the French language dominated, because Creole appeared amid the plantation system, and because those who study this language—Creolists—affirm that its substance is French, one tends to neglect first, the presence of operative African languages such as Congo and second, the linguistic complexity in these colonies. In attempting to understand what took place in the Caribbean to provide it with its characteristics, Martinican theorist Édouard Glissant suggests that the slave boat is the central space where all things African disappeared, including language—one of the most fundamental constituents of identity. According to Glissant, all things original disappearing, the slave boat even becomes the womb giving birth to a new category of beings Africans were to become in the New World:

> For, the center of the slave boat is the place and the moment where African languages disappear, because, just like in the plantations, they never put together on the same slave boat those who spoke the same language. The being was bereft of all sorts of the daily elements of their life, and especially, of their language.[2]

First, if all African languages disappeared, then African modes of thoughts are unlikely to be manifested. Second, if the slave boat is the motherly womb, then its product is not likely to equate the qualities of a human "person" endowed with thought and expressed through human speech. The French *Code noir* will ensure that the conceptualization it advances of the enslaved Africans reflects that perspective since, article 44 labeling them "meuble" (furniture, chattel), it is supposed to determine their existential reality and comportment as nonpersons and as disincarnated, disembodied inanimate beings. Using examples from the French African Creole-speaking Caribbean today (and as it relates to the past), I want to contest this account of what took place in the Caribbean historically and complicate the approach to the metaphysical dynamic that might have unfolded. This enables me to highlight the significance of the persistence of a thought such as the one contained in the Creole "moun," springing from the African (Bantu) "muntu," and to specify even more the philosophical proposition made by Africans even in the Caribbean plantation site.

Given the circumstances under which a moun-based paradigm of thought emerged, its resulting totality and core specificity appears today not as "African" per se but logically as African Caribbean, which itself is a component of what is termed "Africana philosophy." However, when considering African philosophy itself, one should not overlook the way African thoughts and epistemology were posited, articulated, performed, and transformed outside of Africa by Africans and their descendants. For, using eighteenth-century Louis-Narcisse Baudry des Lozières's and nineteenth-century François-Achille Marbot's texts, I will first underscore the processes by which the slaving system used language per se and all spoken languages of the plantation—including French, Creole, and African languages—to attempt to subdue the mind of enslaved Africans and bequeath the latter a sense of *plantation—meuble*—humanness and personhood. Then, I will show how the said Africans, especially the Congos, replied and used the same means of language and the mind to assert a diverging concept—moun—defining the human person and stating plainly what they knew of themselves and what they refused to forsake: their *human* humanness and personhood. We will see how in the plantation, reformulation or translation is used to either enslave or emancipate epistemologically and how, apart from the official legislative codes issued by the royal and state administrations, ordinary members of the colonial and enslaving system also issued myriads of individual texts (taken in its broad sense) officiating as micro-*Codes noir*, making the ordeal endured by the enslaved, but also their inevitable consequences, even more complex. Ultimately, I will demonstrate how in the face of such a determined apparatus to dismantle them through dehumanization and as evinced by the Moun paradigm of thought and ethics, these enslaved Africans proffered an axiological proposition on behalf of the integrity of humankind and its humanity and their ability to convey personhood and an ethically grounded Caribbean discourse that I otherwise name *Pawòl*.

LES BAMBOUS: EXPLOITING LANGUAGE, CREOLE, AND TRANSLATION

François-Achille Marbot's 1846 written Creole text, *Les Bambous. Fables de Lafontaine travesties en patois créole par un vieux commandeur*, is praised[3] for being one of the first texts ever written in Creole, the sole new language that was born on plantation ground and that, today, characterizes the existence paradigms of those who speak it in the Caribbean: Haitians, Martinicans, and Guadeloupeans. It is also celebrated because it interrupts the practice of archival and administrative writing of the colony to situate itself in the bosom of "the arts," namely, literary writing, a specificity that can place *Les Bambous* in a privileged and inceptive genealogical position for Caribbean literature and, in particular, in Creole. However, its overlooked hermeneutics casts light on both an unethical discourse and act that must draw our attention to critical questions pertaining to the philosophy of language as it relates to this part of the world. Centered on the use of language to implant a preset ontology and world vision, Marbot's text provides an enlightening example of the modus operandi for metaphysical enslavement making use of Creole to provoke a certain type of self-destructive comportment in the Africans as well as a cognitive, mental, and moral inertia on their part, a state favoring their acceptance of the plantation order. *Les Bambous* is a Creole rendition of seventeenth-century French Jean de Lafontaine's fables in which socio-behavioral prescriptions are articulated. Although Martinican-born François-Achille Marbot is known to be the author of *Les Bambous*, he kept his name silent to highlight his plantation role as a "commandeur," a noun that means "overseer" but springs from the verb "commander," that is, "to give orders." The tone and objective of his text are captured through the choice to underline his plantation status and role rather than his name, all the more so as on the plantation, the "commandeur" stands as much for ultimate power and violence as he "commande"—gives orders to—the enslaved. This is exactly what Marbot does in *Les Bambous*, whose cynicism is made crude from the outset in the contrasting opening dedication, where he genders his relationship with Creole and associates this language with femininity, even anchoring it in a romanticized and lyrical idealism drawing on an affectionate and structuring nostalgic childhood reminiscence—doux parler/sweet language: "To those of my cute female compatriots who have not forgotten the sweet language of our childhood."[4] In fact, as indicated in an 1869 edition of *Les Bambous*, Marbot translated de Lafontaine's fables to "récréer un petit cercle d'amis," that is, to entertain a small circle of friends.[5] The satisfaction of his fellow enslavers urges the publication of his text and does not fail to indicate the consensus around the perception they hold of the enslaved, which in turn indicates that Marbot's group is a community of ideology advancing a "parler," a shared discourse.

Creole is not "doux"—sweet—for the enslaved since it is the instrument that is used to convey *semantology*[6] to them. If the "parler"—Creole—is "doux" for the class of enslavers, it is because it allows them to foment metaphysical enslavement and to deploy a procedure of epistemological destitution of the Africans in the form of enslaving language and translation. Creole is then underscored as invested with an unethical charge aiming at besmirching the human person and especially the African. Marbot's dedication is addressed to his white compatriots as he entertains and speaks to his friends. However, *Les Bambous*' content is also addressed to the enslaved as much as it is about them. It is in this double paradigm of destitutive speech about the enslaved, directly articulated to them, that the process of metaphysical enslavement builds its deconstructive power. Through addressing his discourse to the enslaved, Marbot hopes that they will internalize and embrace it, thereby making it pass from a *shared* discourse among enslavers to an indelibly *universal* discourse common to both the enslaved and enslavers.

In this way too, he hopes to annex the enslaved as members of the community of ideology against them. Using a tool extraneous to the colony—de Lafontaine's fables—he sharpens it with the most plantation *symbolization-ism*,[7] that is, with modes of representation displaying exclusively aggressive signs, symbols, and discourses about the Africans. Seeking irreversible power over the person subjected to it, symbolizationism wants to be the mirror projecting to them their ontological truth. This symbolizationism relies on plantation parameters, that is, it is *creolized* to impose upon the enslaved ideas, concepts, and a vision of the world and of themselves differing from human precepts.

What is at stake with symbolizationism is *perennial and deeply anchored self- and cross-representation*, that is, the way the enslaved Africans will end up cementing within their own selves an explicit destructive vision and comprehension of said selves on the one hand, and on the other, an implicit deep-seated highly positive vision of the enslaver. The *meaning* appended to the representation constitutes an active factor ensuring power or disempowerment, for what is important to semantology is the *meaning* and existential value it gives the identity it goes to great lengths to represent negatively. Symbolizationism is intentionally de-existentializing. Epistemology also sits at the core of symbolizationism since it purports to teach the sets of values and knowledge the person who endures its process is to hold of themselves and the world. It aims at destitution and sowing confusion about the self. Since it draws on semantics and ontology, I call its intention *semantological* and its result, *semantology*. The inferiorizing meaning it assigns to the identity of the subject it maligns is astutely active, consciously or unconsciously. Semantology is utter political, moral, and symbolic harassment that, in the plantation, purports metaphysical enslavement. In the plantation, symbolizationism and creolization are mutually inclusive and the concept and practice they form is the enslaver's sense of modernity. The latter considers the Africans and especially the Bossals—newly arrived enslaved Africans— unadapted as they are for the norms of the plantation, whence the necessity to reform them via the processes of symbolizationism and creolization construed as transmutating.

Marbot's written text is published two years before the abolition of enslavement, which means that such an applied strategy is already well advanced. It also means that the slaving power is under the pressure of anti-abolitionist actions propelling them to exacerbate their discursive propaganda against the enslaved. Essentially oral, Creole was an established part of the devices used to perfect enslavement. Here, however, the strategy appears in the formalizing written format in Creole,[8] in a genre that is not administrative but "creative"—tale/fable—and through an authoritative means—translation—which formalizes the use of Creole as a powerfully dismantling instrument as much as it makes the communication or linguistic strategy complete and posits a political and symbolic statement about the extent of the enslavers' determination. This is all the more striking since even though they are accustomed to various levels of translation due to the linguistic complexity of the plantation, the African group cannot read and access Marbot's written text in the language that has then become in the nineteenth century almost exclusively associated with the enslaved. The readers are likely to be the white readership, which implies that while the tales are reported in the written form, they are delivered to the Africans orally. It is therefore worth casting light on the way, in *Les Bambous*, Marbot uses language, speech, symbolizationism, and creolization to impart this semantology to enslaved Africans and the way what he claims to be modernizing creolization reveals itself to be, in fact, enslaving translation.

MARBOT AND HIS CREOLE SPEECH

Marbot's ideology is stipulated early in his 208-word prologue to the fables. Critical analysis and close reading further down unveil how paradigms and notions essential to human existence, especially as the latter relate to persons and their sense for where they fit in the world, are exploited to form enslaving categories and systems of human oppression. Such notions include the arts, language, translation, knowledge, pedagogy, meaning, epistemology, conceptualization, and activities such as philosophy. The discourse conveyed in the prologue indicates that indeed, *Les Bambous* "travestit"—distorts—these paradigms, which then become active agents of assimilation to enslavement on the plantation. This points to the extreme density of the plight of the enslaved Africans who, in addition to the severe existential question denoted by semantology, also face crude axiological questions. The distortion of these crucial human paradigms into inhuman instruments adumbrates some of the critical areas where these Africans will have to act for redress:

All of you, slaves of my master, get together:
I have tales to recount
To you. You must listen to them attentively
If you want to save yourselves from chagrin.
What I am asking you to listen to
Are words made for the Béké.
The man who wrote these words
Was no fisherman of crabs
Nor was he an eater of mackerels
(. . .)

Since thanks to the Lord I know how to read
I am coming to you to tell you
All I found in them
To prevent you from being evil.
If this stays in your heart
You will not want to be so evil:
(. . .)
All evil niggers make a point
In hampering their master.
You will see as clear as day light
That people are miserable all over the world.
How you must be patient:
Since in Guinea just like in France
All Christian people suffer
As if they were from a cursed race!
(. . .)
Niggers, Békés, everyone has to suffer:
(. . .)
That is the way through which we can access
Paradise when we die[9]

Marbot is not even the owner of the plantation; he is the overseer and his doing and speech, articulated with a debonair and anodyne tone, illuminate the multiple layers of lethal agents ensuring that the enslavers' project against the enslaved in the plantation is concretely perpetrated. Speech to Marbot does not consist of translateral interaction, as it engages his sole voice as a transmitter of the general slaving discourse. He advances himself as a vessel and intermediary, receiving (divine) words—de Lafontaine's—to pass on like the Gospel to a lost flock of evil souls. And, the charge passed on is erected as a gift apparently satisfying what the enslaved are supposed to be yearning for: *les contes*—storytales. It goes without mentioning that Marbot is pater- nalistic and declares himself an owner of the mode of expression for and of reception—of the sacred—"I know how to read thanks to God." In this logic of his aptitude bestowed by God, the value of his words is made unquestion- ably sacred. That is why this mode of expression and of knowledge reception through the written form are meant for "békés" which, he explains in his Notes, means "maître" or master but in reality, means "white." As meant for the whites, the words bear an edifying essence and the tales themselves are cast as the holy Host and an enlightenment able to annul the "nèg's"—nig- ger's—evilness. Marbot talks to the enslaved about themselves—"All of you, slaves of my master, get together/I have tales to recount/To you"—and con- structs for and about them a set of personality traits he holds as absolute and constitutive of their identity. They are first and foremost, "slaves of (his) master," a definition opposing them and capturing their place and status within the levels of hierarchized relations. The identity of the Africans that he projects back onto them is one that holds them as "si mauvais"—"so evil"—which is a defect they ought to want to correct. Marbot opposes de Lafontaine's nature to that of the "nèg" and, while the former is "yon nhomme com i faut"—a man as one should be, the latter are "mangè macriau"—eaters of mackerel. In the same way as he does this, he establishes the racial division and therefore identity categories and values prevailing in the plantation in his discourse. Indeed, what he puts forth is the method for ameliorating the most despicable traits of the "nèg" who continuously sully the peace of the "békés" through a series of active vices: "Drinking alcohol, marooning. Playing the sorcerer with quinbois. Poisoning the master's livestock/Eating dirt/ Doing all sorts of evil things."[10] Of course, Marbot establishes his kind's moral superiority, and the enslaved are portrayed as active enemies and attackers of the békés, but also as animated with a corrupt mind-set and a decadent moral structure. One needs to note how, through their respective moral descriptions, de Lafontaine is defined and named as a human person, as he is referred to by "nhomme" which is "man," while the *nèg* are bestialized with the hyperbole in the meaning of the verb "manger"—to eat—that makes them appear as rending monsters. Not only are they not human but by contrast to de Lafontaine, they are not refined since they are "eaters of mackerel." Further, they are also dehumanized with what they eat—"dirt"—impairing the peace of the békés and not part of the human foodstuff.

The bearers of such a semantology ought to renounce their evil; the enslaver's request for ontological correction, progress, and modernity is amplified by the fact that Marbot explicitly orients the thoughts and actions of those he addresses with an imperative goal to pursue: "If you want to save yourselves from chagrin." The commandeur gives orders in the form of the imperative mode—Get together!—and modals—you must listen/you must be patient—first to convince the flock that they share with the "békés" racial equality since there is equity in their respective sufferings and second, to tell them what must be done for absolution. "Nèg" and "békés" must suffer in the same way for, if in France the white person suffers how then can the "nèg" of the American plantation think that those in Guinea should not? Thus, Marbot goes beyond the geographical boundaries of the colony to encompass the African and European continents, implying the universal truth of his statement and exhorting the enslaved Africans to fatalism, resignation, and conformity to reality and the modernity enslavement procures them. Naming the plantationed Africans—eaters of mackerel—and adjudicating on what they are not—nhomme com i faut—normal men / human beings—what Marbot delivers to the enslaved through his non-mediated Creole speech is a *semantology* to internalize, an authoritarian teratological ontology and a program for the mental disarticulation of their selves.

LANGUAGE, THE "PHILOSOPHER" AND PHILOSOPHY AND/IN THE PLANTATION LOGIC

The intention to continue to command over and shape the Africans' state of mind, mental production, and behavior facilitating their own psychic decomposition is also to be seen in the process and method used by Marbot. The vocabulary and references are directly extracted from the plantation's mores as the "Notes" of his prologue offer clarifying remarks for the neophyte.[11] Marbot does not just use the Creole language and Creole words to achieve his goal. He also creolizes the meaning of de Lafontaine's texts to infuse them with a plantation logic. Having used the term "philosophe"—philosopher—in several of the fables, Marbot makes a point to explain the plantation meaning of the term in the "Notes": "A *philosopher* is a smooth-talker, a man who pretends to be above his condition."[12] So, a philosopher is defined by the notion of "parole"—speech or statement—and by the nature of and reaction to the said "parole." The statement itself is specified. A philosopher is someone who "parle"—speaks—and emits a "parole"—speech—that is deemed unacceptable. He is a subject vain in essence, not able to proffer any legitimate and seriously substantive discourse, which is why the plantation reviles him. Bearing the trait of "philosopher" as an identity triggers aggressive dismissal. Given that, to determine who counts as a philosopher according to the laws of the plantation, speech content must be examined to draw conclusions about the person's nature and henceforth their validity.

So, Marbot and the plantation logic go as far as stating a discourse on "parole"—speech—thereby inducing critical questions pertaining to the philosophy of language. They also establish an ontological hierarchy related to function and status relegating the "philosopher" to inferiority. An implicit self-representation appears as, in fact, Marbot articulates an ontological statement about himself insinuating that, although also in the domain of "parole," his speech and de La Fontaine's are superior, for they are no "philosophers." As a matter of fact, given the definition of "philosopher," it ensues a symbolizationist portrayal of the Africans whereby, in the plantation, all enslaved Africans are "philosophers," that is, inferior subjects whose "parole" is illegitimate and unacceptable. However, if we apply a more ethical set of values to examine Marbot's "parole" vis-à-vis the plantation definition of "philosopher," then, it surfaces that the "philosophers" of the plantation are the enslavers. The plantation definition of "philosopher" poses a serious epistemological problem to whatever is to come in terms of (Caribbean) philosophy since the evaluation of the speech and of the person emitting it relies on plantation values and criteria which are at their core unethical and antihuman. Any speech against these values is doomed to be labeled that of a "philosopher," a naturally dismissible subject.

Consequently, in alluding to terms of the philosophy of language, axiology, and ontology, Marbot's speech contains its load of risks, the first of which being linguistic and lexical and anchored in the very use of the word "philosopher." If enslavers are named "philosophers" per the unethical nature of their speech and plantation definition, the confusion likely to issue from the amalgamation of the name "enslaver" with the qualification of "philosopher" presents a high epistemological and axiological risk for the entire space of the Caribbean. Another risk is posed by Marbot's definition of the act of philosophizing as negligible. Here, one sees two of the grave metaphysical problems enslavement and the enslaver's sophism have posed to the said space. In any case, the meaning and deficiency attributed to "philosopher" are exactly what the content of Marbot's speech reveals about him. His speech is questionable to the very extent that he places himself above his human condition while at the same time he pretends to address human questions such as ontology and the philosophy of language. This makes even more important, on the one hand, the question related to the nature and value of his own speech as expressed in *Les Bambous* and, on the other, the reaction enslaved Africans will oppose to this plantation logic for the restoration of a more ethical value to language, philosophizing and to the word and meaning of "philosopher."

CONGO

In 1803, as the Haitian Revolution is at its apogee and nine months before Haiti is to emerge as a land free of slaving tyranny, former St. Domingue enslaver, Louis Narcisse Baudry des Lozières, who had ambitions to publish an *Encyclopédie coloniale* but lost his work during his flight from the St. Domingue Revolution to France, publishes instead, *Second voyage à la Louisiane* in which he inserts a *Dictionnaire ou Vocabulaire Congo—Congo Dictionary or Vocabulary*, a list of independent Congo words and phrases collected in the colony of St. Domingue. Through the epistemological charge of language, this time an African language, *Congo Dictionary* too seeks to impart a sense of plantation personhood to the enslaved Africans. Largely contributing the foundation of the Congo person's existence, the Congo language is used in an attempt to de-existentialize the Congo person and creolize him and her, that is, to mold them with the set of plantation codes and values. Here, contrary to *Les Bambous* where they are silenced, the voices of the enslaved are present but neutralized by the enslaver's interpretation, which is used to apply symbolizationism and enunciate plantation translation.

Already, one must note the pretention of the plantation site's enslavers to simulate knowledge patterned after what is produced in the motherland—France—in the realm of philosophy and "science." Des Lozières's dictionary is published only thirty years after the last volume of the *Encyclopedia, or a Systematic Dictionary of the Sciences, Arts, and Crafts* of prominent philosophers of the Enlightenment, Diderot and D'Alembert. The critical nature of the (metaphysical) plight of enslaved Africans, just like their response to their lived experience of enslavement, is also to be measured against this fact of the enslavers' utter cynicism and resolute will to portray themselves as encyclopedists and attempt an intrusion in the world of philosophy.

The dictionary pretends to facilitate a transformation the enslaver equates with modernity. Being "aggressively for the interest of the planters,"[13] Baudry des Lozières believes that St. Domingue will be returned to the enslavers and claims to be establishing his *Congo Dictionary* with the explicit aim of providing both enslavers and doctors who, respectively, command and treat the enslaved, with the appropriate words and "parole" to achieve their defined goals. Des Lozières takes questions related to language further than Marbot since he views language as assuming a critical importance in the wealth-generating business of enslavement. According to him, not knowing the language of the enslaved causes the enslaver to lose many of them.[14] Communities of the Bantu people, including groups of the Congo family, composed the bulk of St. Domingue's Africans. Of course, des Lozières does not specify the subgroups and simply refers to "le langage des Congos"—the language of the Congos—already establishing elliptical simplification.[15] Therefore, what he creates is an intentional instrument whose interest is not solely in the linguistic tools it provides but also in the fact that it highlights the place of the recipients—enslavers and doctors—and the (metaphysical) plight of the enslaved. The recipients' position seeping through the vocabulary points to the fact that the condition of the enslaved lies in exploitation and vulnerability. Des Lozières estimates his enterprise to be progressive as, according to him, he seeks to fill in a gap and provide enslavers with a missing tool he deems "useful" to carry out their task of controlling the enslaved. His intention is pedagogical. He also wants to provide his fellow enslavers with a strategic methodology to gain the trust of the enslaved. Entertaining the enslaved, he claims, is a means to build their trust and having knowledge of their language allows for a twofold result: "know how to speak to them and you will cheer them up and inspire trust in them . . . soon, they will see you but as a man superior to them, as a benefactor."[16] It is here that he also sees his endeavor as philanthropic—as speaking to the Africans in their language, according to him, is a way to give them "espérance," that is, hope, and to dissipate their "crainte," their fear vis-à-vis their condition as enslaved. The dictionary is published in 1803 at a time when enslavers themselves, challenged by the grand freedom action of the Haitian Revolution, are no longer mastering the facts of the colony of St. Domingue. However, of course, the dictionary can benefit the enslavers of Martinique and Guadeloupe where, respectively, the colony has been restituted to France and enslavement is legalized again in 1802 after England supplanted the French, whose Revolution had led to a first abolition.

Furthermore, the *method* should be noted. Just like Marbot uses Creole and orality associated with the enslaved, des Lozières uses the Congos as a source and extracts from them the resource for their subjection. This could give the impression that, contrary to Marbot's, his is a translateral transaction where speech and language account for all parties, emitters, and receptors, but one must not forget that the plantation logic exerts upon the enslaved multifaceted visible and invisible pressures that negate their ability to exercise free choice. Moreover, translation is also the means and by itself, it is important in its unveiling the state of mind of the enslaver who first translates African words, (complex) thoughts, and paradigms within the limits of his own knowledge about and understanding of Congo matters and who second, treats the Africans' thoughts and paradigms reductively. The limits of des Lozières can also be deciphered in the fact that what he seeks to translate is based on his needs as an enslaver. The isolated French words he asks the Congos to translate into their language serve the unsophisticated reality of plantation life, one that does not cater to expansion but to narrowness. Furthermore, he reconstitutes the dictionary from recollection, given that his original ten years' worth collection of words from the plantation of St. Domingue vanished with the Revolution—which introduces the issue of its reliability.

Second, the *intention*. Very much like Marbot after him, des Lozières purports to put forth a *proposition*, one that apparently bears the marks of phenomenology in its ambition to structure the mind of the enslaved and underpin their judgment, perception, and emotion. Most important, although it is construed for the entire group of enslaved people, the dictionary is also to serve as a method for creolization. One intention is to provide the enslavers with effective instruments to creolize, that is, to neutralize the enslaved's own African paradigms. It is also meant to provoke in the newly arrived African—the Bossal—the internalization of the assigned *semantology*, a new mode of relationship with himself and a self-vision incarnated in the ways he is to henceforth judge himself, think about and see himself, and ultimately, feel about himself. In his explanatory introduction, des Lozières articulates the ideology guiding his perception of the Africans and their behavior as well as his conception and use of knowledge as the latter relates to the said Africans:

> This work . . . has been made principally for the planters of the colony. Most of them buy niggers and they do not know their language hence an aspect of the

impediments that bring them to lose their niggers. These wrètched slaves often die soon after their arrival because they cannot be understood. Being a planter myself, I felt the usefulness of this type of science and in my spare time, I did it. I sought to know just enough to understand my bossals and be understood by them. Nothing is sadder than the nigger put on a boat . . . but know how to talk to him and you will brighten him up and inspire confidence in him. His hope sparkles . . . and very soon he sees in you but a man superior to him, only a benefactor who saves him from death, impoverishment and human degradation. Thus, everyone will see that a colonist can be a philanthropist . . . this dictionary or Vocabulary is also of great use (*) to doctors and barbers who can but treat the new niggers poorly if they cannot ask them questions . . . chance left me some notes on the language of the Congos; these notes help me remember and compose a nearly complete Vocabulary.[17]

Des Lozières is not interested in learning the Congo language as a sign for mutual linguistic exchanges or to give that language a valuable status and he declares that he extracts from Congo only what supports his intention. Des Lozières is interested in re-lation through trans-lation as long as this transla-tion supports his enslaving epistemology. His design is to unilaterally use plantation pedagogy to extirpate specific Congo words from the Congos' minds and communicate them back to them with new plantation meanings and concepts. This is all the more consequential since des Lozières departs from the French language (not Creole) and needs to wait for the Bossals to have acquired a smattering of that language to be able to understand the trans-lations that are requested. This departure from the colonial language to arrive at the Congo language as an instrument conditioning the Congo person to the precepts of the plantation is another dimension of the epistemological and metaphysical plight awaiting the Bossals and nothing less than an example of epistemic and metaphysical violence. In its content and aim, the dictionary itself is as much a vector as it is a practice and enforcement of the epistemic violence meant to lead to metaphysical enslavement.

Let us note that, in this imposed linguistic transaction, the result is a translation whose accuracy depends on des Lozières's perception and own ability to understand what the enslaved transmit to him. As guided by his racialized and plantation subjectivity, limits, reductionism, and ignorance are also factors governing the process. Des Lozières additionally sets forth his understanding of the power of language and the power of knowing the African language in the plantation through what is no less than a *method-ology* to achieve the submission of the Africans. Although he claims that learning the Congo language serves the mere purpose of simple commu-nication in the interest of the enslaver, knowing the African language is vested with an underpinning paramount usefulness since it enables the goal of transforming the vision the Africans have of the enslaver to be accomplished. It is part of both the strategy and methodology that des Lozières shares with his fellow enslavers. The dissemination of ideas and expected behavior ensuring the order of the plantation is an objective transpiring through des Lozières's explanations. This is even more important given that the process concerns the identity of the enslaver and syllogistically, that of the enslaved, respectively, categorized as superior and inferior with the latter's behavior having to demonstrate trust toward the former. The Congo language appears as an instrumental accessory whose fulgurant significance is to be seen in the fact that it is utilitarian and does not live long in the colony since the newly arrived Bossals the author refers to rapidly learn the plantation language—Creole.

Des Lozières does not fail to draw a portrait of what he believes is the Congo person's moral character, since the latter's sadness is said to come from their not being understood. The childish naïveté that is insinuated here as a characterizing trait is the context allowing des Lozières to state that language is also important for the Congo person to such an extent that, on the one hand, the reason for their sorrow is not their lucid understanding of their new lived experience of injustice in the plantation, but a mere sadness at not being comprehended linguistically. On the other hand, what saves them from sadness is not simply speaking to them but knowing how to speak to them in their language, that is, knowing how to manipulate words and convey meaning and ideas that may not be truthful. The value the Congos are said to grant to language is devalued by the results of the enslaver's projected outcome which is to bring the Congo to believe that he, the enslaver, is a philanthropic savior destined to receive gratitude for saving the Congo from an assured death and human degradation in Africa.[18] The symbolizationism that the Congo person's character undergoes lies in this constructed belief and discourse about their conception of language and speech and their fate in Africa. The impact of this new knowledge, imparted to the Congo speaker, is measured by the strategic moment when it is transmitted to them; in other words, immediately at their inception in the colony where they are not yet Creolized enslaved, but Bossals.

The devalorization of the concept the Congos attribute to language through its relegation to simplicity, conjoined with the enslavers' misuse of language in general and the Congo language in particular to mystify the Congos, does not augur any emancipatory approach and practice of language, speech, and semantics in the plantation. To des Lozières, his Congo dictionary is complete, suggesting that it contains all that is necessary to achieve the set project. And indeed, despite its relative brevity, the resulting dictionary, made of a series of crude affirmations, exclamative statements, questions, and imperative orders, comprises all that the enslaver needs to arrive to a rapid and simple subjugation. It targets the mind of the Bossal.

MINING AFRICAN LANGUAGES FOR CONFUSION

Des Lozières uses the "vous" form of the subject pronouns, which signifies either the plural or formal respect for a singular person such as "allez vous coucher. ïenda leka koinda"—"go to bed."[19] Although it is not always clear whether only one person or a group are addressed, it is unlikely that the "vous" translates formalism and respect when addressing an enslaved. Actually, "vous" translates authority and power. What is even more critical to pinpoint is that the dictionary articulates phrases meant for interpersonal communication between an enslaver and an enslaved or a doctor and an enslaved. Consequently, the informal "tu" is used. But it is used not so much because of familiarity, which entails the existence of a consensual positive relationship, but rather because of the political and power hierarchy that "tu" can convey, for example, as in the hierarchy between a child and an adult. This same epistemological and metaphysical charge carried by "tu" can be performed by "vous," in which case the dismissal or obliteration of the person that this enunciates is much more operative. Des Lozières also reproduces this in his dictionary as shown in, "allez chercher mon aiguille. miakou koinda vouka"—go look for my needle.[20] The linguistic choices des Lozières opts for are not to be taken lightly as they also contribute to the political and power design governing the setting up of the dictionary.

Congo words that interest des Lozières are those pertaining to language itself, such as, on the one hand, "langage. binbon"—speech; "langue. loudemi"—language; "Parler. sonsa"—to speak; and, on the other hand, words in the same communicative semantic family as "parler" such as "dire. Kambezi.—soukoula—konvoula"; "écouter. ziboula matou"; or "ecrire. sonika"; respectively, "to say," "to listen to," and "to write."[21] Despite the complexity of the Congo's concepts, which might be indicated by the existence of three different ways to express the verb "to say," for des Lozières, the Congo word for "parler"—to speak—equates to "injure. finga," which means, "insult."[22] Given the fact that speaking encodes and signals humanity in the human world as much as it underscores power, it is not surprising that des Lozières opts for reducing the complex perspective from which the Congos conceive of the fact and practice of speaking to an indignity—injure/insult. With this respect, as implacably per the plantation logic, a sizable portion of the vocabulary and phrases concern chiefly the human person, about whom concepts are conveyed, although Baudry des Lozières

never explicitly uses this expression when he posits a certain human identity
as absolute both for the enslaved and the enslaver. Here, it is interesting to
see how symbolizationism is played out in the dictionary to articulate an
enslaving semantology and a plantation discourse regarding the enslaved.
Des Lozières frames the plantation for the enslaved as a place populated
by only two human types. Thus, he lays out the principles by which the
said types will exist in this place, forcing the enslaved to understand what a
human person is in the plantation and how they themselves are irreversibly
relegated within this plantation kind or category. In fact, they are provided
with a social teaching since they are taught that the plantation is populated with two kinds, each of which is labeled through a rank and category
advanced as objective:

blanc (homme). mondélé. (113)	white (man)
captif. m'vika.—gouagni (116)	captive
esclave. vika. (123)	slave
maître. foumou—bakala. (132)	master
maitresse. foumou kinto. (132)	mistress
monsieur. moenné. (133)	mister
nègre. montou. (134)	nigger
négresse. inkinto.—fioté kinto. (134)	nigger (female)

Of course, as the one element to specifically neutralize through definition,
the emphasis is laid on the enslaved to leave a severe imprint in their mind.
Social and gender specifications support the process of symbolizationism that
establishes the mental semantology of the Africans. The latter can then derive
syllogistically the axiological and ontological specification of the "mondélé"—white man—as the "foumou"—master—and his female counterpart,
the "foumou kinto"—mistress. Already, the way des Lozières receives the
complexity of the Congos' answers can be seen through the simplification
of his translations. This is very apparent in the formation of feminine nouns
such as "foumou kinto" and "fioté kinto." If, according to the pattern, "kinto"
refers to the feminine and may perhaps mean "femme"—woman—then, the
translations should not be simplistically "maitresse" and "négresse," but
more complexly "kinto who is foumou" and "kinto who is fioté." Thus, the
translation itself, together with its process, and in its intricate relation with
the translator and the plantation paradigms by which he was shaped, makes
the question of speech, concepts, and epistemology highly critical indeed.
Apart from using single words bringing a moral judgment such as "laid.
m'bi" which means "ugly," "anthropophage. lianga banou." translated by
"cannibal," or "paresseux. mongui lititi uga salé.—guéïé sala bénéko" standing for "lazy,"[23] enslavers use the Congo language to tell the enslaved Congo

what and who they are with a series of graphic descriptive and affirmative sentences in which they anchor what they see as an objective moral determination of the enslaved:

bonne personne. montozambi. (114)	good person
tu es une bête. guéi ïoba. (115)	you are a beast
fils de femme débauchée. kounou goua kou. (115)	son of a whore
comment vous appelez-vous? deziné liakou. kom-bo a kou? (119)	what is your name?
tu es une dinde. guéïé pilou. (122)	you are such a goose.
tu es un empoisonneur. guéïé n'doki. (129)	you are a poisoner
ta mère a mis au monde un cochon. mamakou oli outa goulonbou. (130)	your mother gave birth to a pig
Que tu es laid! guéïé manbéné m'bi. (131)	how ugly you are!
quel navire t'a porté? kia kombi nata guéïé? (135)	what boat brought you?

"Bonne personne" combines two fundamental words that proffer a category for personhood. The reverse phrase is not furnished, which makes "bonne personne" even more critical in the plantation context, as it is likely to refer to what the enslaved has to understand of herself or himself—which is that she or he is not a "good person" and that she or he has to become so according to the terms outlined by the enslaver.[24] The moral characterization is coupled with one that devalues the humanity of the Congos and places them in the realm of infrahumanity. While one can give his or her name when asked, what it stands for is defined as being part of bestiality—bête, dinde, cochon/beast, goose, pig; perversion—fils de femme débauchée; ugliness—laid/ugly; evilness—empoisonneur/poisoner. The ontological determination now takes the form of an existential set of parameters, since the person being defined is one whose chances to belong to plain humankind are nil, not just because of their physical and moral inappropriateness, but because the core root of their provenance not only exemplifies decadent social mores—débauchée—but above all, produces mere animals. The mother indeed gives birth to pigs. This is why despite the name that they may be proffering when asked, they cannot be seen to spring out of any normal human procedure but solely out of a corrupt and infected[25] inanimate entity such as the holds of the slave boats through which they were deported; hence the said boat is ultimately held as the origin defining their true identity. Here one finds an echo to Glissant's perception of the slave boat being the womb birthing Africans meant to become Caribbean: "what boat brought you?"

Having defined the existential root identity of the enslaved, the enslaver also determines their place, function, and fate in the plantation as the ones who are beaten, who work, and who receive executive orders:

anneau pour le pied. m'longa. (109)	chain for the feet
aller coucher. ïenda leka.—koinda. (111)	go to bed (or piss off)
battre. nouana. Boula (113)	beat
canne à sucre. mousinga (116)	sugar cane
chaîne. panga. (117)	chain
prends garde au fouet. bika m'singa lakota. (124)	beware of the whip
prends la houx. sinba cingo. (128)	take the hoe
si tu ne travailles pas je te battrai. guéïée	
salako filam	if you do not work,
singa akona matkaou	I will beat you
tiakou (145)	

Thus, the Congo person belongs to the kind of the working beast which syllogistically defines the enslaver as the epitome of the humankind and category. It is therefore worth pointing out the question: "m'aimes-tu? menou zozé guéié?"—"Do you love me?" the enslaver asks the enslaved.[26] It may appear at first bemusing that such a question is even posed in the explicit context of a plantation that is antithetical to "love." However, educing emotion is in fact a component of the system of domination and the question manifests the affective reaction and confusion the dominant seeks to extort from the dominated person receiving the stimuli, namely, the concepts, symbols, and political structure conveyed through the linguistic apparatus. In addition to implying through his speech that he is of the sole type able to arouse the positive emotion of "love" because he is a "bonne personne"—good person—the enslaver seeks from the enslaved confirmation that his strategy of making him docile and infrahuman is successful to its inner core. Perhaps it is this unique question that captures the most, the magnitude of the social, moral, dehumanizing, and existential project embodied in des Lozières's dictionary and that articulates the crude tensions brought about by the general and profound confusion the plantation system seeks to instill in the enslaved. This is amplified by the declarative sentence, "nous sommes bons. béfo miévésé"— we are good people—a sentence likely to have been asserted by the enslaver as a self-portrayal and referring directly to des Lozières's discourse about the enslaver's philanthropy.[27] The confusion sought is of the kind illustrated by the contradictory orders and statements thrown at the enslaved such as "va te déshabiller. guéïé koinda bolola m'lélé tiakou."—go undress yourself—and, "habillez-vous, vous êtes indécent"—"vouata psété tiakou."—get dressed, you are indecent.[28] Such an order can be given in a variety of circumstances on a plantation but, apart from rhetorically indicating the epistemological and metaphysical nakedness and starkness the enslaver expects of the enslaved and that stipulates them as socially and morally repulsive, "va te déshabiller" is a demand likely to be made by the doctor for the needs of the medical examination. However, anchored in the way the enslaver sees the body of the enslaved as exhausting their identity, the value judgment regarding the result and ensuing the compliance of the enslaved to the order of the plantation is of a nature likely to create disarray on their part, as they have to put on new (figurative) clothing to be plantation decent—"habillez-vous, vous êtes indecent."

MONTOU/MUNTU

"Montou" is one of the terms of des Lozières's dictionary that should not leave one indifferent, because of its bold political signification in the context of plantation facts. It is the equivalent of the form "Muntu" that is mostly used today among Bantu peoples. The formalized discussion on "Muntu" started when a Belgian priest officiating in the Congo, Placide Tempels, published his 1945 *La philosophie bantoue*[29]—*Bantu Philosophy*—in which, comparing the Baluba people's vision of the world to that of the Europeans', he articulated the Bantu concept paralleling the European comprehension of the "being":

Force is inseparably linked to the being and this is why these two notions remain related in their definition of being. This must be received as the basis of the Bantu philosophy. This is the least one can admit if one wants to understand the Bantus. Thus, the Bantus have a composed notion of the being that can be formulated as such: the being is what possesses force . . . for the Bantu person . . . the being is force, force is the being. Our notion of being is "what is," theirs is "the force that is." Where we think about the concept "to be," they use the concept "force."[30]

The human being is central to the universe and is manifested as a God-given force that is vital and represents what he is and is otherwise called, "muntu." This is to such an extent that the human person is "muntu":

According to Bantu ontology, man is at the center of the created universe. The "muntu," his vital force is the wonders of the Divine creation. Life is a gift from God. . . . The human vital force is the force element among the multiplicity of beings. This ontological order emanates from the "muntu." The ontological norm as well as the ethical norm for Good and Evil is the vital force. It is also at the basis of human rights.[31]

Additionally, force is not static and can expand or deplete depending on the muntu's set of personal conditions: "Any force can consolidate or become weaker. That is to say that, all beings can become stronger or weaker."[32]

Tempels seeks to demonstrate that, contrary to what the colonial discourse holds, due to the colonizer's lack of knowledge of the African ontological principles, Africans produce philosophy. Nevertheless, his ambition is to use knowledge about the Bantu peoples' inner specificities and thoughts to compel a more fluid and permanent reception of the colonial religion and faith, Christianity, one that according to him, reflects modernity. In this, serving the same colonial project and even though on one hand, in the Caribbean, this colonial project is de facto enslavement and the material enrichment it provides and on the other hand, in the Congo, it is symbolic, religious, with an immaterial and metaphysical gain, the methodology he advocates to Christianize the Bantu people through their own vision of cosmogony, the universe and spirituality, is in direct continuity with that articulated by des Lozières during the enslavement period in America:

> This said, one must admit that, through the direct and global study of these living documents, i.e., the black person and their way of living, one can succeed in penetrating their soul, to assimilate it. If it is developed enough, this assimilation could allow us to understand, immediately and strikingly, all of their religious and magical practices, their political organization, their clan life, their moral, their laws and even language.[33]

What is more is that, according to Tempels, since "language is spoken wisdom," studying the Bantu peoples' language can lead to a more profound seizure of their inner mental complexus. He also affirms that one can explain the logic of the Bantu languages' rules only through the Bantu's mentality and philosophy.[34]

Tempels's theory sparked a discussion among African thinkers over two generations during which one sought to determine whether there was such a thing as an African philosophy per se or simply wisdom and ethnophilosophy. Corrective studies such as Alexis Kagamé's 1956 *La philosophie bantu-rwandaise de l'Etre* were conducted, to nuance some of Tempels's abrupt and absolute statements. The discussion goes as far as to the twenty-first century when Senegalese philosopher Souleymane Bachir Diagne offered another reading of Tempels's propositions in his 2013 *The Ink of the Scholars*. To Diagne, the contestable points that Tempels's work contains do not preclude the fact that it "marked the beginning of African philosophy as an academic discipline."[35] It remains true indeed that Tempels has brought to light, in a formal way, "muntu," a critical aspect of the principles governing the way Bantu people tend to view the human person who animates and makes the universe intelligible, a way that is not contested by these Bantu people. What also serves our reflective purpose here is the fact that language, in itself, has been an operative instrument of colonial designs largely applied by European languages which de facto become colonial languages mediating the same instrumentalization. Besides, whether in Africa or in America, Africans have been subjected to the effects of these linguistic operations in a determining manner. It is also the case with Creole, which served as a vehicle for colonial subjugation. However, of the two languages spoken in the French Creole Caribbean, it is not anodyne that it is in the one translating the space of Haiti, Guadeloupe, and Martinique the most, that is Creole, that one finds what is perhaps the most relevant and significant testimony to the way enslaved Africans posited a philosophical principle in direct opposition to the ideology governing the enslavers' motivations and actions and drawing very directly on an African vision of "person" and "personhood" as rendered by "muntu." Despite the unilateral approach to language and speech action observed by the carriers of the plantation logic, enslaved Africans operate a translateral counteraction shedding light on their philosophical positions regarding ontology and axiology as assumed by language. Through what it signifies, "moun" redresses the plantation's social, moral, human, and existential phenomenology imposed by des Lozières's and Marbot's discourses. It complicates the plantation outlook on both the "philosopher" and the act the latter performs.

MOUN

In the context of this epistemic and metaphysical violence, which attempted to redefine what a human person is and especially excluded them from this definition, many plantationed Africans certainly observed a comportment reflecting submission, contradiction, and disarray. However, one can also identify constant gestural and verbal behaviors positing their refusal to accept the *plantation proposition* and categories that the enslaver advances as the paradigm for existence and that they inscribe, among other vessels, in language to form a neutralizing linguistic apparatus. Given that the African had little control over the handling of his or her own body, apart from the multifaceted physical revolts and contests and even though, as we have seen, the mind is under attack on the plantation, many signs, discourses, and actions systematically held by enslaved Africans signal that the mind was also an important site for protest and refusal of the enslaving categories.

The African languages did not survive the linguistic assault and complexity of the plantation, to the extent that indeed, the Creole lexicon largely derives from French. This fact might, at first, imply that the worldview that Creole assumes is primarily French. However, I want to argue that despite the loss of African words, a vast number of fundamental African concepts and world-views were absorbed by French African Creole and critically, in the very way it envisaged, comprehended, signified, and practiced what epistemic violence has sought to extinguish: the human person and its human integrity. In the same way as Marbot and des Lozières used African modes to subdue, symbolizationize, and attempt to reassign ontology into plantation semantol-ogy, the enslaved too drew on their African modes to create alternatives, *counter-propositions*, and *emancipatory categories* the first of which residing in *meaning* and, particularly, in what the human person is and is not.

If there is one prominent term in Creole, it is "moun"—person, people, human being—which springs from the Congo "muntu" or "montou," the latter arguably being the sole word of des Lozières's vocabulary list found in today's Caribbean Creole language. Des Lozières translates "montou" by "nègre"—"nigger," a plantation referent unveiling his limited and reductive way of comprehending what the Congos were conveying to him about their selves.[36] For in fact, "montou" carries a radically differing epistemology.

The presence of "moun" in Marbot's 1846 *Les Bambous* to mean "person" or "people" and even earlier in Moreau de Saint-Méry's 1797 observation on Haitian vaudou: "Canga moune dé lé." indicates how anchored the word and its meaning are in the Creole language and Caribbean critical thought.[37] That French African Creole spoken today features this one term—moun—found in des Lozières's dictionary is not of interest because that dictionary would have made this retention possible. Rather, I want to stress how this mere fact enunciates the fundamental importance of "moun" as a word, but especially a word that is instrumental in carrying what is arguably the single concept and meaning that most sustains Caribbean thought and values. I am arguing that it is an African word in Creole that symbolizes and provides *meaning* and ethical value to what the enslaving categories, paradigms, and practices had severely and relentlessly targeted: the human person and the human meaning that human paradigms convey to it. "Moun" is a Congo word in the contem-porary Caribbean that testifies to the significance of the philosophical work accomplished and the metaphysical approach mobilized by the African group to assert their own propositions, statements, and discourse on behalf of what the word signifies: the central position of humanness in the world of humans. The central presence of this word despite the inhuman assaults demonstrates the African will and intent to not allow the centrality of the human person in all matters human to be sacrificed. In retaining this one word in America they state what matters to them and the value they grant its meaning.

One should not take lightly the fact that of all of the words appearing in des Lozières's Congo dictionary, only one—"montou"—has found an effec-tive place in Creole—"moun"—to qualify exactly what the apparatus of the plantation sought to question and inhibit in the enslaved group: an edifying

conception of themselves as human as well as of the universe. The epistemological and ontological significance of both the retention and the concept
should not be neglected for it points to one of the ways metaphysical enslavement is kept in check. Creole is a site of memory for the epistemological locus
where these Africans situated their resilience and choice to build a modernity-
oriented society from which the meaning and practice of plantation modernity
had been exorcised. Creole is a site of epistemological tension as it is used
on one hand by the enslaver to creolize, which amounts to epistemological
and existential dismantling for the enslaved, while the latter uses the same
language to Africanize it and through this, ethicalize it and the realities it is to
say, bring to thought, and make manifest. I take this fundamental presence of
"moun" and its ethical meaning in the Caribbean context and language as sig-
naling that one of the prime domains of resilience as much as resistance to the
antihuman colonial project has been the mind and its production as determining not just beliefs but also convictions. Through enslavement, the colonial
project severely endangered humankind and its humanity to the point that the
main question concerned the type of substance and epistemological paradigms
those conditioned by the plantation paradigm must use to found the basis for
thought and action. The very existence of "moun" as offered by the enslaved
Africans responds to that question. It subtends the refusal of the enslavers'
paradigm and offers a category for the thought and especially critical thought
that Africans contributed to establishing as a fundamental point of departure
for thought and praxis in the Caribbean. Not only does it articulate an ethical discourse and ethicalize language and the use of language per se, but it
also contributes to the redress of enslaving paradigms in paramount human
domains such as the arts, language, epistemology, meaning, or pedagogy.

"Moun" stands for "person" and "people" with, "an moun" meaning, "a
person" and the plural "moun" meaning "people." Given the part played in
Creole by the French lexicon, it is indeed striking that the French phrase "une
personne"—a person/someone—that would be "an pèsonn" in Creole—simply does not exist in this latter language. What exists is "pèsonn" to mean "no
one" that serves as an alternative to "piès moun" also meaning "no person"
or "no one." "Moun" comes in radical contradiction to "meuble"—furniture/
chattel—which is the term and declarative meaning that the colonial ideology
inscribed in article 44 of the *Code noir* to reference the African human person. It also contradicts des Lozières's portrayal of the Congos as beasts, pigs,
and geese/turkeys. Here we are seeing how, through and within language, an
axiological counterpoint was advanced to the speech or discourse proffered
by the enslaver, as well as what the African valued and deemed paramount to
save and anchor indelibly: what they believe the human person to be in the
human universe and especially, what they are convinced they themselves are
in the same universe.

When translating how the Congos conceived of "language" and "speech," affirming that it sufficed to know how to speak to them to elicit an expected reaction, des Lozières was irretrievably wrong. He was far from capturing the complex dimensions of the Congos' response when he asked them for the equivalence of "nègre" and they answered "montou." If "montou" is actually "muntu" then it is only logical that the Congos' rendition of what the enslaver sees as "nègre"—nigger—is one that reflects their own representation of their selves. Much more than a simple counter-translation, what the Congos asserted is self-translation and emancipatory translation from firm epistemological knowledge. It is not so much the term "nigger" and the plantation meaning appended to it that is primarily relevant to them, but rather the fact that it is supposed to identify those who know themselves to be "mountu." When des Lozières asks them how they refer to themselves in Congo he uses the term "nègre." But the Congos' answer shows that they do not recognize their person as "nègre" but as "mountu." It is in this epistemic transaction and tension concerning a fabricated knowledge—plantation—and an intrinsic and original knowledge—Congo—about the Congo self and the fact that the Congos themselves effect an action onto meaning and onto meaning of the self as ontological paradigm, that their answer and contribution are not to be overlooked. In their Congo paradigm, "mountu" does not mean "nègre." It does mean "human" and "person" as a vital force, and this is also a paradigm that they succeed in imposing as a mode of (self-) perception and thought in the midst of the plantation system, as the presence of "moun" to mean "person"/"people" in today's Creole attests. The complex meaning and metaphysical operation that des Lozières is unable to seize and that the enslaved Africans boldly assert through retention (of words and meaning) is a lens through which one might attempt to understand the scope of the African contribution in America. Already, des Lozières writes "mon" for the first syllable but the derivation of the Creole "moun" is closer to the "mun" of "muntu," a pronunciation that must have also been practiced in the plantation.[38] It is therefore rational that, under this African epistemological and metaphysical operation, "nègre"—infrahuman, nonhuman—ends up meaning in Creole "moun"—person, human being.

Indeed, in Creole, "an nèg" is "a person" and especially, "a black person" or "a black man."[39] Even the association the plantationed Congo draw here between themselves and a color or even what is conceived as "race" in the plantation on the basis of a skin color may not necessarily participate in the same dynamic as that of the enslaver and consequently may not stand for a resulting internalization of plantation modes. For, in des Lozières's dictionary, one pinpoints that "nègre" (black man) is also translated with "fioté iagala," "négresse" (black woman) as "fioté kinto" and that "fioté" means "noir."[40]—"fioté-fiota" (134)—black. Des Lozières does not specify whether "fioté" refers to a color, as he had distinguished the person white "mondélé" (113) and the color white, "pinba.—banda.—ouavinboka." (113). However, the Congos are very much aware of the notion and concept of "color" since "négresse" is not translated with "montou" but with "inkinto" and "fioté kinto" (134).[41] The plantation's racial paradigm exacerbates the Congo's urgent necessity to make taxonomic choices. However, here it is apparently not the core root of the epistemological sense that provides them with perception on skin color.

AFRICAN EPISTEME IN CARIBBEAN
THOUGHT PARADIGMS: MOUN AND FÒS

The enslaving and European systems are not the sole categorial parameters through which plantationed Africans envisaged the world to come. In fact, as language permits to underscore, the African thought categories have been much more operative than one estimates in the process of providing the New World with a critical thought system in the first place and then, one that would not present itself as detrimental to humankind and humanity. The mere presence of "moun" as an operative and signifying term in one of the languages spoken in the Caribbean elevates a deep ethical meaning, qualifies the type of *proposition* that the Africans make in in response to and in opposition to that of des Lozières's, and in the same domain—related to the definition of the human person. These Africans propose the advent of and placement in a corrective Modernity excluding unethical values. Drawing on my own inner knowledge of Creole as a native speaker as well as on moral philosophy paradigms, I want to focus on the semantic dimension of "moun" in the Caribbean and underline other examples of epistemic and metaphysical paradigms springing from African epistemes.

Again, the significance of the inscription of the Africans' response through the form of a product of the mind—a thought process leading to critical thought—a conviction and an ethics, is to be measured in relation to the enslaver's discourse and definition of the African. It is not because the enslaver's speech and their ability to make it effective are more powerful and dominant that no African precepts exist and operate in that domain of ontology and axiology. For the enslaver, the African is a "meuble" and a "corps" or "kò"—"body"—in Creole. But a Creole saying inherited from plantationed Africans asserts that, "Sé lèspri kò ki mèt kò"—it is the mind of the body that is the master of the body.[42] The frequency of this saying in appropriate contexts today reveals not only its relevance in the paradigm of thought but also its guiding impulse for everyday actions and decision-making processes as these relate to convictions regarding individual freedom and personhood. The

predominance granted to the mind over the body does not erase the importance of the body but places it in a locus where its seizure does not affect
what is supreme: the mind and its freedom to determine individual actions as
it pleases. The importance of this conviction is exacerbated with the fact of
the constant violent manipulation of the African body at the time of enslavement. "Moun" therefore, that is, the human person, is his or her mind. This is
to be understood with the additional thought that "moun," the person, is also
thought to be a "kadav doubout" as affirmed in, "moun sé kadav doubout"—
we, humans, are corpses standing up. Here, the finitude of the human person's life is what is invoked as a corporeal object which will inevitably be
depleted of its "fòs"—force, strength—and die. "Moun sé kadav doubout"
is a statement on existence and the (moral) choices the human person must
make in front of this existential reality. Marbot underlines that among the
enslaved, "On dit cadave (cadavre) en parlant du corps même animé"—
"They say corpse to talk about the living body."[43] Their consciousness about
the particularities of the body and syllogistically, of the mind, is acute and
circles back to the concept and practice of "moun," that is, what one believes
a human person to be. For the term "moun" is not deprived of substance and
of a consensual meaning. This is shown through a response that is systematically made when one questions the actions of another person and is answered
with yet another question: "É ben, i pa moun?"—"excuse me? Is he/she not
a human person?" or, "Sa i yé? i pa moun?"—"what is he/she? Is he/she
not a human person?" The question is a reminder of the category in which
the person questioned finds themselves, a category which according to this
paradigm of thought is human and as such should make this person neither
more nor less than another. It also explains their behavior, whether proper or
unbecoming. This leads directly to the thought that "tout moun sé moun"—all
human beings are human beings because they are human beings or "all people
are people."[44] Apart from the notion of equality this thought puts forth, it
insists on the category from which the person is seen and therefore thought
through and of. In other words, the question means: "what other behavior can
one expect from a human person if not a human behavior, good or bad?" It is
implied that one should not be surprised by the action questioned. Through
this transpires the fact that one possesses sure knowledge and conviction of
what the human person is. It also means that the integrity of the person as a
human is preserved even though one might decry their integrity as a (social)
individual carrying questionable values. This person may be judged as a bad
social person with a poor morality and lose their social standing, but not the
humanity making them human.

   Actually, "moun"—people—have according to their "fòs"—force—the
set of interior factors that determine them. The Creole word "fòs" springs
from the French "force" and means either force or strength and refers to

intrinsic and mental capacity and individual identity. Springing from a French term, "fòs" is invested with the Congo "muntu" epistemology and metaphysics.[45] The word often appears as a statement, "Sé wou ki konnèt fòs-ou"—You are the one who knows your force—or a question, "ki fòs ou?"—what type of person are you? Who are you? Tell me what is inside of you that gives you the capacity to be you? This question can be asked as a plaisanterie or very solemnly and seriously when two persons are engaged in a transaction and one leaves the other the choice to determine how they will behave toward a given phenomenon and determine the relation paradigm. This is a challenge and a tacit request for an axiological positioning, implying that the parties' relation paradigm should be based on an ethics that the challenged party must clarify. It is in the clarification of the ethics set for the transaction that the said party's identity will be revealed. It is also implied that, human comportment and individuals' identity depending on their sense of responsibility and determining whether their "fòs" exercises ethics or not, they must choose judiciously. Here, identity is largely a function of ethics. In particular, "ki fòs-ou?" can mean "Are you able to do this?" or "Show who you are, how your actions are going to unveil what animates you and who you are intrinsically?" "Your actions" stands for "what you have inside," in other words, your values. All of that is "fòs," that is, what makes the person who they are. Fòs is evidently comprehended as existing within the person in different degrees hence the question "ki fòs-ou?" It is also acknowledged that not all persons share the same fòs and subjectivity is centered.

Another context in which "fòs" appears in the thought process that indicates a perspective on human identity is in "plis fòs"—more force—a departing salutation bestowed upon those whom one leaves. It means "good bye." This "good bye" is a wish; what you send your party away with is the wish to see their "fòs" become stronger.[46] "Plis fos" in this context means, "I wish that what animates you grows and becomes stronger until we meet again." Very interestingly, Théodore Theuws comments on a Congo analogy from which this Creole episteme may be springing: "En saluant on se souhaite la force: *Wakomapo*, que tu sois fort! . . . En faisant ses adieux à un enfant, l'aïeul dit: *Enda biyampe, ukakoma,* vas bien, tu seras fort!"[47] "As greetings, one wishes force to one another: *Wakomapo*, may you be force! . . . Saying good bye to their grandchild, the grandfather says: *Enda biyamoe, ukakoma,* go, you will be force!"

In that they constitute epistemological pillars of the way Haitians, Guadeloupeans, and Martinicans may envision themselves in the world as evidenced by the systematic recourse to "moun" and "plis fòs" in fundamental aspects of the quotidian that engage ethical positioning, these two dimensions of Caribbean thought and episteme should draw attention to the extent of the African influence in America and the place and contribution of African

Caribbean critical thought systems and discourses in the thought systems of the world.

"Moun" and "Fòs" show how enslaved Africans and their offspring are at work philosophically, metaphysically, in a domain that is not visible, to promote an *idea* and *vision* of the human person in America that would ensure the *human* existence of that said person, that is, an existence defined by what elevates, dignifies, and builds instead of what diminishes what is human. In America, Africans did not simply accomplish the forced monetary and material erection of individuals and countries in America and outside of America. Facing the a-human ideologies and practices of the enslaving party, they made, for the New World and the larger world, a philosophical and ethical *proposition* that concerns the very nature and fate of the human person and consequently, of humankind and its humanity in the aforementioned worlds. They formulated and anchored in language for thought and praxis, structuring epistemic values that can allow us to envisage an ethical way of conceiving of and experiencing *moun*, the human person, in all geographies and temporalities, past, present, and future.

NOTES

1. Hanétha Vété-Congolo, "Caribbean Interorality: A Brief Introduction," in *The Caribbean Oral Tradition: Literature, Performance, and Practice*, ed. Hanétha Vété-Congolo (Switzerland: Palgrave MacMillan, 2016), 2.

2. My translation of: "Car l'antre du bateau négrier est l'endroit et le moment où les langues africaines disparaissent, parce qu'on ne mettait jamais ensemble dans le bateau négrier, tout comme dans les plantations, des gens qui parlaient la même langue. L'être se retrouvait dépouillé de toutes sortes d'éléments de sa vie quotidienne, et surtout de sa langue." Édouard Glissant, *Introduction à une poétique du divers* (Paris: Gallimard, 1996), 16.

3. Especially by pundits of creolization.

4. My translation of: "A celles de mes jolies compatriotes qui n'ont pas oublié le doux parler de notre enfance." All subsequent translations of *Les Bambous* are mine.

5. François-Achille Marbot, *Les Bambous: Fables de la Fontaine travesties en patois créole par un vieux commandeur* (Fort-Royal, Martinique: E. Ruelle & Ch. Arnaud, Imprimeurs du gouvernement, 1846), 3.

6. This word is defined further down.

7. Process of representing a person with aggressive and negative signs, symbols, and discourse.

8. A non-written language, but one to which a first published text—a poem—attests in 1757: "Liset quitté La plaine," by the Saint Domingue enslaver, Duvivier de la Mahautiere.

9. Zott toutt, nèg maîte moin, semblé:
   Moin ni conte pou moin conté

Ba zott. Faut couté yo bien,
Si zott vlé sauvé chagrin.
Ça moin ka dit zott couté
C'est bagage faite pou béké.
Nhomme qui, les autt-fois, fè ça
Pas té yon péchè couquia
Ni yon mangè macriau,
C'était yon nhomme com i faut
Yo té crié Lafontaine.
(. . .)
Com, grace a Dié! moin savé li
Vini oti Zott pou dit
Tout ça moin trouvé ladans
Pou empêché zott méchans.
Si dans khé zott éa rété
Zott pas ka lé si mauvais:
(. . .)
Toutt mauvais nég tini soin
Fè, pou baille maîte yo tintoin.
Zott va voué, tout clè com jou
Moune malhéré tout-patout.
Combien zott doué prend patience:
Piss dans Guinein com en France
Toutt chritien, yo ka souffri
Com si yo té race maudit!
(. . .)
Nèg, béké, toutt doué souffri:
(. . .)
C'est moyen pou nous rendi
Quand nous mò dans Paradis
Marbot, *Les Bambous,* 10–11.

10. Marbot, *Les Bambous,* 10, 11. "boué tafia, marron dans bois. Fè sòcié avec quinbois. Empouésonnein bèf béké/Mangé tè, /Fè toutt métié."

11. Marbot, *Les Bambous,* 127–137.

12. "Un *philosophe* est un beau-parleur, un homme qui affecte de se montrer au-dessus de sa condition." Marbot, *Les Bambous,* 134.

13. "tout de feu pour les intérêts des Colons" Marbot, *Les Bambous,* 4.

14. Baudry des Lozières, *Second voyage à la Louisiane*, vol 2. *Dictionnaire ou Vocabulaire Congo* (Paris: Charles, 1803), 72. All translations into English of des Lozières's French and Creole are mine.

15. Baudry des Lozières, *Second voyage à la Louisiane*, vol 2. *Dictionnaire ou Vocabulaire Congo* (Paris: Charles, 1803), 74.

16. ". . . sachez lui parler, vous l'égayez, vous lui inspirez de la confiance . . . et bientôt il ne voit plus en vous qu'un homme supérieur à lui, qu'un bienfaiteur

. . ." Baudry des Lozières, *Second voyage à la Louisiane*, vol 2. *Dictionnaire ou Vocabulaire Congo* (Paris: Charles, 1803), 73.

17. Cet ouvrage . . . a été principalement fait pour les planteurs des Colonies. La plupart achètent des nègres, et ils n'en connaissent pas le langage. De là une partie des inconvénients qui leur en font perdre autant. Ces malheureux esclaves périssent souvent peu de temps après leur arrivée, parce qu'ils ne peuvent pas se faire comprendre. Etant planteur moi-même, j'ai senti l'utilité de cette espèce de science, et dans mes moments de loisir je m'y suis livré. Je n'ai cherché à en savoir assez que pour entendre mes bossals et en être entendu. Rien n'est plus triste que le nègre pris à bord . . . mais sachez lui parler et vous l'égayer, vous lui inspirez de la confiance. Son espérance naît, . . . et bientôt il ne voit plus en vous qu'un homme supérieur à lui, qu'un bienfaiteur qui l'arrache à la mort, à la misère et à la dégradation d'homme. Ainsi l'on verra qu'un Colon sait faire un ouvrage philanthropique. . . . Ce Dictionnaire ou ce Vocabulaire est encore d'une grande utilité (*) pour les médecins, pour les chirurgiens qui ne peuvent que traiter mal les nègres nouveaux, s'ils ne sont pas en état de leur faire des questions. . . . Le hasard m'a laissé quelques notes sur le langage des Congos; ces notes, remettant ma mémoire sur la voie, me permettent de composer un Vocabulaire assez complet. Baudry des Lozières, *Second voyage à la Louisiane*, vol 2. *Dictionnaire ou Vocabulaire Congo* (Paris: Charles, 1803), 72–75.

18. Baudry des Lozières, *Second voyage à la Louisiane*, vol 2. *Dictionnaire ou Vocabulaire Congo* (Paris: Charles, 1803), 73.

19. Baudry des Lozières, *Second voyage à la Louisiane*, vol 2. *Dictionnaire ou Vocabulaire Congo* (Paris: Charles, 1803), 120.

20. Des Lozières, *Vocabulaire Congo,* 124.

21. Des Lozières, *Vocabulaire Congo*, 130, 137, 122.

22. Des Lozières, *Vocabulaire Congo,* 129.

23. Des Lozières, *Vocabulaire Congo*, 130, 109, 137.

24. Des Lozières claims to have lost the manuscript he was preparing—"Encyclopédie coloniale" in the midst of the Revolution and to be reconstituting this dictionary from memory. Perhaps he has forgotten the Congo phrase for "bad person." However, he also claims that his dictionary reconstituted out of his memory is fairly "complete."

25. In addition to being the place where Africans were held captive against their will, the slave ship holds were a place where diseases spread systematically.

26. Des Lozières, *Vocabulaire Congo*, 111.

27. Des Lozières, *Vocabulaire Congo*, 135.

28. Des Lozières, *Vocabulaire Congo*, 122, 128. Des Lozières writes, "habillez-vous, vous êtes indécemment?" using an adverb instead of an adjective but this may be a mistake, the adverb not making sense here.

29. Originally published in Flemish.

30. My translation of:

La force est inséparablement liée à l'être et c'est pourquoi ces deux notions demeurent liées dans leur définition de l'être. Ceci doit être reçu comme base de la philosophie bantoue. C'est un minimum qu'il faut admettre, sous peine de ne pas comprendre les Bantous. Ainsi les Bantous auraient une notion composée de l'être que l'on pourrait formuler : l'être est ce qui possède la force . . . pour le Bantou . . . L'être est force, la force est être.

Notre notion d'être est "ce qui EST," la leur "la force qui est." La où nous pensons le concept "être," eux se servent du concept "force." R. P. Placide Tempels, "L'être est force: Extraits de 'La philosophie bantoue'." *Présence Africaine* no. 7 (1949): 249.

31. My translation of: "selon l'ontologie bantoue, l'homme est le centre de l'univers créé. Le 'muntu', sa force vitale est la merveille de la création divine. La vie est un don de Dieu. Toute science n'est autre que force vitale, force de l'esprit qui pénètre la nature intérieure des êtres. La force vitale humaine est l'élément d'ordre dans la multiplicité des êtres. Cet ordre ontologique émane du 'muntu.' La norme ontologique aussi bien qu'éthique du Bien et du Mal est la force vitale." R. P. Placide Tempels, "L'étude des langues bantoues à la lumière de la philosophie bantoue." *Présence Africaine*, no. 5 (1948): 757–758.

32. "Toute force peut se renforcer ou s'affaiblir. C'est-à-dire tout être peut devenir plus fort ou plus faible." Tempels, "L'être est force," 250.

33. My translation of: "Ceci dit, il faut admettre également que par une étude directe et globale de ce document vivant, le Noir et sa façon de vivre, on peut arriver à pénétrer son âme, à l'assimiler. Cette assimilation, suffisamment poussée, permettrait de comprendre immédiatement, d'une manière éclatante, toutes ses pratiques religieuses et magiques, son organisation politique, sa vie de clan, sa morale, son droit et même sa langue." Tempels, "L'étude des langues bantoues," 756.

34. Tempels, "L'étude des langues bantoues," 756.

35. Souleymane Bachir Diagne, *The Ink of the Scholars: Reflections on Philosophy in Africa,* trans. Jonathan Adjemian (Senegal: CODESRIA, 2016), 10–11.

36. Des Lozières, *Vocabulaire Congo*, 134.

37. Marbot, *Les Bambous*, 11; Louis-Élie Moreau de Saint-Méry, *Description topographique et politique de la partie espagnole de l'isle Saint-Domingue avec des observations générales sur le climat, la population, les productions le caractère et les mœurs des habitants de cette de cette colonie et un tableau raisonné des différentes parties de son administration accompagné d'une nouvelle carte de la totalité de l'Isle*, Vol 2 (Philadelphie, 1796), 57.

38. Both pronunciations exist; that is, "montu" and "muntu."

39. Hanétha Vété-Congolo, "Caribbean French-African Creole and African Metaphysics," in *Tracing Language Movement in Africa,* ed. Ericka A. Albaugh and Kathryn M. de Luna (UK: Oxford University Press, 2018), 365–386.

40. This will be the subject of a subsequent research of mine.

41. Of course, I do not forget that the translation is mediated by an enslaver whose gaze, level of understanding, and intention are motivated by a racist outcome. I apply prudence in the analysis and its conclusions.

42. I am using Martinique as an example.

43. Marbot, *Les Bambous,* 132.

44. Vété-Congolo, "Caribbean French-African Creole and African Metaphysics," 365–386.

45. My intention here is to introduce "fòs" in its relation to "moun" and not to offer an extensive account of its metaphysical meaning in the French African Caribbean world. I am devoting a long study to this notion soon to be published.

Hanétha Vété-Congolo

46. Perhaps this needs to be considered with the Jamaica reggae/dance hall values enunciated with "big up."
47. Théodore Theuws, "Philosophie Bantoue et Philosophie Occidentale." *Civilisations* 1, no. 3 (1951): 56.

BIBLIOGRAPHY

Des Lozières, Baudry. *Second voyage à la Louisiane,* vol 2 *(Dictionnaire ou Vocabulaire Congo)* (Paris: Charles, 1803): 72–146.
Diagne, Souleymane Bachir. *The Ink of the Scholars: Reflections on Philosophy in Africa.* Translated from French by Jonathan Adjemian (Senegal: CODESRIA, 2016).
Glissant, Édouard. *Introduction à une poétique du divers* (Paris: Gallimard, 1996).
Marbot, François-Achille. *Les Bambous: Fables de la Fontaine travesties en patois créole par un vieux commandeur* (Fort-Royal, Martinique: E. Ruelle & Ch. Arnaud, Imprimeurs du gouvernement, 1846).
Moreau de Saint-Méry, Louis-Élie. *Description topographique et politique de la partie espagnole de l'Isle Saint-Domingue avec des observations générales sur le climat, la population, les productions, le caractère et les mœurs des habitants de cette colonie et un tableau raisonné des différentes parties de son administration accompagné d'une nouvelle carte de la totalité de l'Isle.* Vol 2 (Philadelphie, 1796).
Tempels R. P. Placide. a. "L'étude des langues bantoues à la lumière de la philosophie bantoue." *Présence Africaine,* no. 5 (1948): 755–760.
———. b. "L'être est force: Extraits de 'La philosophie bantoue'." *Présence Africaine* no. 7 (1949): 249–251.
Theuws, Théodore. "Philosophie Bantoue et Philosophie Occidentale." *Civilisations* 1, no. 3 (1951): 54–63.
Vété-Congolo, Hanétha. "Caribbean Interorality: A Brief Introduction." In *The Caribbean Oral Tradition: Literature, Performance, and Practice.* Edited by Hanétha Vété-Congolo. (Switzerland: Palgrave MacMillan, 2016).
———. "Caribbean French-African Creole and African Metaphysics." In *Tracing Language Movement in Africa.* Edited by Ericka A. Albaugh and Kathryn M. de Luna (UK: Oxford University Press, 2018): 366–386.

Chapter 9

Nelson Mandela and the Topology of African Encounter with the World

Chielozona Eze

Perceptive African philosophers have decried the state of philosophy or critical thinking in Africa with moving metaphors.* For example, V. Y. Mudimbe compares the situation of the African elite to a person "trapped in an elevator that perpetually goes up and down."[1] Mudimbe's observation, made in the mid-twentieth century, applies with little qualification in the twenty-first. In the assumption that the world has yet to understand the real Africa, African intellection is largely engaged with explaining Africa to the world. Cameroonian philosopher Jean Godefroy Bidima captures the dilemma of the African elite today, which is the elite's critique of Africa's violent encounters with the West, and the subsequent uses of this critique as its own source of power as Africa's mouthpiece. "'Postcolonialism' has become a commodity to be marketed and sold," he writes. "In the North American higher education machine, it serves as an alibi, sometimes blurring the boundaries between critique and resentment, and absolving the failures of an unjust social system" in Africa.[2]

Philosophy, understood as a quest for wisdom or an articulation of a people's attitude to reality, is old in Africa—every ethnicity has its own form of quest. As a rigorous academic discipline, however, it is relatively young, and, as Dismas Masolo has aptly captured in his book, it is yet in search of identity.[3] Having gone through debates ranging from the validity of ethnophilosophy to various articulations of African nationalism as resistance to Western epistemic framing of Africa, philosophy in Africa had been, with a few negligible exceptions, concerned with refuting Western (mis)conceptions of Africa. In a way, therefore, Africa is still answering questions raised in European capitals in the nineteenth century. What is produced in the process is nothing short of litigation discourse, whose goal is not to explore the human condition, but rather to indict the assumed interlocutor and to invent what is believed to have been denied: the authentic Africa. Thus, discourse in or about Africa circles the same old issue of encounters with the West, like an unending carousel (Mudimbe's elevator!). In this carousel, the West must retain its imperial identity, because that is precisely where the African elite derives its moral and intellectual legitimation. Ironically, the West is the implicit audience of such discourse—even when it purports to be educating Africa, as Chinua Achebe claimed about his novel, *Things Fall Apart*.[4]

Indeed, because much of African encounter with the world is still dictated by the need to answer questions raised in Western capitals, Africans know more about what the West thinks about Africa than what Africans think about themselves; they know what Africans are to the West more than they know what Africans are to one another. This critique of the West dispenses with recognizable introspection on the part of the African elite—and as Bidima argues, without going to the root of things and observing "how symbols are produced and the threads of dependence that bind us,"[5] Africa might not exit the circuitous discourse that is anchored in the judgment of the past and sanctimonious disbursement of responsibility to the West.[6]

Whereas the twentieth century presented the African elite with an urgent task of political and intellectual liberation, which required them to write back to the center—and justifiably so—the twenty-first century has exposed a new set of challenges. The most outstanding is the absence of the conditions for the practice of justice. The challenge is that of survival and human flourishing in Africa, as it is in every part of the world today. The new global order, which includes increased migration and ease of (mis)communication and physical and cultural interaction with the world, poses another challenge. Thus, although there might have been some merit in phrases such as "African solutions for African problems," such an attitude today is not only contradictory but also self-defeatist. Africa must encounter the world anew and with a radically different paradigm. But every true encounter with the world begins with oneself; hence Bidima's insistence that self-reflection is the only thing that can "cut the fuse" of African "powder-keg."[7] I read this metaphor as an urgent plea for Africa to recalibrate its modality of encounter with self and the world, and its attitude to history.

Mudimbe's metaphor of the African elite trapped in an elevator is certainly not unique to Africa. It can be applied to all cultures, and perhaps civilizations, that enter into intermittent periods of comatose existence until a genius among them lights a spark of change—or until it is conquered (colonized) by other civilizations. Mudimbe wonders why the elite does not understand that the initiative to escape belongs to them, and so provides a practical suggestion: "In principle, a single gesture would be sufficient to stop the machine, get out, and rent an apartment or a room; in sum live and experience the reality of the world."[8] I suggest that Nelson Mandela has shown the African elite how to stop the elevator, step out of it, and be the kinetic force of one's own actions in the world. In short, Mandela provides Africa new modalities for encounter with the world. In my uses of Mandela as a theoretical prism to examine the conditions of encounter, I pursue some guiding questions: How can we read Mandela as possibly initiating a new diacritical relation with history, which is best conceived as a living organism that constantly adjusts itself in the present with the relevant genetic residues of the past? How does Mandela provide lineaments for understanding Africa's existence in the world in the twenty-first century? What exactly does Mandela mean for the humanities (philosophy and literature) in Africa?[9]

To address these questions, I discuss two anecdotes about the life of Mandela and their philosophical implications for human encounter today. I then proceed with a reflection on two scenes from Africa's premier postcolonial narrative, *Things Fall Apart*, as emblematic of the African elite's engagement with Africa. I conclude with thoughts on how philosophy can help us engage a runaway world of today.

MANDELA AS A METAPHOR

The first anecdote: Mandela's most favorite of Aesop's fables has it that one day, the sun and the wind had a debate on who was the stronger. While they are disputing, a traveler passes along the road, wrapped in a cloak. The sun says: "Let us agree that he is the stronger who can strip that traveler of his cloak." The wind takes the challenge and right away blasts a cold gust against the traveler. As soon as the traveler feels the cold blast, he wraps his cloak tightly around him. The harder the wind blows, the tighter he holds the cloak to him. The wind grows angrier and blows with greater force, but all its effort is in vain. It is now the turn of the sun. It begins to shine. At first, its rays are gentle. The traveler is happy; he unties his cloak and lets it hang loosely from his shoulders. As the sun's rays grow warmer and warmer, the man takes off his cap; he finally pulls off his cloak and throws himself down in the welcome shade of a tree by the side of the road.[10]

The second anecdote: When Mandela was released from jail, he went to the Cape Town Parade, shook hands with F. W. De Klerk, and addressed a large crowd, calling on all South Africans to start working for peace and reconciliation.[11] It was one of his many handshakes that went round the world and reassured the nervous nation that the future held better promises. He was called a "man of many handshakes."[12] With the handshake, he set the tone for reconciliation and its legendary notion of forgiveness. Enfolded in Mandela's gesture of handshake is the notion of forgiveness with which he had become closely associated, and which I address shortly. He forgave his torturers and consequently appealed to his fellow South Africans to forge a common community by responding to the pain of others. Some of his former jailers remembered him as a friendly person.[13]

The centrality of the above Aesop's fable in Mandela's thinking can best be appreciated in the context of the long history of anticolonial struggle in Africa, of which Mandela had been an important part. Recall that he was the founder of *uMkhonto we Sizwe*, the military arm of the African National Congress (ANC). He had thus subscribed to Frantz Fanon's revolutionary violence as a means of liberating his people, and he owed no one apologies for that. The postapartheid period, however, brings a new set of questions, the most central of which is: how do we enhance human well-being in the country? Mandela asks through Aesop: how do we coax goodwill and cooperation from all South Africans so as to rebuild a nation torn apart by hatred and racial violence? This question is obviously rooted in the urgency of the moment in relation to the life of the people, but even more particularly, the survivability of South Africa as a political entity. This required that Mandela jettison ideology, and, as Martha Nussbaum has read, exercise practical wisdom. Mandela, she argues, has demonstrated that the most important task in dealing with the other party is to get it "to work with you rather than against you. Progress is impeded by the other party's defensiveness and anxious self-promotion."[14] Hence the wisdom of the sun is getting the wayfarer to do the sun's will without the wayfarer knowing it—and even if he knew, he still complied because doing so was in his self-interest.

If we apply the above anecdotes to the African condition and Africa's relation to the larger world, one wonders what is more consequential to Africa as a place of human flourishing: to litigate the West with the goal of proving its culpability in the African condition or to encounter it with the goal of enhancing a better life for all? Judging from the history of postcolonial African discourse, it is difficult, if not impossible, to engage in both; one cannot encounter the world one seeks to indict. One cannot even encounter oneself if one possesses the mind-set that only judges and condemns the other.

My use of encounter relies heavily on Martin Buber's exploration of the same. Buber states that all actual life is encounter between humans. I understand that Buber modeled his notion of human relation on that between humans and God. I read him not in a religious, but rather in a purely phenomenological (existential) sense of openness to being. Buber differentiates between experience and relation; we experience the world of things, but we stand in relation to the world of humans. Relation is not a one-way attitude; it is reciprocity, which recognizes the other as an end rather than a means to an end. Experience is "remoteness from you," but relation reduces that remoteness. If the remoteness between the two individuals is nullified, there is then the possibility of encounter. It is to treat the person as if you were standing in the person's position, as if you were relating to yourself. In this encounter, the individual, 'I,' could meet the other, *You*, as "my You." The phrase "my You" seeks to present the other, who is otherwise an indifferent entity, as very close to the subjectivity of 'I' to the degree that there is no longer an estranging distance caused by abstractions such as ideology. Ideology prevents an "I" from relating to the other as "Thou"; rather, the "I" relates to the other as an "It"—a thing to be used.[15] To engage the other as "Thou" rather than an "It" is to affirm the totality of the person's being. In Alexander S. Kohanski's reading, "this relation is love, that is, I stand in relation to [the other] as a whole. If I single out any aspect of him for observation or classification, or for some use, he is no longer Thou."[16] Underlying Buber's conception of encounter is the notion that humans are not finished products; their being is not exhausted in the definition we give them. Individual humans are infinitely unknowable; they are full of possibilities, aspects of which could enrich other people's lives. This condition necessarily calls for openness in relating to them.

Aware of the colossal duty of nation-building in a society of diverse races and ethnicities, Mandela chose not to define these races and ethnicities and the individuals who identify with them; rather, adopting a cosmopolitan attitude, he chose to relate to them, to encounter them. The most obvious trope of this readiness is the handshake, a phenomenological gesture that acknowledges the facticity of the other body and all the ethical obligations it assumes. As Richard Kearney has argued in his exploration of what he called carnal hermeneutics, "the first act of civilisation was a handshake, which was already an act of hospitality by putting out an open hand rather than reaching for the sword."[17] It is the fundamental task of choosing either "hostility or hospitality."[18]

Kearney's insight into the phenomenology of the handshake gives us some working vocabularies with which to approach Mandela's philosophy. In showing an open palm rather than a clenched fist, in reaching out to shake the other, Mandela demonstrated that he was not holding anything back in terms of human relations; he was not clutching a stone. We must acknowledge that his gesture entailed some degree of risk. Indeed, in a handshake, an open palm meets another open palm in a demonstration of vulnerability.[19] The reward is, however, worth the risk. Mandela's hand reaching to shake the other's, especially De Klerk's, states resolutely: I recognize that you are present. I affirm you. Interpreted against the backdrop of Euro-modernist philosophy—or indeed, the apartheid ideology that conceived the black body and personhood as an absence (i.e., as subhuman), and therefore unworthy of being related to—Mandela establishes a new modality of encounter in South Africa. It is one rooted in a fundamental openness to the other. This, I think, is South Africa's greatest gift to the world, and which has not yet received its due attention.

Mandela's handshake is also a clever sociopolitical move, understood as
an open invitation for cooperation toward making the new nation better. It
is no secret that white people in South Africa possessed the technological
and even political know-how that the postapartheid society cannot do without. Mandela knew that the ANC and black people, having been in opposition for as long as South Africa existed, would need enough white people
of good faith to help keep the country up to par with the technologically
and democratically more developed parts of the world—a condition that
would be forfeited were black people to pursue retribution and vengeance.
To be sure, he and the Truth and Reconciliation Commission (TRC) have
been criticized for not pursuing justice in the typical Western retributive
format.[20] Despite its weaknesses, the ritual of the TRC, which he initiated
and which could be seen as an extension of his personality and political
masterstroke, marked the formal end of the oppositional conception of reality and posed the challenge of constructing universal moral frameworks for
conviviality. For one, Mandela did not waste time litigating the past—not
only because of the inherent ethical and political futility of the exercise, but
also because of the more urgent moral imperative to create a functioning
society for all.

Though Mandela is now inextricably associated with the South African
notion of forgiveness, Nussbaum notes that he never made it the centerpiece
of his philosophy. It was rather Archbishop Desmond Tutu who gave the
notion an extensive interpretation; being a Christian leader, he made the term
recognizably Christian.[21] Nussbaum rather understands Mandela as embody-
ing "generosity and forgetfulness of past wrongs."[22]

I do not intend to import Archbishop Desmond Tutu's religious interpretation of forgiveness. Nor do I rely on Jacques Derrida's famous reading.[23]
I read the South African (TRC) forgiveness in terms of generosity guided
by Mandela's larger goal of human flourishing for all—a goal which, seen
through the prism of his favorite fable, is getting South Africa to shed the
coat of hatred and to reach out hands of cooperation for nation-building. I
admit that it is possible to read the Mandelean gesture as a pure political
calculation, rather than with the often abstract moral superiority with which
the world has come to associate him. A quick answer would be that political
calculations are not inherently devoid of moral content. Much depends on
the goal in relation to the common good. Of importance here is the question
implicit in Mandela and the South African gesture: what kind of society do
we want and how best can we achieve that? Thus, the Mandela way is not
without moral force. I see him as exhibiting wisdom that every successful
leader (even parent) must possess. Of significance, especially to the state
of the discourse in Africa, is that Mandela has broken from the traditional
litigation of the West that had characterized the politics of such leaders as

Robert Mugabe, and rather initiated an age of cooperation through his richly symbolic postprison life.

Even if we understand forgiveness as generosity, it does not mean forgetting or doing away with the past. Nor does it mean leaving intact the economic status quo that keeps a majority of the black population in poverty. It also does not imply not addressing the legacies of the evils of the past. Forgiveness suggests not allowing the past to be the measuring scale of today's encounter with the world. It means encountering humans from the standpoint that takes their dignity as a given and proceeding to consider conditions that can enhance their lives, which include a pursuit of justice and fairness. Forgiveness therefore dispenses with cheap moral judgment deriving from the past in which one is cast as a victim—an implicit psychic recourse that has sustained postcolonial African discourse.

Mandela's prison guard Christo Brand, who was an eighteen-year-old man when he was sent to Robben Island in 1978 to guard Mandela, gives an account that contains some insight in relation to his philosophy of friendship and its potential political implication. Brand had been instructed that he was going to guard the most dangerous terrorists, but when he met Mandela he was surprised by the latter's friendliness. "To his surprise, Prisoner 46664, then aged 60, asked him about his family, his upbringing, his fears for the future."[24] Mr. Brand came to his job with his mind already poisoned by the typical ideological narrative of the powerful, which is to demonize the powerless. Mandela defused the narrative by taking interest in Mr. Brand's humanity; he eventually won him over with his friendship. Mandela let him know that he (the jailer) was there not because of any personal animosity toward blacks or Mandela in particular. The guard was merely doing his job. The prison guard responded in kind; he accorded Mandela preferential treatment not because of his royal heritage, but because of Mandela's humanity. He undertook to preserve Mandela's life, rather than treat him as a criminal and enemy of the state. Mr. Brand could have decided to make Mandela's life extremely difficult.

Friendship has advantages, the most obvious of which is that it not only preserves life, it makes it easier to live as well. Friendship, or true encounter, makes it easy for humans to put themselves in the shoes of others. Friendship necessarily expands our hermeneutic horizon, if only for the simple reason that it disposes one to engage with the world of others, rather than dismiss it offhandedly. Encounter allows humans to hear one another's stories; the more stories we hear, the more our imaginations expand and necessarily embrace the indisputable diversities of all the life there is. This is also the lesson learned from the ritual of TRC during which people told their stories, as Antjie Krog has eminently documented in *Country of My Skull*.[25]

Expanding one's hermeneutic horizon through encounter with others and hearing their stories often keeps one morally alert. For one, it reminds individuals that, in the same way that meaning is not generated by an individual all alone and that others have intrinsic meaning in one's life, so does one arrive at the awareness that one cannot live meaningfully without respect for the dignity and comfort of others. This sentiment hews close to the South African notion of Ubuntu—the idea that a person is a person through other persons—and which I have explained elsewhere.[26] It helps, however, to mention an instructive reading provided by South African philosopher Thaddeus Metz. For him, the Ubuntu expression is a normative account of what we ought to value in life: becoming fully human. For him, "one's ultimate goal in life should be to become a (complete) person, a (true) self or a (genuine) human being."[27] The emphasis is on becoming, and this is actuated only in a community of other persons. "One becomes a moral person insofar as one honours communal relationships."[28]

Understood within the spirit of Ubuntu, encounter suggests a compelling moral framework by the force of which all individuals who take themselves seriously bind themselves to the survival and flourishing of the community even while retaining the freedom to be individuals. The individual understands morality as a binding duty, as Harry Frankfurt states; morality in this regard is "essentially designed to put people *on* the hook. Whether or not a person adheres to the moral law is not supposed to be independent of the kind of person he is."[29] We put ourselves on the hook not because we choose to make our lives intolerable, but because our survival as humans depends on every one of us overcoming ourselves so that we can work together for the benefit of all. Seen through the prism of Mandela's philosophy of encounter, to extend the hand of friendship is to put oneself on the hook; it is simply a testament to the fact that one compels oneself to live within a given framework that takes the humanity of the partners as the starting point of the encounter.

To the degree that the offended person does not seek to extract retribution from the offender, to the degree that he or she has reached out a hand of friendship or cooperation, he or she has signaled his or her readiness to go beyond that hurt and enter into dialogue with the other. This gesture, of course, assumes a quantum of humility that is rooted in the knowledge that no single individual is ever self-sufficient or without flaws. He or she is incomplete per se and requires the presence and cooperation of others to achieve some measure of completion. He is a dependent rational being, as Alasdair MacIntyre expresses in *Dependent Rational Animals*.[30] In the same way, no culture or society is ever self-sufficient; cultures necessarily borrow or appropriate ideas (or inspiration) from others. This has been the case ever since recorded history. Every culture builds its greatness with incentives from others. The refusal to become entangled in judgment of the West in relation to the African present is, therefore, not a naïve act or a sign of weakness; it is a tactical sociopolitical move with profound ethical and existential implications. For one, it directs the mind to search for solutions and to expand the axis of friendship rather than to luxuriate in false moral rectitude.

THINGS FALL APART AND THE STRUGGLE FOR RECOGNITION

I suggested elsewhere that African literature can provide us with grounds in which to root questions about the human condition in Africa.[31] We read these narratives not as a source of ethnological knowledge about Africa, nor even in the belief that they might provide answers to ontological or ethical questions, but rather because they help us formulate questions that are autochthonous to the African condition. While the questions might sprout from the African soil, the answers need not also. I am of course not being innovative in suggesting literature as a handmaid of philosophy; literature has always preceded philosophy as a rigorous discipline. It is not an accident that Plato, the father of Western philosophy, claimed that Homer, the father of Western literature, was the supreme teacher of the Greeks. Philosophy broadly conceived is, essentially, a story.

Things Fall Apart is one of the most influential postcolonial African novels. Okonkwo is a respected leader in Umuofia who achieves his fame by defeating Amalinze, another tribe's hero, in a wrestling match. When British colonialists and missionaries invade his country, he champions strong resistance against the invaders. He commits suicide when he realizes that his clan is not willing to join his crusade against the colonial invaders. His death is ultimately thought to have conferred on him the honor of tragic heroism and is a signifier of African anticolonial resistance. The novel gave Africa its most eloquent, unifying narrative that anchored postcolonial African culture and identity in resistance to the West. Owing to the overwhelming need to address the colonial master—part of which I have already addressed above—not much attention has been paid to the contours of human encounter in Africa, especially as structured in the novel. Fundamental questions such as those that analyze the ethical assumptions of human interactions, and even the question of the conditions of justice and the dignity of individual lives in Africa, are largely ignored. If broached, the answers are packaged in a hackneyed collective ethnic chorus that yield no knowledge, such as "The Igbo notion of . . ." the "African conception of . . . ," and so on. Most responses to the novel express glowing admiration of its role in redeeming and shaping African culture.[32] My interest is in examining the image of the human as portrayed in many significant scenes, such as the fate of the members of the *osu* caste, who are considered by the Igbo to be inferior humans and are therefore segregated against in every imaginable way. What are the ethical, social, and political implications of the caste system? Did the caste system and similar feudal social cultural structures in African societies contribute to the society falling apart? Did they prevent the evolution of modern societies in the first place?

In my aforementioned essay, I discussed the depressing scene of the killing of Ikemefuna, the boy originally from Mbaino, who was taken as ransom for his people killing a woman from Umuofia, and raised in Okonkwo's household. The Umuofia oracle dictates that the boy be sacrificed; without challenging the oracle, Okonkwo leads him to the jungle where he is killed. I asked a question I believe I did not address adequately in the essay: What exactly was Ikemefuna's life to Umuofia people in general and Okonkwo in particular? I return to the killing of Ikemefuna in the conclusion, when I compare the circumstances surrounding the killing of the boy with those of Abraham's intended sacrifice of Isaac.

In his discussion of justice and otherness in Africa, Nigerian philosopher Uchenna Okeja argues that the primary condition for justice in society is the unconditional acceptance of the humanity of the other. Justice is based on deliberation, which in itself is "contingent upon the intersubjective affirmation of a basic principle, namely, the principle of humanity."[33] Recognition is the basis for justice, without which no society can function in a somewhat acceptable civil manner. Recognition from our fellow humans is essential—primarily for our self-perception as humans, and secondarily for our exercise of citizenship. Even when we are aware that we possess dignity as humans, we still need our fellows to affirm it in their relation to us. Postcolonial politics in Africa and racial politics in America have been largely about the right to recognition. The colonizers denied the colonized humanity and thus related to them in a typical Hegelian master/slave dialectic. The master does not recognize the slave because the slave does not possess self-consciousness. The same logic applies to racist societies. But the master/slave dialectic is not restricted to Western exercise of power on the colonized or racialized peoples of the world. In precolonial Africa, the same dynamics took place in the relationship between the privileged and the less privileged, between the powerful and the powerless. The same goes for sexist and patriarchal societies.

The *osu* caste system is a sociopolitical order rooted in ancient religious practices in which certain people are dedicated to deities in Igboland as *pharmakós* (scapegoats) to appease the gods. In *Things Fall Apart* an *osu* is defined as

> a person dedicated to a god, a thing set apart—a taboo forever, and his children after him. He could neither marry nor be married by the free-born. He was in

fact an outcast, living in a special area of the village, close to the Great Shrine. Wherever he went he carried with him the mark of his forbidden caste. . . . An osu could not attend an assembly of the free-born, and they, in turn, could not shelter under his roof.[34]

The descendants of those dedicated to the deities inherit their ancestors' fate in the same way that the descendants of black slaves (and indeed all blacks) in America inherited the scourge of racism. As the carriers of the communities' evils, the *osus* are regarded as *efulefu*—worthless—and are ignored by the clan not only in matters of social and political relevance but also in daily encounter. There is indeed no encounter between them and the so-called free-born. The closest analogy is the condition of blacks during the Jim Crow era. In *Things Fall Apart*, the *osus* are featured mainly in relation to the advent of the new religion. When they saw that "the new religion welcomed twins and such abominations, [they] thought that it was possible that they would also be received."[35] They were thus among the first Igbo to convert to Christianity, together with some of the women whose twin children were wrenched from them and thrown away into the jungle because the Igbo considered twins anomalous. The *osus* could, of course, not launch a revolution for recognition, or begin a civil rights movement, given their negligible numerical strength. Nor could the women mourning the senseless killing of their twins. The new religion gave to these people what the old order denied them: a sense of worth, recognition as humans, albeit supported by the colonial power.

The *osus* were not only the first people to welcome the white man and convert to Christianity. Visiting Okonkwo in his place of exile, Obierika tells him how Umuofia has changed during the seven years of his absence; the white man has established missions, and the people of Umuofia have abandoned their old ways of life. The saddest news is that Nwoye, Okonkwo's first son, has joined the missionaries. Later in their discussion, Obierika observes that the white man has "put a knife on the things that held us together, and we have fallen apart."[36] Earlier in the story, Obierika has been called the "thinker" of the tribe. It is not accidental that he pronounces the judgment on the white man as the cause of their community disintegrating. I call him the archetypal postcolonial elite. The most consequential questions we ought to ask in regard to his judgment include: why was it rather too easy for the members of the *osu* caste to join the new religion? Why could Okonkwo, who wanted to fight the colonial master, not prevent his own son from joining his religion? Why was it easy for the society to collapse even without the white man firing a shot, without any combat?

Attempts to answer these questions objectively must first issue from the perspective of the outcasts, the grieving women, and Okonkwo's son. Of course, we already know the official answer from the perspective of

Obierika—the elite of that society for whom the only cause of their falling apart was the white man's knife that was put on the *things* that held had them together. Let us begin with Nwoye, who converted to Christianity as soon as he received the opportunity. The reason for his turning his back on his father and everything he stood for was not only because he was attracted by the poetry of the new religion; he was disappointed in his father for failing to protect Ikemefuna, a boy he had begun to see as a brother. Indeed, he saw in his father someone who could possibly also kill him. Okonkwo (and the culture) could not give Nwoye something to defend or something to love—universal human values of love, justice, mercy, fairness, truth, and so on. The same could be said of the people of Umuofia about the *osus*. In the same way that Okonkwo failed to protect the life of Ikemefuna, the elite of the people failed to establish conditions for the practice of justice, or conditions that would allow these people to perceive themselves as humans.

We identify with a culture precisely because it is what or where we feel affirmed. The outcasts had nothing in common with the rest of society because there was no basis for justice: they were not recognized. For them, therefore, things did not fall apart—they never stood together in the first place. To ignore these groups' concerns is to make the mistake of relating to society in the abstract. From their perspective, it appears that the white man could not have come at a more auspicious time; the white man's arrival was therefore a gesture of liberation. They formed a new society to protect their lives and to live with dignity. It appears, however, that the situation had not much to do with the white man per se. If the Chinese had arrived at the time the Europeans came and had offered the outcasts the requisite recognition, they would still have abandoned the old order. Strictly speaking, therefore, things fell apart for the privileged members of society who lost the power to control the narratives in that society.

To be sure, I do not dismiss the specificity of European imperial power. But Umuofia fell apart not only because of the colonialists' gunboats, but precisely because there were fissures in society that prevented a certain degree of cohesion and moral framework. There were scant grounds for an enriching human encounter. This is surely not peculiar to Africa. Despite his excesses, Napoleon Bonaparte is still lauded in many parts of Europe for having liberated them from the last clutches of feudalism over two hundred years ago.

In many ways, we might take *Things Fall Apart* as a cautionary tale for every society in which a section of the populace is denied recognition because of their phenotypical, anatomical, religious, or cultural difference to the normative group. This, I think, is a plausible interpretation and a line of serious intellectual inquiry. Sadly, though, the overwhelming need to litigate the white man, who, according to Obierika, "put a knife on the things that held us together," has overshadowed the need to engage in creative thought that would enhance conditions for better human encounter. There are two possibilities regarding Obierika, representative of the elite of his people: either he is not being honest, or he had a severely limited moral imagination. It is for the same reason that postcolonial discourse is an elite discourse among Africans or people from the formerly colonized world who now reside in the West.[37] To be sure, all this is not to ignore the violence of the colonial encounter. But after Mandela, philosophy in Africa can no longer crawl back into the cave of blind and abstract speculation.

MANDELA IN THE WORLD, OR HOW TO PHILOSOPHIZE LIKE AESOP

I return to the killing of Ikemefuna, one of the most disturbing scenes in *Things Fall Apart*. For a proper ethical and perhaps political reading of the scene, I propose what I call the Rawlsian test for the judgment of the African condition—indeed, the condition of every modern society. John Rawls's thought experiment is a hypothetical condition called the original position, or more popularly, the veil of ignorance, and which I paraphrase here in particular regard to two stories of human sacrifice ordered by Oracles: Abraham's intended sacrifice of Isaac, and Okonkwo's killing of Ikemefuna—and also in regard to the *osu* caste system: Imagine you were an embryo, unaware of which society you will be born in; you were asked to choose between an Isaac society and an Ikemefuna society. You would most likely wish to be born into a society that finds a way to save a life rather than vanquish it in the name of faithfulness to an oracle. Another version: which kind of society would you like to be born in if you did not know in which condition of health or ability you would be born—the one that respects the dignity and difference of every individual, or one that regards difference and disability as a nuisance and anomalous? Since there is always the "possibility that you might be one of the disabled members of society, you would be compelled to choose principles that extend justice to the disabled."[38] We would rather choose to be born in societies that not only have a place for people with disabilities, but also help them to live to their utmost capability. However, since we are all born into imperfect societies, and given that we might be privileged to not be born with disability or not to belong to those traditionally excluded from power, the greater and nobler task is how to create societies in which all lives can be appreciated and helped in their pursuit of happiness. The nobler task is to create a condition for the practice of justice. This, I think, is the most urgent challenge facing African elites. It is the challenge of asking Aesopian questions: what is the best way to enhance human flourishing in Africa? The lesson from Mandela suggests that it is more rewarding for the dignity of black people and for the pursuit of well-being to extend an open hand to the world rather than indulge in extracting guilt from it for colonialism and racism.

Knowing what a leader (elite) wants to achieve often dictates how he or she goes about it. As simple as the above truism is, it does seem that much of postcolonial philosophizing in Africa has yet to catch up with that. Mandela might have picked this obvious principle from the simplicity and profundity of Aesop's fable, in addition to his native intelligence and wisdom. In practical terms, this Aesopian wisdom consists of not letting his eyes off the more encompassing goal of creating a better society. If creating a better society that fulfills human encounter and well-being is the ultimate prize African elites can win for not obsessing over the evils of the West, then it is worth following the South African (TRC) example. Mandela's undisguised effort to learn from all sectors of South African society must be seen as a sign of political strength rather than of weakness. His generosity toward his former jailers and his refusal to condemn them is nothing short of moral and political ingenuity.

The Euro-modernist construction of the world, which we identify as the culprit of much of the world's problems today, was characteristically devoid of self-reflection and humility. Mandela turned it upside down with his cosmopolitan moral compass. He therefore set the frames for new encounter in the emergent democratic society, and for the world: Encountering others in mutually enriching ways might indeed be the only thing that saves the world, in which all lives are now inescapably interconnected physically and virtually. The outbreak of COVID-19 is just a sad, yet apt example of how interconnected the world has become and, therefore, can only survive by recognizing the mutuality of interest and dependence.

*This paper benefitted from suggestions by Dr. Oritsegbubemi Anthony Oyowe. I am so grateful.

NOTES

1. Cited in Bennetta Jules-Rosette, "Speaking About Hidden Times: The Anthropology of V. Y. Mudimbe," *Callaloo* 14, no. 4 (Autumn 1991): 948.

2. Jean Godefroy Bidima, "Staging Africa: The warning and the promise," https://www.eurozine.com/staging-africa/.

3. Dismas Masolo, *African Philosophy in Search of Identity* (Bloomington, IN: Indiana University Press, 1994).

4. Chinua Achebe, *Things Fall Apart* (Portsmouth: Heinemann, 1958). To be sure, the issue is not just with litigating the past, or that critiquing the past is to be discouraged; it is that the critique of colonial subjection has formed the basis of postcolonial African thought—the result of which is that Africa has failed to enhance knowledge of self, except to the degree that it is seen as a victim of history. As much

as it is important to critique domination, it is even more expedient to invest in ethics, in ways we can rebuild just communities.

5. Bidima, "Staging Africa."

6. What is said about the condition of the African elite goes for postcolonial African political leaders, from Mobutu Sese Seko, to Robert Mugabe, and even to Yoweri Museveni of Uganda—all start out with a critique of the West, proceed to make themselves life-presidents, and end up impoverishing their people.

7. Bidima, "Staging Africa."

8. Bennetta Jules-Rosette, "Speaking About Hidden Times," 948.

9. I am aware that some South Africans do not see Mandela as a hero. I recognize the concerns of the younger generation of South Africans about the present social and economic inequality. Some of them see in Mandela not a savior, but rather a sellout. Some expected Marxist economic policies that would have nationalized everything. It is true that Mandela's government was not perfect, but calling him a sellout is a stretch.

10. This is a paraphrasing of the story as rendered in Martha C. Nussbaum, *Anger and Forgiveness: Resentment, Generosity, Justice* (New York: Oxford University Press, 2016), 229.

11. Frederik Van Zyl Slabbert, "Truth without Reconciliation, Reconciliation without Truth," in *After the TRC: Reflections on Truth and Reconciliation in South Africa,* ed. Wilmot James and Linda Van De Vijver (Athens: Ohio University Press, 2001): 62.

12. Tom Cohen, "Nelson Mandela: Man of many handshakes." https://www.cnn.com/2013/12/05/world/africa/nelson-mandela-handshakes/index.html.

13. Alex Perry, "Mandela's Jailer: 'He Was My Prisoner, But He Was My Father'" https://world.time.com/2013/12/06/mandelas-jailer-he-was-my-prisoner-but-he-was-my-father/.

14. Nussbaum, *Anger and Forgiveness*, 230.

15. Martin Buber, *I and Thou* (New York: Simon & Schuster, [1923] 1970), 60–62.

16. Alexander S. Kohanski, *An Analytical Interpretation of Marin Buber's I and Thou* (New York: Barron's Educational Series, Inc. 1975), 49.

17. B. O'Rourke, "Intercultural Encounters as Hospitality. An Interview with Richard Kearney," *Journal of Virtual Exchange* 1 (2018): 33. Research-publishing.net. https://doi.org/10.14705/rpnet.2018.jve.2.

18. Richard Kearney, "The Wager of Carnal Hermeneutics," in *Carnal Hermeneutics*, ed. Richard Kearney and Brian Treanor (New York: Fordham University Press, 2015), 17.

19. At least since the COVID-19 pandemic we now know that an ordinary handshake can lead to life-threatening infection.

20. Archbishop Desmond Tutu has provided a fitting defense of the TRC and South African restorative justice. See Desmond Tutu, *No Future without Forgiveness* (New York: Image Doubleday, 1999).

21. Nussbaum, *Anger and Forgiveness*, 242.

22. Nussbaum, *Anger and Forgiveness*, 235.

23. Jacques Derrida, *On Cosmopolitanism and Forgiveness,* trans. Mark Dooley and Michael Hughes (New York: Routledge, 2001).

24. Alex Perry, "Mandela's Jailer: 'He Was My Prisoner, But He Was My Father.'"

25. Antjie Krog, *Country of My Skull* (New York: Three Rivers Press, 1998).

26. Chielozona Eze, *Race, Decolonization, and Global Citizenship in South Africa* (New York: University of Rochester Press, 2018).

27. Thaddeus Metz, "Ubuntu as a Moral Theory and Human Rights in South Africa," *African Human Rights Law Journal* 11, no. 2 (2011): 537.

28. Metz, "Ubuntu as a Moral Theory," 547.

29. Harry Frankfurt, *Taking Ourselves Seriously* (Stanford: Stanford University Press, 2006), 22.

30. Alasdair MacIntyre, *Dependent Rational Animals: Why Human Beings Need the Virtues* (Chicago: Open Court, 2001).

31. Chielozona Eze, "African Literature as a Handmaid of African Philosophy," in *African Philosophical and Literary Possibilities: Re-reading the Canon*, ed. by Aretha Phiri (New York: Lexington Books, 2020).

32. See, for instance, C. L. Innes and Bernth Lindfors, eds., *Critical Perspectives on Chinua Achebe* (Washington: Three Continents Press, 1978); Patrick Nnoromele, "The Plight of a Hero in Achebe's Things Fall Apart," in *Chinua Achebe's Things Fall Apart*, ed. Harold Bloom (New York: Bloom's Literary Criticism, 2010).

33. Uchenna Okeja, "Justice Through Deliberation and the Problem of Otherness," *Angelaki: Journal of the Theoretical Humanities* 24, no. 2 (2019): 10.

34. Achebe, *Things Fall Apart*, 113.

35. Achebe, *Things Fall Apart*, 113.

36. Achebe, *Things Fall Apart*, 124.

37. Arif Dirlik thinks that the term 'postcolonial' began when Third World intellectuals arrived, and made their voices heard, in First World Academe. Arif Dirlik, "The Postcolonial Aura: Third World Criticism in the Age of Global Capitalism," *Critical Inquiry* 20 (1994): 329–332.

38. I am grateful to Dr. Oritsegbubemi Anthony Oyowe for helping me to clarify this point.

BIBLIOGRAPHY

Achebe, Chinua. *Things Fall Apart* (Portsmouth: Heinemann, 1958).

Bidima, Jean Godefroy. "Staging Africa: The warning and the promise," https://www.eurozine.com/staging-africa/.

Buber, Martin. *I and Thou* (New York: Simon Schuster, [1923] 1970).

Tom Cohen, "Nelson Mandela: Man of many handshakes." https://www.cnn.com/2013/12/05/world/africa/nelson-mandela-handshakes/index.html.

Dirlik, Arif. "The Postcolonial Aura: Third World Criticism in the Age of Global Capitalism." *Critical Inquiry* 20 (1994): 329–332.

Derrida, Jacques. *On Cosmopolitanism and Forgiveness,* trans. Mark Dooley and Michael Hughes (New York: Routledge, 2001).

Eze, Chielozona. *Race, Decolonization, and Global Citizenship in South Africa* (New York: University of Rochester Press, 2018).

———. "African Literature as a Handmaid of African Philosophy," in *African Philosophical and Literary Possibilities: Re-reading the Canon*, ed. by Aretha Phiri (New York: Lexington Books, 2020).

Frankfurt, Harry. *Taking Ourselves Seriously* (Stanford: Stanford University Press, 2006).

Innes, C.L. and Bernth Lindfors, eds., *Critical perspectives on Chinua Achebe* (Washington: Three Continents Press, 1978).

Jules-Rosette, Bennetta. "Speaking About Hidden Times: The Anthropology of V. Y. Mudimbe," *Callaloo* 14, no. 4 (Autumn 1991): 944–960.

Kearney, Richard. "The Wager of Carnal Hermeneutics," in *Carnal Hermeneutics*, ed. Richard Kearney and Brian Treanor (New York: Fordham University Press, 2015).

Kohanski, Alexander S. *An Analytical Interpretation of Marin Buber's I and Thou* (New York: Barron's Educational Series, Inc., 1975).

Krog, Antjie. *Country of My Skull* (New York: Three Rivers Press, 1998).

Masolo, Dismas. *African Philosophy in Search of Identity* (Bloomington, IN: Indiana University Press, 1994).

MacIntyre, Alasdair. *Dependent Rational Animals: Why Human Beings Need the Virtues* (Chicago: Open Court, 2001).

Metz, Thaddeus. "Ubuntu as a Moral Theory and Human Rights in South Africa." *African Human Rights Law Journal* 11, no. 2 (2011).

Nnoromele, Patrick. "The Plight of a Hero in Achebe's Things Fall Apart," in *Chinua Achebe's Things Fall Apart*, ed. Harold Bloom (New York: Bloom's Literary Criticism, 2010).

Nussbaum, Martha C. *Anger and Forgiveness: Resentment, Generosity, Justice* (New York: Oxford University Press, 2016).

Okeja, Uchenna. "Justice Through Deliberation and the Problem of Otherness," *Angelaki: Journal of the Theoretical Humanities* 24, no. 2 (2019).

O'Rourke, B. "Intercultural Encounters as Hospitality. An Interview with Richard Kearney," *Journal of Virtual Exchange* 1 (2018): 33. Research-publishing.net. https://doi.org/10.14705/rpnet.2018.jve.2.

Perry, Alex. "Mandela's Jailer: 'He Was My Prisoner, But He Was My Father'" https://world.time.com/2013/12/06/mandelas-jailer-he-was-my-prisoner-but-he-was-my-father/.

Tutu, Desmond. *No Future without Forgiveness* (New York: Image Doubleday, 1999).

Van Zyl Slabbert, Frederik. "Truth without Reconciliation, Reconciliation without Truth," in *After the TRC: Reflections on Truth and Reconciliation in South Africa*, ed. Wilmot James and Linda Van De Vijver (Athens: Ohio University Press, 2001).

Conclusion

Jean Godefroy Bidima

Like Being in Aristotle, *transition* is said in many senses where African philosophies are concerned. Initially, the question of transition is *kinetic*. It arises most often in the context of seeing a transition and evaluating its speed. Speed itself has become a great preoccupation of philosophers, inasmuch as it stages the notion of "transport." In Paul Virilio's words: *"We are transports which carry and which carry away."*[1] What carries African philosophy and African philosophers away in this transition; what do they carry, and at what speed? Following from this, transition is a *matter of topology*. From (*unde?*) and toward (*quo?*) what places are we displaced? How are transitory and transitional spaces constituted? The question here is one of knowing what discursive, political, anthropological, and economic sites African philosophies have been able to mark off in order to constitute themselves, to gain consistency, and to continue in speaking and acting?

In these transitions, the relations between the formulation of these African philosophies and the *economy* are stressed less often than their connections to theology, linguistics, literature, ethnology, and politics, which have taken the upper hand. How do funding, the politics of book promotion, the imposition of new heroic and thematic figures, the intrusion of media into these philosophies' choice of words and reception, the way that some topics are "prioritized" or highlighted and what remains unsaid regarding what was "put aside" for later, the game of philosophical supply and demand, the politics of research centers in Africa, the interaction between philosophers and NGOs, and the hide and seek which such actors play with states and their policies determine the creation of such sites? How to cross over from one site to another and who plays the role of border control between locations?[2]

Transition is also a *matter of style* (*quomodo?*). How does one move around within African philosophy? Voluntarily, *motu proprio*, or involuntarily (pushed by emergencies in the domain of academics, mass media, or politics)? How do these philosophies, which in the end are nothing but discourses expressing diverse styles of individual and common life, manage various contingencies when they come into contact with events which give rise to other kinds of historical upheavals? Transition could also be a *transmission*, as one finds in a relay race. What counts in such a race is both the *contact* of the baton's passing from one hand to another, its *acceptance* by the runner who continues into the next phase, and its *speed*, which will vary from one runner to the next. How do African philosophies conjugate such acts of transmission and what relationships do they establish between contents of tradition, which are frequently out of date,[3] and the void of new appearances? What articulations are woven between stories, experiences, and their recycled bits as well as the refuse of this transmission? What misfortunes can such acts of transmission undergo? How are the contents of these African philosophies communicated? Finally, transition is an *optimistic, critical, and self-critical wager* that accompanies the becoming of things, ideas, and societies: *"Every transition begins with the conviction that things could be different. . . . Every transition begins with a wavering of ordinary convictions."*[4] "Transitional acts" will also be those that bring the question of the commons into discussion.

In Latin, *transire* means *to go beyond*, to cross over. This does not mean leaving immanence behind, but rather inscribing it in the historicity of ideas and practices. Traversing also means looking at something awry (*regarder de travers*), escaping the "homodoxy" (Plato) of thought-spectacles and the rhetoric of academic slogans. Problems related to "race" and to the "colony/postcolony" have a political and heuristic importance that must be recognized. But it remains to be demonstrated that they are the "unsurpassable horizon" of our time as claimed by Africanist and African ideologies.[5] Perhaps transition could encourage African philosophies to grow toward other horizons instead of being preoccupied uniquely with these problems. The first such horizon would involve elaborating some thoughts regarding the *commons*. It will no longer be possible to define the commons in terms of a slight "aloofness" whose psychological-political business is treated with the same legitimacy as the victim who claims claim his or her dignity, experience, and memory, but rather like the one who, on the edges and against the diversity of interests and choices, decodes and promotes the "common good."[6]

We should not decline the "commons" as a spin-off of communitarianism, which conjugates the common in a confrontation between "us" and "them," between what "they" do and what "we" do. "They" and "we" belong to one common humanity that suffers; doubts; introduces divisions, multiplications, subtractions, additions, divisions; and which also dies. The "economicist" vision of the world with its abstractions and financial speculations is perhaps authorized by a ruse, namely, to elicit an internal, symbolic, noisy, visual opposition by which each group claims its historical and ethnic interests in the violent atmosphere of opposition between "races." The never-changing constant in these cases is the *struggle of interests belonging to each sector* in the frame preconceived by capital and its metamorphoses; in other words, what remains permanent is *competition* and *consumption*. Every "race" struggles for its interests, its visibility, and its stories, like every business struggling for its own interests, its visibility/publicity, and its narratives (the gospel of profit/prosperity gospel/good news of profit). What remains unquestioned in this atmosphere is the notion of interest itself and the surpassing of this agonistic view of history.

As important as they are, "racialist" and "decolonialist" visions of the world—which are integrated into African philosophies—risk becoming a sort of theology of history if they renounce the philosophical moment of *self-reflection*. Just as Teilhard de Chardin, the Catholic theologian and philosopher, made Christ the motor of the *noosphere* (the Earth's thinking envelope) and the biosphere (the sphere of life surrounding the Earth) and consequently also the motor of evolutionary history and the only kind of lens through which the steps of world history could be deciphered, so too a vision of the world in terms of "race" and the "colony" risks constituting these as the sole motors and lenses through which African history—or indeed world history—can be viewed. In their *passages/transits*, African philosophies should take care not to let themselves be trapped in the conceptual ghetto where true critique and self-critique are set aside for the benefit of a critical spectacle, one delivered sometimes with the air and tone of a spotless prosecutor. Adorno quite rightly reminds us of the modesty that philosophical critics and prosecutors of social idiocy must assume: *"the distances that one takes with respect to the gears of the system represent a luxury that is only possible as a product of the system itself."*[7]

Transit is also a *site of waiting and of change*, a crossing over [*traversée*]. Sometimes transit is the *site for reflection*, where changes of orientation feed the very urgency with which the path is pursued. This enrichment and this new orientation are offered to African philosophies in transit toward their own reflection regarding [and by means of] *digital transitions*. How is Africa going to bring the digital revolution into line? What does this digital revolution imply about Africa's anthropological, cognitive, and political choices? How does the "fetishism of miniaturization" where communication instruments are concerned come into contact with the fetishism of traditions and of gods? How will artificial intelligence, technological conformism, and post-national narratives be articulated for the benefit of Africans? How, in this network logic that inaugurates the digital era, could the relationship between *new virtual communities* and unforeseen forms of *symbolization* be conceived?[8]

In this vein, how are processes of subjectivation and of individuation functioning? At the cultural level in which everyone is interested: *"are we dealing with a simple change of dimension and scope or are we really confronted with a true change of nature/kind?"*[9] How to reconceptualize the question of "cognitive justice" so that it would no longer be a confrontation between North and South but between those who have and those who have nothing or very little? The *ecological transition*, on the other hand, will pose African philosophies with questions regarding humanity in its fragility and its transformations. Ecology and the environment will no longer be the new faces of apocalyptic discourses (we fear the worst!), economicist discourses (save the resources of biodiversity!), or crypto-theological discourses (we must protect the goddess Nature!), but places where we are called to *question alliances* (between humans and their Other, between humans and other humans) and *consistencies* (the cult of Life, but which life? the question of labor and its transformations, etc.). The questioning of alliances will be able to explore the relations between the production and distribution of knowledge and new forms of spirituality. It will also be able to interrogate our ways of "dwelling in the world."

Finally, the *pedagogico-existential transition* of African philosophies will set them free from the academic straitjacket of well-salaried (and subsidized) philosophers and their concepts, so that the former can describe and prefigure the utopia of a life liberated from mutilations and pretenses. African philosophies will pose a "transitional act" in abolishing the division of intellectual labor that assigns places to those who speak, conceive, object, propose, cite (and are cited) and sanctions them for becoming those who listen, observe, and learn to mistrust their own symbolizations. Philosophy is "en route" (Jaspers) but could also be "attuned," even to the "world's idiocy." Calling on Walter Benjamin, Adorno made the remark that "to every respectable thought belongs a respectable portion of stupidity as well."[10]

The "transitional acts" of African philosophies with respect to the themes evoked here do not cover all the problems occupying the public sphere in Africa and elsewhere. Meanwhile, these reflections of Péguy give us something to think about: "A great philosophy is not one which pronounces definitive judgments, which installs a definitive truth. It is one which introduces a disquiet, which opens a shudder . . . a great philosophy is not one whose reasoning is invincible. It is not even one that was victorious at one time. It is one that fought in its time. And the small philosophies . . . are the ones that only pretend to fight"[11] or which fight among themselves over definitions and propositions and citations while leaving the battles of the world to others. African philosophies fight to create and to maintain exacting words and actions that will ward off the violence of warnings, fortunes, slogans, and cannons from its own heart and from those of its societies.

NOTES

1. Paul Virilo, *La pensée exposée* (Paris: Actes Sud, 2012), 244.

2. In his own era, Michel Foucault described the "discursive politics" of discourses which determine and control their rules and the procedures fated to mark out their limits, to guarantee their validity and to legitimate the exclusion of other forms of discourse. See Michel Foucault, *L'ordre du discours* (Paris, Gallimard, 1971), 37ff.

3. Walter Benjamin had apt words for this obsolescence of certain traditions and above all for the difficulty of transmitting it. He mentions Kafka's letter to his father, in which he reproached the latter for handing on nothing but his irony, his scorn, his silences, and his sarcasm. Kafka thought this explained why he lacked "*soil, air, law. To create them [therefore became] his task.*" In Franz Kafka, *Carnets*, trans. Marthe Robert (Paris: Cercle du Livre Précieux, 1957), 96. In his June 12, 1938, letter to Gerhard Scholem, Benjamin mentions the real dilemma which sometimes divides transmission between truth and transmissibility: "*He (Kafka) renounced truth for the sake of transmissibility.*" Walter Benjamin, *Correspondance, 1929–1940*, vol. 2., trans. G. Petitdemange (Paris: Editions Aubier-Montaigne, 1979), 251.

4. Pascal Chabot, *L'âge des transitions* (Paris: Éditions Aubier-Montaigne, 1979), 251.

5. It should be said somewhere that Africa existed before the colonial and postcolonial adventures and it will exist after such adventures. It is therefore reductive to only read Africa in light of the twin concepts of race and the colony/postcolony. Race, as a category for explaining African history, is blind with respect to the material culture revealed to us by archeology. The practices and symbolic acts to which ceramics and ironwork and its effects on African agriculture testify, the technologies of irrigation and iron forging, copper and the decorative arts, and wood and its many uses are entire chapters in African history which do not involve talk about "race" or the "colony/postcolony."

6. As Pierre Dardot and Christian Laval indicate, the notion of the "common" has been the object of theological, political, and philosophical reflection. One could affirm today that the destruction of nature and its biodiversity, the debt imposed on people's future, peace, and security by the machine of wealth production/reproduction and financial speculation are part of discussions to be held around this very notion of "common goods." For example,

The *common* of Latin origin resonates with the conception of the institution of the common (*koinôn*) and of "putting in common" (*koinônein*) in Aristotle. According to the Aristotelian conception, it is for the citizens who deliberate in common to determine what is appropriate for the City and what is right to do. . . . "Living together" is not, as in the case of cattle, "grazing in the same place" . . . it is "producing, through deliberation and legislation, similar morals and rules of life for all those who pursue the same goal. . . . The institution of the common (*koinôn*) is the effect of a "putting in common" which always supposes a reciprocity.

See Pierre Dardot and Christian Laval, *Commun. Essai sur la révolution au XXIe siècle* (Paris, La Découverte, 2014), 23.

7. Theodor W. Adorno, *Minima Moralia*, trans. E. Kaufhoz and J. R. Ladmiral (Paris: Editions Payot, 1980), 23. In the same vein, Edouard Glissant seems to have no confidence whatsoever in the elite of the Third World: "*As almost everywhere in the Third World, what terrifies, considering its lightness, is its assurance, its placid bad taste, its serene servility, its chronic lack of productivity.*" Edouard Glissant, *Le discours antillais* (Paris, Gallimard, 2002), 826.

8. On this subject, read Antoine Garapon and Jean Lassègue, *Justice digitale* (Paris: Presses Universitaires de France, 2018), 134 ff.

9. Rémy Rieffel, *Révolution numérique, révolution culturelle?* (Paris: Gallimard, 2014).

10. Theodor W. Adorno, *Critical Models : Interventions and Catchwords*, trans. Henry W. Pickford (New York: Columbia University Press, 2005), 134.

11. Charles Péguy, "Notes sur M. Bergson et la philosophie bergsonienne," in *Oeuvres en prose, 1909–1914* (Paris: Gallimard, 1961), 1338–1339.

BIBLIOGRAPHY

Adorno, Theodor W. *Minima Moralia*, trans. E. Kaufhoz and J. R. Ladmiral (Paris: Editions Payot, 1980).
———. *Critical Models: Interventions and Catchwords*, trans. Henry W. Pickford (Columbia University Press, 2005).
Benjamin, Walter. *Correspondance, 1929-1940*, vol. 2., trans. G. Petitdemange (Paris: Editions Aubier-Montaigne, 1979).
Chabot, Pascal. *L'age des transitions* (Paris: Éditions Aubier-Montaigne, 1979).
Dardot, Pierre and Christian Laval. *Commun. Essai sur la revolution au XXIe siècle* (Paris: La Découverte, 2014).
Foucault, Michel. *L'ordre du discours* (Paris: Gallimard, 1971).
Garapon, Antoine and Jean Lassègue: *Justice digitale* (Paris: Presses Universitaires de France, 2018).
Glissant, Edouard. *Le discours antillais* (Paris: Gallimard, 2002).
Kafka, Franz. *Carnets*, trans. Marthe Robert (Paris: Cercle du Livre Précieux, 1957).
Péguy, Charles. "Notes sur M. Bergson et la philosophie bergsonienne," in *Oeuvres en prose, 1909-1914* (Paris: Gallimard, 1961).
Rieffel, Rémy. *Révolution numérique, révolution culturelle?* (Paris: Gallimard, 2014).
Virilo, Paul. *La pensée exposée* (Paris: Actes Sud, 2012).

Index

generosity, 27, 188, 189, 196. *See also* friendship; hospitality

Geschiere, Peter, 56, 58, 64n8, 66n34

Glissant, Édouard, 89, 91, 141, 152, 167

globalization, 2, 5, 17, 91, 95–98, 100–101, 116, 184; and the arts, 55; and feminism, 6, 37, 39, 46–48

Haiti (St. Domingue), 4, 10, 91–94, 98–100, 127, 160, 162, 171–72, 177; SOHA, 78–79

handshake, 10, 11, 185, 187–88

Hegel, G. W. F., 90, 91, 94, 192

Heidegger, Martin, 126

history, 11, 56–57, 110–12, 122–23, 138–39, 191; African, 43–44, 48, 110–11; Caribbean, 91–94, 152, 171–75; and philosophy, 1–2, 10, 22, 184–86, 188–89, 203; of science, 75, 121; of slavery, 135–39. *See also* tradition

Horkheimer, Max, 97, 108

hospitality, 7, 53, 57–59, 61–63, 65, 187. *See also* generosity

Hountondji, Paulin, 125, 135

humanism(s), 6, 93, 142; and animism, 9, 141–45; and anti-humanism(s), 8, 9, 12, 89–91

humanity: denied, 167, 173, 175; of enslaved persons, 10, 154, 162, 170–75; and relationships, 19, 137, 186–87, 190; in relation to nature, 105–10, 112, 114, 123, 140, 142–45; as value, 6, 12, 94–97, 143–44, 153, 158, 169, 172–74, 176–78, 190, 192, 194

Humboldt, Wilhelm von, 73–75

ideologies: African, 186–87; Althusserian critique of, 90–91; of maternity, 20–21, 41, 43; racist, 154–56, 171–73, 178, 202

Igbo people, 39, 61, 191–93

independence, of African nations, 2, 54, 59, 92–94, 135–36, 140

individual, as concept, 17, 21–22, 25, 110, 176–77, 187, 195, 197

infertility, 26, 41–42, 61

injustice, 7, 10, 35–36, 42–43, 45–48, 92–94; cognitive, 72, 75–79, 81–82; in Haitian history, 92–94, 151–69, 171; risk of, 117

intelligence, artificial, 79, 203

Internet and social networks, 30, 203. *See also* digital world

Ivory Coast. *See* Côte d'Ivoire

Jacobins, Black, 89, 93–94

Jacotot, Joseph, 73

James, C. L. R., 89–90, 100

Jonas, Hans, 114

justice, 10, 36, 53, 56, 72, 188–89, 192, 195; and climate change, 107; conditions for, 193–95; epistemic, 12, 72, 84, 101, 112, 115, 124, 204; and recognition, 192–94. *See also* injustice

Kagame, Alexis, 170

Kant, Immanuel, 9, 57–58, 94

kinship, 7, 17, 18, 28, 38–40, 53, 55–63; and exchange, 56–57, 61. *See also* family

knowledge, 117, 124; African forms of, 28, 55–56, 71–72, 111; as capital, 75–80; decolonization of, 4, 20, 109–12, 124–25, 135–37; and ethics, 55–56, 117, 190; linked to colonization, 138–39, 161, 174; Non-Western/ Southern, 77, 80–81, 124–25, 139; positivist, 73–77; as world-system, 78–79, 84. *See also* epistemologies; research; universities

Kourouma, Ahmadou, 7, 26–27, 29

labor. *See* employment; work

Lafontaine, Jean de, 153–59

language: philosophy of, 89–92, 159, 170–78; site of social memory, 40, 173–74; and social power, 5, 7, 10,

About the Contributors

Delphine Abadie is an associate professor in the Department of Philosophy at Cheikh Anta Diop University in Dakar. She defended a dissertation in African philosophy in 2018. Her main research interests include the epistemology of decolonization and reconstruction of the philosophical canon and the development of a social and prospective philosophy for the African continent. Her interest in issues of gender justice in Africa is inevitably linked to the latter research area. She has published several articles and, with Ernest-Marie Mbonda, coedited a special issue on African philosophy for the journal *Philosophiques* (vol. 26 no. 2, Fall 2019). She is also an associate researcher at the Laboratoire des Logiques Contemporaines de la Philosophie (U. Paris 8).

Jean Godefroy Bidima earned a PhD at Université Paris I Panthéon-Sorbonne (Philosophy Department) and a Diplôme d'Etudes Approfondies in Aesthetics and Sciences of Arts (Plastic Arts Department-Université Paris I Panthéon-Sorbonne). A former visiting associate professor at Bayreuth University (Germany) and directeur de programme at the Collège International of Philosophie (Paris), he has been since 2004 full professor with tenure and Yvonne Arnoult Chairholder in French Studies at Tulane University (New Orleans, USA). His research includes continental philosophy, literatures and arts of the Francophone world, African philosophies, juridical anthropology, and medical ethics. His publications include numerous articles and books: *Théorie Critique et Modernité négro-africaine: De l'Ecole de Francfort à la "Docta spes africana"* (Publications de la Sorbonne, 1993); *La philosophie négro-africaine* (PUF, Collection Que sais-je? 1995); *L'art négro-africain* (PUF, Collection Que sais-je? 1997); and *La palabre: Une juridiction de la parole* (Editions Michalon, 1997), translated as *Law and the Public Sphere in Africa* (Indiana University Press, 2014); and *Philosophie africaines:*

Traversées des Expériences (Editor), Special Issue, Rue Descartes, no. 36, Collège International de Philosophie de Paris, Presses Universitaires de France (2002). With Lavou Zoungbo Victorien, he coedited *Réalités et représentations de la violence dans les postcolonies* (Presses de l'Université de Perpignan, 2015) and with Aline Alterman, *L'Histoire à l'épreuve de l'histoire* (Paris, Editions Mimesis, 2021). He was a laureate 2011/2012 of Eurias (European Institutes for Advanced Studies).

Tanella Boni (Docteure ès Lettres, University of Paris-Sorbonne) was born in Abidjan and currently holds the post of full professor of Philosophy at Félix Houphouët-Boigny University, Abidjan, Côte d'Ivoire. She is a poet and a writer. She has been program director at the Collège International de Philosophie, Paris (1992–1998); vice-dean of the Faculty of Letters, Arts and Human Sciences at Université de Cocody, Abidjan, Côte d'Ivoire (1993–1997); and visiting professor in Paris and Toulouse. Currently, she is a member of the Steering Committee of International Federation of Philosophical Societies, a member of the International Institute of Philosophy, and a member of the Academy of Sciences, Arts, Cultures of Africa and African Diasporas. Author of papers in philosophy, literature, and interdisciplinary research; novels, essays (*Que vivent les femmes d'Afrique?* Karthala, 2011; *Habiter*, Museo, 2018); and many books for young people; she has also published numerous poetry collections (*The Future Has an Appointment with the Dawn*, University of Nebraska Press, 2018 and *Where It Is So Clear in Me*—forthcoming at Nebraska Press, both translated by Todd Fredson).

Chielozona Eze is a professor of African and African American literary and cultural studies at Northeastern Illinois University, Chicago, where he is also Bernard J. Brommel Distinguished Research Professor. He earned his PhD in English and Philosophy from Purdue University. He has written extensively on such topics as cosmopolitanism, empathy, human rights, social justice, and so on. He is the author of *Race, Decolonization, and Global Citizenship in South Africa* (University of Rochester Press, 2018), *Ethics and Human Rights in Anglophone African Women's Literature—Feminist Empathy* (Palgrave Macmillan, 2016), and *Justice and Human Rights in the African Imagination: We, Too, Are Humans* (Routledge, 2021). He is currently working on a book titled *The Wisdom of Mandela: Anger, Forgiveness, and Friendship in African Political Thought*.

Laura Hengehold, professor of philosophy at Case Western Reserve University, USA, teaches and researches political philosophy and philosophy of feminism and sexuality studies using perspectives from continental European and African thought. She is author of *The Body Problematic: Political*

Imagination in Kant and Foucault (2007), *Simone de Beauvoir's Philosophy of Individuation* (2017), and coeditor of the *Blackwell Companion to Simone de Beauvoir* (2017). She has also edited and translated *Law and the Public Sphere in Africa*: *La Palabre and Other Writings* by Jean Godefroy Bidima (2014), and translated *Kafka's Monkey and Other Phantoms of Africa* by Seloua Luste Boulbina (2019).

Séverine Kodjo-Grandvaux is a philosopher and associate researcher with the Laboratoire d'études et de recherches sur les logiques contemporaines de la philosophie at Université Paris 8. She is the author of *Philosophies africaines* (Présence Africaine, 2013), which won the Louis Marin Prize of the Académie des Sciences d'Outre-Mer, and *Devenir vivants* (éd. Philippe Rey, 2021). She is coeditor of *Droit et colonisation* (Bruylant, 2005). Séverine Kodjo-Grandvaux is also the scientific officer of the Fabrique de Souza (Cameroon), an institution for research and experimentation bringing together scientists, artists, and farmers to conceptualize and actively realize a utopia in which human beings think of themselves in terms of their relationship with the living world.

Nick Nesbitt is a professor of French Literature at Princeton University and senior researcher in philosophy at the Czech Academy of Sciences. Most recently, he is the editor of *The Concept in Crisis: Reading Capital Today* (Duke UP 2017), and the author of *Caribbean Critique: Antillean Critical Theory from Toussaint to Glissant* (Liverpool UP 2013). His next book, entitled *The Price of Slavery: Capitalism and Revolution in the Caribbean*, is forthcoming with University of Virginia Press, Fall 2021.

Florence Piron was an anthropologist and ethicist, professor in the Department of Information and Communication at Université Laval (Québec) where she taught critical thinking through courses on ethics, democracy, and *vivre-ensemble* (collective life). Founding president of the Association Science et Bien Commun and of the *boutique des sciences et des savoirs* (science shop) Accès Savoirs at Université Laval, director of the Éditions Science et Bien Commun, she was interested in the links between science, society, and culture (ethics), both as a researcher and as an activist for a more open, more inclusive, socially responsible science, focused on the common good, which she interpreted as the fight against injustice and environmental degradation. She spoke and wrote on these topics in a wide variety of settings, both inside and outside academia. From January 2015 until her death in 2021, she led the SOHA project (Open Science as a Collective Tool for Cognitive Justice and Empowerment in Haiti and Francophone Africa: Towards a Roadmap/*La science ouverte comme outil collectif de justice cognitive et de développement* *du pouvoir d'agir en Haïti et en Afrique francophone: vers une feuille de route).*

Hanétha Vété-Congolo is Henry Wadsworth Longfellow Professor of Romance Languages and Literatures at Bowdoin College, Maine, chair of the Department of Romance Languages and Literatures and president of the Caribbean Philosophical Association. She is a member of the Africa Academic Hub Initiative and affiliated to the Africana, the Latin American, Caribbean and Latinx and the Gender, Women and Sexuality Studies Programs of her institution. She is also Membre d'Honneur of the Research Group on Black Latin America at the Université de Perpignan Via Domitia, France (CRESEM/GRENAL, Languages and identities). Her scholarship focuses principally on Caribbean and African critical thought, philosophy, literature, culture, and orality and, on discourses by women and about women of the Caribbean and West and Central Africa. She is author of *Nous sommes Martiniquaises. Pawòl en bouches de femmes châtaignes: Une pensée existentialise noire sur la question des femmes* (2020), *L'interoralité caribéenne: le mot conté de l'identité (Vers un traité d'esthétique caribéenne)* (2016), and editor of *The Caribbean Oral Tradition* (2016), *Léon-Gontran Damas: Une Négritude entière* (2015), and *Le conte d'hier, aujourd'hui: Oralité et modernité* (2014).

www.ingramcontent.com/pod-product-compliance
Lightning Source LLC
Chambersburg PA
CBHW021346290326
41932CB00043B/198